CREATING THE
NEXT GENERATION

ıll College

EDWARD GROSS

&

MARK A. ALTMAN

B🌿XTREE

First published in the UK 1995 by
BOXTREE Ltd
Broadwall House
21 Broadwall
London SE1 9PL

10 9 8 7 6 5 4 3 2 1

This publication is not licensed by, nor is Boxtree affiliated with, Paramount Pictures. This is a scholarly work intended to document the development of a television series

No photos appearing in this book are copyright Paramount Pictures

Front cover photo copyright © David Strick/Onyx

ISBN 07522 0843 8

Typeset by SX Composing Ltd, Rayleigh, Essex
Printed and bound in Great Britain by
Butler & Tanner Ltd, Frome and London

A catalogue record for this book is available from the British Library

CREATING THE NEXT GENERATION
AN INTRODUCTION

By 1995, the television series *Star Trek: The Next Generation* had ended its seven year run, but had proven so successful that it inspired a big screen version titled *Star Trek: Generations*, and two spin-offs, *Star Trek: Deep Space Nine* and *Star Trek: Voyager*.

While all of this seems pretty commonplace now, back in October of 1986 when *TNG* was initially announced, no one was sure if it was going to work. Would the audience accept a *Star Trek* without Kirk or Spock? Could these new adventures match those of the 1960s? Would the phenomenon support two distinct versions of the same show? Naturally, as history has shown, the answer to all three questions was a resounding yes.

Creating the Next Generation is a somewhat episodic look back at the genesis and first season of the series. We begin with a look at the early development from its announcement on October 10, 1986 through its first few months of gestation, where much of the groundwork was laid down. From there, we provide an overview of the first season episodes, featuring the commentaries of the show's cast and crew. This is followed by a "script to screen" look at the first few episodes, detailing how the stories transformed from initial concepts to aired versions.

There is another side to the early days of *Star Trek: The Next Generation*; a dark history of politics, manipulations and power-struggles. Frankly, that material would fill a book of its own and its exploration is not the intent of *Creating the Next Generation*. For a taste of what went on, it's recommended that you purchase Joel Engel's biography of Gene Roddenberry, *Gene Roddenberry: The Myth and the Man Behind Star Trek,* which looks to the dark side of the Great Bird of the Galaxy.

What you are getting in this book, though, is a previously unexplored chapter in Star Trek history: an exploration of the birthing process of *The Next Generation*.

Edward Gross
Mark A. Altman
Summer, 1995

PART I
THE PROCESS OF CREATION

On October 10, 1986, the Earth shook.

If it didn't, then it must have been a movement of damn near equal proportion. It was a day that proved to be unlike any other as far as Trekkies and Trekkers around the globe were concerned, as Paramount Pictures made the official announcement: *Star Trek* would be returning to television via first run syndication, and Gene Roddenberry, "The Great Bird of the Galaxy" himself, would be serving as executive producer.

Rumors of Star Trek's return to television had been going on for some time, with *The Hollywood Reporter* stating that the three networks as well as Fox Broadcasting were interested in the proposed series. One story had it that an all new cast would be utilized, another that it would be set at Starfleet Academy, while still another had the supporting cast members of the original series put in the center seat, with newcomers filling out the starship bridge. William Shatner and Leonard Nimoy would make occasional guest appearances as Captain James T. Kirk and Mr. Spock.

Paramount studied all of these possibilities carefully, ultimately deciding to produce the series themselves and syndicate it to local stations still carrying the original. "In the end," explained Mel Harris, then President of Paramount Television, "we realized that nobody else was going to care as much about *Star Trek* as we did."

The announcement was ready to be made as early as September of 1986, but was held off in the belief that it would take away some of the luster from the original show's 20th anniversary celebration.

Titled *Star Trek: The Next Generation*, the series would be guaranteed twenty-six aired hours of episodes, budgeted at over a million dollars per hour. Joining Roddenberry behind the scenes would be producers Eddie Milkis and Bob Justman (both of whom had been involved with the original series). In front of the cameras would be a brand new cast of characters, none of which had any relationship with members of the original Enterprise crew.

"I'm still in the process of laying there, staring at the ceiling and trying this, that and the other idea out," said Roddenberry at the time. "I don't think we need a retread crew with people playing the same kind of roles. I'm not at all sure we will have a retread Vulcan. I would hate to think our imagination is so slender that there aren't other possibilities to think about."

"Twenty years ago," Harris added, "the genius of one man brought to television a program that has transcended the medium. We are enormously pleased that that man, Gene Roddenberry, is going to do it again. Just as public demand kept the original series on the air, this new series is also a result of grass roots support for Gene and his vision."

Generally unknown is that Roddenberry was actually third on Paramount's list of potential producers for the series. First they had gone to producer Sam Strangis, and when that attempt didn't work out, they went to actor-director Leonard Nimoy, who had scored so successfully with the third and fourth *Star Trek* features as director.

"I didn't want to do it," said Nimoy, "but not because I don't think it's a good idea or anything like that. I just don't want to be doing that for the next two or three years of my life. I do have mixed feelings about the series. Of course anything is possible. It's a tough challenge. There are going to be constant comparisons."

Reaction to *Star Trek: The Next Generation* was immediate. Fans either loved or hated the idea. The former because it presented the opportunity to go beyond the original series, and the latter because it would not feature the original cast, who, many felt, made *Star Trek* as successful as it was.

"Things grow and *Star Trek* has grown too," Roddenberry said in response to criticisms. "Let me say that I'm going to miss like hell the original characters and the very clever people who brought them to life. How could I not miss them when all of these characters are my children? They're blood of my blood. I will say that I've talked this new series over with George Takei, Nichelle Nichols, Jimmy Doohan and all the rest of them and they've said to me, 'Gene, you've got to strike out fresh now. We'll be doing the movies and all of that, and go with God. We understand, Gene.' We are a family. They're supporters of this as if I had struck out to get myself a new job somewhere. My determination is that the new *Star Trek* will reflect that same kind of love between all the members of the cast."

Despite these words to the contrary, the original cast was quick to respond to *The Next Generation*, and the reaction was not all that favorable.

"It's a mystery to me why they are doing it," said DeForest Kelley, best known as Dr. Leonard "Bones" McCoy, who, ironically enough, would cameo in the premiere episode. "I assume Paramount thinks they can hold on to the *Star Trek* phenomena. There's no doubt we can't go on forever, so they're trying a way to keep it going. But there's only one *Star Trek*, and that's ours."

James "Scotty" Doohan, who would also guest star on the series, exclaimed, "I just regret that they are calling it *Star Trek*, when we know what it is, which is the characters. They are trying to fool the public, and that's bad business."

William Shatner, who would ultimately co-star in the first feature based on *The Next Generation* nearly a decade later, said he didn't "feel good about the new series. I think without the cast as we know it and not in the time we know it, it's hard to understand why they are calling it *Star Trek*. In addition, there's a risk of overexposure."

Shatner's final concern was par-

ticularly valid. The fans normally built up their appetite for a new *Star Trek* adventure over the course of two years, and within that time they merely placated themselves with reruns of the original series. With a new adventure *every week* on television for free, how willing would they be to pay for a feature version? It's undeniable that the box office of the fifth and sixth films were impacted by the ultimate success of the series.

Following the October 10th announcement, the public had to wait for details regarding the new show, and they were slow in coming. All that was known was that the series was to take place 150 to 200 years beyond the current *Trek* time-frame (ultimately reduced to 75), and that the Enterprise, albeit in updated form, would be the mode of transportation for the crew. In addition, there would be *no* Vulcans, Klingons or Romulans, as this series was going to be completely fresh, and the military atmosphere of the feature films would be greatly downplayed.

Writer David Gerrold recalled that October day when *The Next Generation* was announced.

"I heard the news and confirmed it with Gene's assistant, Susan Sackett," Gerrold explained. "Then I dropped a note in the mail that said, 'Congratulations, this is great news. . . .' The kind of thing that said you worked hard and deserve the best. Gene and I for twenty years had been friends, despite the fact that we had never really specifically worked together on anything. We'd always sort of just missed. I'd be at conventions and follow the party line that Gene was a terrific person because he said

all the right things in public and seemed to be on the right side of the issues. So at that time I assumed that Gene was this terrific guy. The relationship was good, and for twenty years we'd be at conventions and Gene would say nice things about me on panels and I would say nice things about him. When you're not working together, you *have* to say good things. I called Dorothy Fontana right away and said, 'It's just been announced,' and she and I jokingly said, 'Okay, when Gene calls me I'll tell him he has to hire you, and when he calls you, you tell him he has to hire me.' As it happened, that's exactly what took place."

"I was very excited about the news," enthused Fontana. "I thought it was a wonderful opportunity to do something new and wonderful. Leonard Nimoy said that it was difficult to catch lightning in a bottle twice, which is true, but the potential of moving it ahead in time with totally new characters gave it a new venue. A new playground. I thought all of those *possibilities* were exciting at the time."

She had been phoned by Roddenberry and invited to dinner with him and his wife, Majel Barrett. At Yamatos Restaurant they discussed the new series.

"Primarily," detailed Fontana, "we talked about things Roddenberry wanted to avoid and a few things he definitely wanted to accomplish the second time around. He implied that I would be a valuable part of the new show, and the subject was left with the implied promise that when the show took on staff, I would be included. At that time, I also suggested that a good person to talk to would be David Gerrold, because of his previous involvement with the original *Star Trek*, his many novels and television science fiction work in the interim, and his excellent knowledge of science. Later in the month I was told that Gene had brought David on the show and that he was serving as a consultant. Early talks about the direction of the new series were taking place. I was told at the same time that there was no place for me yet, but I began to receive copies of memos sent to Gene Roddenberry from Bob Justman and David Gerrold. I was invited to comment on all memo suggestions, which I did in early November."

At the time, Gerrold had not yet been *officially* offered a staff position.

"Gene and I went out to lunch," he said, "we sat, talked and he said, 'What would you do with *Star Trek*?' He did not say, 'I want to hire you.' I nonetheless outlined my ideas for *Star Trek*, which were to shift the show to a first officer and let the captain stay on the ship. This allows you to simultaneously run shipboard stories and planetside stories. Before, the focus of the story always stayed where Kirk was. If you break it up and have a captain who's always on the ship, then you can stay with him if there are reasons to cut back to the ship, and yet you don't have him putting himself in danger on the planet. If your first officer is strong, then you have a focus there. So you have two heroes instead of one hero and a sidekick. I pitched it pretty hard; it's an idea I've had since way back in the early seventies.

"He thought that was a good idea," Gerrold elaborated, "and then I suggested a Klingon first officer, which he was adamantly against. It was that kind of discussion. At that point, I came right out and said that I wanted to be story editor of the series, but he didn't say yes or no."

Roddenberry proceeded to tell Gerrold that he, Milkis, Justman, Fontana and himself would screen science fiction films released over the past ten years so as to get a feel for living in the future as opposed to the 20th century.

"It was really an attempt to charge our batteries," Gerrold smiled. "Every day after the screenings, we'd all troop over to the Executive Dining Room, which is a big board room where you get personal service of the highest caliber and you have to reserve it. Well, Gene had it for three weeks straight, and we'd come marching in and you'd hear the conversation stop. People were saying things like, 'There goes thirty million dollars.' Like we had a blank check. It was kind of a neat feeling. We'd sit down and talk about the movie we'd just seen and spark ideas. Like after *Aliens*, Gene said, 'Jenette Goldstein created a new style of feminine beauty. We should have something like that in *Star Trek*.' So we started off with a character named Macha Hernandez, who eventually became Tasha Yar because in Spanish Macha was short for gay women.

"What also happened from day one is that Bob Justman and I started generating pounds of memos. Bob's memos were mostly 'how tos' and mine were 'what tos.' I did memos on the look of the ship, technology of the ship, warp speed, star dates, casting . . . everything about what the show should be. Gene kept telling me how thrilled he was with all the work I was doing. The studio execs were receiving copies of the memos and they would stop me on the lot and tell me how thrilled they were with the work I was doing. They were so enthusiastic and so delighted, and I was thrilled, because at that point I was at an interesting mental state. I made up my mind that this was the most incredible opportunity in the history of television, and that my job was not about making David Gerrold look wonderful or about being right. My job was totally to see that *Star Trek* turned out to be the best that we could make it.

"With everything I did, I would ask myself the question: is this good for *Star Trek*? There was a weird realization one day. I told Gene about it, although I don't think he quite got what I was saying. I said, '*Star Trek* to me was not just a TV show. It was a vision that says, "Life as it is today is not necessarily the way that life has to be lived. It is a statement that says we can build a world that works for everyone, with no one and nothing left out," and that's what the vision of the show is.' I'd say something like that to Gene and he'd look at me and say, 'Sometimes I think you understand *Star Trek* even better than I do.' So we had this great working relationship then in the planning stages. Gene would say to me, 'You're going to be a great Executive Story Consultant.' "

Optimism ran high in those early formative days of *Star Trek: The Next Generation*, as did the general level of creativity. It truly seemed as though this show would be unlike any that had ever been aired before. Although Gerrold still did not have an official position, he was confident that it would only be a matter of time, so he continued generating memos and aiding in the creative process.

Between October 17th and October 20th, Justman generated numerous memos, some of which would eventually play significant roles in the series. First off was his "Noah's Ark" premise, which basically said that a greater thread of realism might be portrayed if whole families were on board the Enterprise so that crewmembers would not have to be separated from their loved ones for long periods of time. This, he felt, would make *Star Trek* a true "Wagon Train to the Stars." Additionally, he was inspired by the film *Soylant Green* to have an area of the Enterprise able to create the home environment of any crewmember. He postulated a story premise in which the captain and several key officers are trapped in this area during a critical moment and cannot be extricated.

Justman also believed that a new alien race would help *The Next Generation* establish its own identity apart from the original series. In terms of the main characters, he stated that a half-human Klingon "Marine" might create an air of mystery similar to the one that surrounded the Spock character; and suggested an android regular who would be able to feature the best qualities of both Kirk and Spock, and he noted that actor Patrick Stewart would be perfect for the part; a female ensign who is trying to live up to the legend of her great-

great grandfather, James T. Kirk; a Latina MP, inspired, as stated previously, by Jenette Goldstein in *Aliens*; and a female science officer who is part Vulcan.

Interestingly, many of these suggestions were incorporated. The new Enterprise did contain large numbers of families; the ship was equipped with holodecks which can create virtually any environment, and in Tracy Torme's "The Big Goodbye," key crewmembers, including the captain, are trapped in it; there is an android character, Data; Patrick Stewart would eventually be signed as Captain Jean Luc Picard, there is a Klingon serving on the bridge, a female security chief and a new alien threat, the Ferengi Alliance. Apparently Justman deserves credit for making so many suggestions that were actually utilized.

Gerrold began meeting with Roddenberry more often, with Roddenberry informing him that he wanted Gerrold to rough draft the show's bible, which is exactly what had been on the writer's mind. This situation would eventually lead Gerrold to file a grievance with the Writer's Guild at a later date, which was ultimately quietly settled. He discusses the subject now, seemingly reflective of his optimistic naiveté at the time.

"When we first began discussing the bible," he recalled, "Gene said to me, 'Who are our characters? Who do you see?' I said, 'I see that our first officer is this, our captain is this, we should have a woman on the bridge who is an adviser to the captain.' He said, 'What about our navigator, helmsman and chief engineer?' I said,

'Our technology is so advanced, let's put all of those in one officer, and come up with other officers with different duties.' At one point, Gene said he wanted to have a disabled crewmember, so I prepared a memo listing various disabilities. Gene fastened on to blindness. I envisioned the character with some kind of eye treatment; maybe just a couple of enlarged lenses that you put over the actor's eyes. Instead they went with this air filter look, which I totally did not like. If you cover up too much of an actor's eyes, he's got nothing to work with. Then I suggested he be named after George La Forge, who was the fan in the wheelchair with Muscular Dystrophy who Gene had made an admiral. Gene thought that was a terrific idea, and then I suggested that in keeping with the ethnic character of the ship, and if neither the captain or first officer were black, then it was perhaps Geordi who should be black.

"I kept making suggestions," he added. "One day during lunch I was talking about Beverly Crusher, who was going to be the ship's school teacher, and in the middle of this I said, 'We don't have a ship's doctor yet, why don't we make Beverly Crusher the doctor?' I wish I'd tape recorded the conversation, because everybody said, 'Nah, that doesn't work,' and then they started discussing it. Eddie Milkis said, 'You know, that saves us a character if she's the doctor.' Then Bob Justman said, 'No, that makes it harder for the captain to have this relationship with the doctor that we want him to have. On the other hand, the fact that it's harder to have this relationship puts more tension . . . you know, Gene, that's not a bad idea.' And then Gene started discussing it. By lunch, Beverly Crusher was the ship's doctor.

"I was very satisfied making those kinds of suggestions and proving myself valuable to the show. We blocked out like three or four of the characters and Gene said to me, 'Okay, go home and do a character profile of each of those. Give me two pages on each of them.' Then the next day we sat down and talked about two more characters and he said, 'Give me profiles of those,' and I did that. I did a rough draft bible for him, then he sat down and did the bible that eventually came out on November 16th. That came out of Gene's computer, but a lot of it was rough drafted in my computer, and Gene sat down and rewrote it. You can see that the relationship between what I did and what he did was very, very close."

After that, Gerrold went back to writing memos, covering such subjects as a new and improved transporter beam, "enlightenment on the Enterprise" and the show's first story premise, "Mind Swarm," which proposed the possibility of implanting a computer into a human brain. What if it's possible for an implanted human to establish radio contact with another human, thus creating electronic telepathy? "Further suppose," he said "that when two or more humans link up in such a fashion, they become a massmind – a swarmed intelligence. Just as a colony of ants or a hive of bees can be thought of as a single entity, a mind swarm is a single entity that lives in many human bodies. Indeed, if an individual body

happens to die, the entity itself doesn't care because the entity continues – it is larger than the sum of its parts."

During the final week of October, numerous meetings were held in the Executive Dining Room, where a variety of issues were discussed. Among them was that they would produce a two-hour "movie" to kick of the series, the possibilities of shooting in stereo, Bob Justman's suggestion that members of the original cast be used in the opening episode, the need for a starship counselor-type, the possibilities of using writers and directors from the first *Star Trek*, a method of obtaining fresh, new writing talent, and Gerrold's suggestion that the crew view episodes of *Hill Street Blues, St. Elsewhere* and *L.A. Law* to get a sense of ensemble shows of the '80s.

On the 29th, Roddenberry issued a memo to Gerrold in which he agreed with Justman's "Noah's Ark" premise, and the idea that their handicapped crewperson be blind, yet able to "see" though a prosthetic device. In terms of armaments and militarism, he noted that on the new series it should be "de-emphasized over previous *Star Trek* series and very much de-emphasized over the *Star Trek* movies. We go back to the flavor of the previous series' first year, when emphasis was on 'strange new worlds' rather than on space villains and space battles. True, our new Enterprise still has awesome powers in its phaser and photon torpedo banks with everything organized for prompt obedience to chain of command decisions, but the flavor of this new *Star Trek* emphasizes not military

efficiency but rather the *maturity* of humanity in our 25th century in which *quality of life* is considered enormously more important than technological advances. Thus, we won't need Prussian Guard uniforms and saluting and all that, except where it is retained as a form of *courtesy* and occasionally as a spot of color in their lives."

The next day, Justman suggested a story idea entitled "Fanta-Sex," in which a hallucinogen allows someone to indulge in sex with whoever they choose, without that person ever being aware of it. The problem would be a person who develops a dependency on this drug, and their sexual obsession becomes a threat to the Enterprise. While there may be an intriguing element to this story suggestion, it unfortunately would be a prelude to the series' preoccupation with sex that would eventually pervade many episodes of the first season.

Also occurring that week was an event that affected David Gerrold, but would prove to be a microcosm of the way that many of the behind the scenes personnel on the series would eventually be treated in its early days. It was a moment which, in retrospect, should have served as an ominous foreboding of what was to come.

"About a week after Gene told me I was going to make a great Executive Story Consultant," Gerrold said, "he told me that he wanted me to keep doing everything that I had been doing. Essentially I had been doing the job of a producer and doing what was necessary in the creation of the show. If I saw a problem that I could fix, I would fix it before it was a problem. I was continually bringing solutions to the show. At the same time, I was being very careful not to step on anyone's toes. I would always communicate with Bob Justman, Eddie Milkis and Gene. 'What do you think about this? Should I do that?' I never did anything I wasn't supposed to. On a Tuesday Gene calls me in to his office and says, 'My lawyer advises me that I shouldn't give you the title Creative Consultant because it gets into all kinds of Writer's Guild stuff. David, I'm not backing off on anything, but at this point we don't have the budget and we don't . . .' I said, 'Gene, my main concern is *Star Trek*, the quality of the show. It's not a big thing to me whether I'm consultant.' He said, 'Fine. We're old friends.' This started to become a theme: 'We're old friends' and 'I knew I could count on you.'

"They finally offered me a deal another week later," he laughed humorlessly. "I did not get a pay-check or a deal negotiated for three weeks. They finally called my agent and offered $750 a week, which is a terrible deal. I went to Gene and told him that this deal was like hiring a writer for below Guild wages, and is quite inappropriate. He said, 'Let me talk to the studio. That's what the studio offered.' And the studio said to my agent that that was what Gene had authorized. At that time, I did not know that his lawyer was running the negotiations angle for Gene. That was coming from him, and that's all he was willing to authorize. So they upped the offer to $1,000 a week for ten weeks. Gene said, 'Come January

first, when this deal expires, we'll get you a proper contract on staff and you'll be here a long time; you'll be working here a long time. It's going to be fine, David.' And I thought, 'Well, I don't know what's going on. Maybe the studio is not going to release big amounts of development money until they see what he is developing.

"So I took the deal against my better judgment. It was not a good deal, but I took it because I thought I could contribute to *Star Trek*, we can still have the very best *Star Trek* and I'll just use this as an opportunity to prove that I'm worth it. I figured, 'Alright, I haven't had a staff job on a show for like five or six years, and maybe I'm rusty. Maybe I need to prove myself.' I'm this kind of a guy where I will internalize everything. I'll say, 'Gee, is it my fault? What did I do? What can I do better?' It's like I'm a product of the '70s."

At about the same time, the creative staff of *Star Trek: The Next Generation* began moving into offices, though the only offices available on the Paramount lot at the time were some located in the *Entertainment Tonight* building. There was an office complex that had previously been used by the research division, Kellem DeForest, and it was considered an attractive set of offices. On one side there were three offices with room for two secretaries. The other side was almost as large, with two offices and room for two secretaries. Justman and Milkis took the offices on the "three" side, while Roddenberry took the offices on the "two."

"Gene said to me, 'You'll take this office here, because I want you

close to me,'" said Gerrold. "It was a very good office and a very good position. It made a lot of people think that I was due to be promoted to a producer. I thought, 'Okay,' but I could see trouble on the horizon because Gene's lawyer kept saying, 'We're going to bring in another producer and he's going to have to have an office too.' Again, things were going so well in all of that start-up period, and we were all enthusiastic."

In early November, Bob Justman proposed a new and improved take on the show's opening credits – a tour of the solar system and beyond. "A new show," he said, "connotates a new Main Title and yet I think we need to have our new different Main Title feel familiar to the audience. The old one worked wonderfully well for us despite the fact that, as we both well remember, it was put together mostly from what few pieces of film we were able to salvage from the first and second pilots. This time, we have a chance to do something that we couldn't do before – put the audience into a place from which they can see the spatial relationship between where the Enterprise (and its crew and the viewers) are coming from and where we all are going. Today, we have filmic techniques we could only dream about when we first started *Star Trek*."

Once again, Gerrold took to writing memos. On November 2nd – which turned out to be a very prolific day for him – he offered one with the heading "who's 'it' this week"? "Twenty years ago," he said, "a writer in *TV Guide* noticed something interesting about the *Star Trek* format. In the teaser, we see Kirk, Spock, McCoy and two crewmen who we've never seen before beam down to the surface of a strange alien planet. Guess who's going to get killed in the next three minutes? Right. I think we have to avoid repeating that mistake. We have four permanent members of our regular team. We should suggest that there are many other members to the contact team, even if they are not always shown. We can imply that in two ways. 1) Even if no one is going to die on a particular mission, we should always show additional team members beaming down with them. 2) We should vary who beams down to the surface, so that sometimes one of the regular team members has to stay aboard at a console and monitor the job his/her replacement is doing – just as the NASA astronauts monitor each other's missions. This would allow us to show our regular team member's grief when a crewmember gets killed on the surface … We should keep ourselves conscious of this, so as to avoid the obvious game of 'Guess who gets killed this week?'"

Gerrold also suggested that the show avoid the Kirk-Spock-McCoy troika of the original series, focusing more on an ensemble as in Bochco's shows. His first reason for feeling this way was that as an ensemble show, it would be easier to tell stories about supporting characters without the feeling of slighting the star. "Because of the contractual need to have Kirk and Spock at the center of every story in the old series, there wasn't as much opportunity for our other characters to be heroic," he said. "This ultimately proved unfair to a very talented

group of actors. [Also], as an ensemble show, it's easier to kill off a character (if necessary) without drastic damage to the format of the series. If a cop dies on *Hill Street Blues*, we mourn for a couple of episodes, and then a new cop takes his place – and then the series goes on."

Another concern of his was *Next Generation* avoiding an inter-character relationship that would mirror the Kirk/Spock one from the original series. "The relationship between Number One and Data, the android, could very well evolve into a new Kirk-Spock relationship," noted Gerrold. "Do we want this, and if so, how should we represent it? If not, how should we avoid it? Could the two have something of an adversarial relationship? We absolutely do need to demonstrate a profound friendship among our regulars to create a family/ensemble feeling. We should probably work very hard to avoid any echoes of the past. This is an area that needs further consideration."

Same day, Gerrold suggested an additional make-up effect for the android crewmember – perhaps a golden shade of skin, or, even simpler, special contact lenses to give him a golden eye color. In terms of casting, he suggested Kim Miyori (*St. Elsewhere, John and Yoko*), and Robert Englund (*"V", Nightmare on Elm Street*).

In a memo titled "Enlightenment on the Enterprise," he informed Roddenberry that he and Justman had been talking about a person aboard ship who serves the function of an emotional healer. Not a chaplain, he said, because humanity has moved beyond mere ritual, but someone

who serves as a "master." "His job," proposed Gerrold, "is to support those aboard the ship in the job of *being* the best they can be. He/she cannot be a healer, therapist, or any kind of a medical officer because that implies that our people have to be sick or damaged to need his/her help. For something of the same reasons, he cannot be a trainer/teacher because that also implies that our people are less than fully trained. He can't be a bartender because that suggests that our people seek solace irresponsibly."

He suggested a Chief of Recreation. On the surface, this character's job would be to re-create the crew of the Enterprise; to create them fresh and new, to re-inspire and re-invigorate them, again and again and again. "In practice," he said, "I could see this fellow sitting down to play chess with a troubled crewperson – and in the course of their conversation, gently and unobtrusively providing all of the appropriate support for that character's emotional growth."

On November 3rd, Dorothy Fontana reminded Roddenberry of an infrequently recurring character she had suggested during a recent dinner. "I mentioned a planet with a Japanese-like culture and traditions," said Fontana, "in particular, the Samurai code – a planet which has been destroyed. Our character (not necessarily Oriental) is one of the few survivors, having been off-planet at the time. He is truly a *Ronin*, a masterless Samurai. In the tradition of *Yojimbo, Sanjuro*, and the 'Babycart' movies, this Ronin will take on any job for money and serve his paying master for the length of the contract – but he has his own complex moral code. He may take a job that isn't so morally savory because he needs the money – and maybe he sees a way to make the job take on moral value. In this way, the character won't always be on the side of our heroes. Story possibilities increase if this character is a woman."

Fontana also addressed the issue of the Vulcan Neck Pinch (also referred to as the FSNP, for Famous Spock Nerve Pinch), which was a solution for a non-violent character to utilize when he needed to incapacitate someone for story purposes. "However, it wound up being used all the time," she noted, "and it *always worked* on whomever (whatever) Spock applied it. I suggest the android character Data could project a special 'tone' that acts as a hypnotic on most humans or humanoid species. (Our crew members would have an implant or would have been conditioned to not respond to it.) This hypnotic tone would not necessarily work on every species. Some aliens would be on other 'frequencies' – or perhaps they might not have ears! Thus Data has something interesting and non-violent to use as a weapon if needed, but it isn't a sure-fire winner every time."

On November 4th another lunch meeting was held, where a variety of topics were covered, including: the Enterprise should have the capacity to separate, either the saucer section breaking away or some kind of two-part ship. A story idea relating to this had "our guys" leaving in one section and returning to find their families and the others hijacked, or held hos-

tage, or totally vanished. At that same meeting, it was noted that Patrick Stewart was being considered as a male lead, and that John Lone from *Iceman* should be kept in mind for Data.

Also that day, Fontana suggested a new character, Mission Specialist Kerry. "Michael Alan Kerry looks like he chews nails and spits out rivets – to quote Jim Croce, 'Badder than ol' King Kong, meaner than a junkyard dog,'" she mused. "Inside, Mike's a teddy bear – thoughtful, sensitive, gentle. He'd really rather be left alone to pursue research, but his knowledge in his field makes him a natural for a good number of contact teams … Mike is an anthropologist with a 'minor' in history. His feeling for people, their culture, societal development, and history is deep and sensitive, sometimes intuitively brilliant. Personally, Mike is a family man with a wife and a young daughter. He is a talented chef, and his dinners and parties are legend. If Mike invites you to dinner, drop everything and go – the cuisine in his quarters is magnificent, and he does all the cooking. His wife, Susan, works in Operations. She is a dedicated officer as well as wife and mother and works hard at all her jobs. Occasionally, her lack of time resulting from her efforts to be good at all of her roles leads to conflict between her and Mike – but mostly they are a happy couple, trying to live a normal life aboard ship and provide a good family atmosphere for their daughter."

During that first week in November a first draft bible for the show was circulated to the staff. Fontana responded on the fourth with some

problems with the document as presented.

"I feel a lack in the characters as proposed," she said, "primarily because I do not see any references to friendships, relationships. Each character proposed seems to have limited communications with others, and each seems to have a lot that will go on inside his/her head or in private. The Captain keeps his emotions private, goes to his cabin and communes with books. Con talks to the Captain, but only to differ with him. She deals with *her* emotions in private. Ops talks to the ship. Number One has disagreements with the other senior officers and heads the contact teams. Who does he talk to, besides the "few women who know him well enough to call him by his real name?" The reference to Data's relationships seem sexual only, Macha deals with her feelings privately and expresses temper or displeasure aloud in dealing with stupidity or intolerance. Who does she *talk* to? Jordy is the only one who seems to have the capability of forming relationships.

"The backbone of *Star Trek* has always been relationships and human stories," she added. "I realize you don't want the buddy system that evolved before, but people do form friendships and trusts, loves and hates in their working and personal lives. Both are contained side by side on this ship, and they must be seen in the characters. A base is there for the Captain and Con. The others are not there yet; and I feel a background should be laid in, both for the writers and the actors. I believe the best area for this is in the contact team, which presumably will always (or almost always) include Number One, Macha and Data. Again, I do not mean to suggest a triumvirate such as was there before. However, the contact team is a team, some members of which work together all the time. If they don't have a relationship – one in which all elements know, trust and depend on one another – that 'team' is not a team. It is in trouble."

On November 6th, Gerrold brought up the subject of bridge design. Noting that the front half of the bridge for the original show was wasted space, he proposed that the helm – perhaps called the Operations Console – be on a raised area at the rear of the bridge. This would give Ops (and perhaps one or two assistants) command of the entire operations area of the bridge without having to be in the center of everything.

"In the center area," he continued, "we put three or four chairs – but not like the current Captain's chair; instead something more like those tall chairs we see on the bridge of an aircraft carrier. Comfortable, but clearly not lounging chairs. These are for our senior officers: Captain, Science Officer, Number One – who else? – and one or two mission specialists, as needed for a particular mission ... We angle the chairs slightly towards each other, and give each chair access to a mini-console or terminal. Now, it's clearly a Command Center, but without all the electronics in the way. The chairs can turn forward for the main viewer. On the raised area of the bridge, we put various work-stations. A science station. A weaponry station. (What

else?) We should probably have enough gingerbread in the bridge design to make it look exciting, but not so much as before, as it tends to pull attention away from the human element of our stories. All of those knobs and buttons and switches and levers are fun to play with, but ultimately make you wonder exactly what our people are doing and why they need to do it. On our new ship, the computer technology should probably handle almost all of that automatically, so our people can concentrate on solving the real problems at hand."

On November 9th, Bob Justman suggested that the opening episode of the series should deal with a sociological experiment that Starfleet Command has undertaken to see if it is feasible for humans to live a normal life in space.

"Can our people maintain familial and/or other personal relationships during an extended voyage?" he mused. "This premise would be premise 'A,' the internal premise of this show. The other premise would be premise 'B' and would have to do with an external threat to the mission. Hopefully, the resolution of the threat of premise 'B' would come about as a direct result of our solution of the problems engendered by premise ... During this first episode, all sorts of conflicts arise which have to do with men and women love/hate, marriage/divorce, friendship/antagonism, adultery, social and professional competition – in other words, all the elements of human drama to which mankind has been subject since the dawn of time. At the end of this first

show, Picard opts to continue with this 'ship of fools' experiment. After all, humans have always behaved in a less than perfect way – but we have also always striven to become better than we are. What right do I or any other person, thinks Picard, have to deny my fellow man the chance to try to evolve into something better, something finer, something approaching a state of grace?"

The following day, Dorothy Fontana brought up the subject of the Romulans, wondering if the Neutral Zone still exists. "Have Starfleet and the Klingons gone around the Romulan Empire and isolated it?" she asked. "Is the Federation still technically at war (or at 'hostile peace') with the Romulans? Are they still (please) as mysterious, remote and in a way, romantic, as last seen? Where did they come in – or did they? – in the proposed struggle with a whole new alien menace? It would be nice to keep the Romulans with their Roman code of ethics and battle as a question mark; a still unreconciled enemy, however highly respected; a still little-known people in spite of the partial information that may have been gained from the Federation/Klingon alliance. The Romulans were never overused, and that is part of their charm and a good reason to keep them alive. What has happened to them in the past 150 years? Because they were so little used on the old *Trek*, the Romulans retain their mystery and intrigue. They also have ears. If you intend to play down the Vulcans, do remember you have a Romulan backup."

The Klingons were another source of curiosity for her, with the writer believing that they must be dealt with one way or another. Her suggestions were to leave them as they were – black-hat villains; ignore them, eliminate them altogether or create peace between the Empire and the Federation. "Solution four sets up several situations that can create stories," she noted. "Depending on when the alliance took place, there are bound to be in Starfleet a number of veterans or children of veterans who opposed the Klingons and who still greatly mistrust the alliance and/or any Klingon in any circumstance. You may not want a regular Klingon crew person on board; but story situations can grow from interaction with ambassadors, trading ships, other 'alliance' vessels with Klingon personnel, important Klingon passengers, Klingon personnel of space stations of planetary centers with whom the Enterprise must deal, half-breed Klingons in any capacity, etc."

She also brought up the subject of Patrick Stewart possibly being cast as Captain Picard. "This is fine," Fontana said, "but I suggest you also consider some actors in their middle to late-forties in addition. The distinguished youthful fifties is alright if we have a short-lived series – but if you go longer (and I know you're hopeful it will be a *lot* longer), there is the fat-and-hairline factor to consider. Remember? The fat expands and the hairline recedes. I believe you can safely go to a man in his middle forties and still have the 'older, experienced' image. Please consider."

On November 19th, David Gerrold dealt with the notion of a detachable saucer section. Having

families with children aboard the Enterprise, he reasoned, would present a problem when it comes to telling stories in which the starship is in direct danger. What would happen to families and children if the ship comes under attack?

"Possible solution: establish that the disk part of the vessel is detachable from the main module," he said. "When we know that we are going to be going into a dangerous sector, the saucer (which contains the main living decks) detaches and retreats to a safe distance from for later rendezvous. The main module and nacelles become a fierce-looking battle-unit. Much of the most fearsome weaponry can be located in the connecting strut. In keeping with Starfleet's demilitarized mission, however, we should also establish that our Captain is extremely reluctant to take this step because even to go to a situation of military readiness is to acknowledge the failure of diplomatic efforts."

That same day, Gerrold brought to Roddenberry's attention a young actor who had appeared on *St. Elsewhere*. "He's a fourteen-year-old doctor. Male," he explained. "Very much like Wesley Crusher as we have described and discussed. Played by the young kid in *Stand By Me* who grew up to be Richard Dreyfuss. Did a very good job. If the character is not a regular, we should take a look at this fellow." That fellow turned out to be Wil Wheaton, who would, indeed, be cast as Wesley Crusher.

On December 9th, Dorothy Fontana brought up to Roddenberry, apparently for the second time, her idea that there needed to be a new

alien threat, and her notion was that these aliens should be shapeshifters. "We may not know what they're really after, at least in the beginning," she proposed. "We would not be able to say for certain what they really look like. We would never be sure that someone we believe we can trust isn't really a shapeshifter. The idea's been used many times in other sf stories, so it's not new – but I'm sure interesting variations on the theme can be found if you think the idea is viable." Interestingly, this very notion would resurface in the 1994-95 television season, when the series *Star Trek: Deep Space Nine* established a race of shapeshifters as the newest threat to the Federation.

Fontana also brought up the notion of sisterhood on the Enterprise, believing that it would be important to have relationships between the women characters as the audience gets to know them. "These women," offered Fontana, "are going to be saying more than, 'Hailing frequencies open,' and 'Yes, Doctor.' We have to let them be as fully fleshed as characters as the men. If they're going to be important – and you've set it up so they will be – they must have feelings, attitudes, and relationships with each other as well as with the men of the crew and outsiders they will meet."

As story ideas came in during those early days, Fontana noticed an alarming trend of focusing too much on the character of Leslie Crusher (later to become Wesley), a problem which would indeed rear its head on the first season of *Next Generation*. Said Fontana, "Aren't we thinking a little too much about this girl and not enough about our other people? I have a gut feeling that too many Leslie stories will drive our audience away because they will perceive it to be a kiddy show. (It won't be, but a hint of that is all it takes.) Perhaps I'm jumping the gun on this, but I hope the next few story proposals I see/hear are centered around the other series leads."

On December 18th, Fontana brought up the subject of Data, and the fact that she and Gerrold had come up with the notion of Data *not* being the only one of his kind in existence. They proposed the idea of a female android. "She was sent away from the planet to guarantee that someone would be left alive to tell the tale (I've been reading Melville again)," she explained. "Now when Data meets this woman, we have a story. How does he feel when he finds he is not alone of his kind in the universe? How does she? What is

their relationship, how do they both feel about the responsibility that was thrust upon them? How does this 'woman' live her life and what is her future? We also batted around the suggestion that Data (and the woman, if you like her) were the perfect products that the aliens created. What about the ones that didn't work as well? Could one of them have survived and escaped? What's wrong with him or her? Can this android be Data's enemy, foil, rival? We thought there were story possibilities here that can be developed." And one notion in particular, that of a "rival" was exploited in the episode "Datalore," which introduced Data's evil brother Lore, who became something of a continuing threat.

As *Star Trek: The Next Generation* ended its first several months of life, and as the year 1986 was coming to a close, the show's bible was being refined, stories were being assigned and scripts written; and the

show's staff began to grow with the addition of veteran producer Robert Lewin, a new breed of writers as represented by Herb Wright, and Maurice Hurley, who had come off of *Miami Vice* and *The Equalizer*. Each of these writers were hoping to bring their particular talents to the show in an effort to combine them with those of Gerrold, Fontana, Justman and, of course, Roddenberry. Another addition – and the only member of the group who remained with the series past the second season – was Rick Berman, who shifted over from being a Paramount executive to the series itself and who, in years to come, would replace Roddenberry as Great Bird of the Galaxy when the series' creator passed away.

Unfortunately, as would become evident as the show unfolded during its first season, *Star Trek: The Next Generation* would spend quite some time as a series desperately searching for direction.

PART II
STAR TREK: THE NEXT GENERATION
Season One Set Visit

The following visit to the set of Star Trek: The Next Generation took place shortly after the airing of the series' premiere episode, "Encounter at Farpoint." The subsequent article was written by Mark A. Altman, from the efforts of Altman, Steven Simak and Mitchell Rubinstein. It is reprinted here with the permission of Galactic Journal magazine, holder of the article's copyright.

"You couldn't imagine how hard it is to get on the back of a box of Cheerios," the publicist representing *Star Trek: The Next Generation* explained to me as he pointed at the back of a cereal box. On it was a picture of a young boy flanked by Jonathan Frakes and Marina Sirtis. In the starfield above them it said you could win a chance to appear in a *Star Trek* episode, and at the very least you could find a sticker with your favorite *Next Generation* star inside. I nodded. It was hardly what anyone would have expected when the cameras first started to roll on the pilot for *Star Trek* way back in 1964, but now, over twenty years later, history was being made again, not only on the airwaves, but in kitchen cabinets across America as well.

I put the box back down on the table next to the water cooler. On the other side of the plywood wall separating us was the bridge of the new Enterprise, where rehearsal was beginning on another scene in the latest episode of the critically acclaimed new syndicated space opera.

"You will jump to warp eight and I will personally lead the Away Team," says one of the episode's guest stars as he struts down to the helm. Patrick Stewart rises from the captain's chair and walks to the ops position and turns. Rob Bowman, the director, shakes his head disapprovingly. He approaches Stewart, they exchange hushed words and all is well again. Stewart and LeVar Burton exchange quips and they prepare to rehearse the scene again. Denise Crosby, who plays Security Chief Tasha Yar, looks somewhat out of place in back of the weapons console in a white halter top as she does her make-up. The cast patiently awaits for the scene to be rehearsed again.

It is here, on Stage 10, that the bridge of the Enterprise is housed along with the captain's ready room and several of the principal personnel quarters. Several soundstages down is Stage 9, where most of the permanent sets for the series are housed. Most are redressed versions of the motion picture sets. The scarred remnants of the battle bridge featured in "Encounter at Farpoint" is now substituting for the USS Stargazer, Captain Picard's former command, and was the original bridge from *Star Trek: The Motion Picture*. Nearby is sickbay, the multipurpose briefing room, the transporter room and engineering. All the gadgets adorning the *Trek* sets have been carefully thought out and are engineered to operate in a certain way.

"The art department has programmed all that stuff," Denise Crosby says. "They know exactly what all of it does. All you have to do is say what does this thing do or how would I launch a photon torpedo? They have all that worked out."

Adjacent to engineering and through one of the myriad of Enterprise deck corridors is an all-purpose area which will eventually serve as the ship's shuttlecraft bay, if need be. It is currently used for storage and was utilized for the holodeck sequence in "Code of Honor."

The holodeck, an exciting new piece of Enterprise technology, was first envisioned during the animated *Trek* episodes, but has been vividly realized in the new series. It will play a vital part in upcoming *Trek* stories, reveals Jonathan Frakes, who plays the new Enterprise's first-in-command and away team leader, William Riker. "Brent and I went on location in the Ferndale area for the holodeck," Frakes notes of its use in "Encounter at Farpoint". In the scene, he encounters Data in the wilds of a Terran forest. It was some of the only location shooting that the series would feature until "Justice," otherwise known as the Edo Planet episode. Rob Legato, who's responsible for the series' visual effects, has found the holodeck sequences some of his most challenging work. "It's all a heavy blue screen composite. He [Frakes] is actually walking on a blue screen floor. We try to keep all the shadows as they actually appear on the floor so they will appear on the exterior location [and] it looks like he's married to it. It's a fairly complex composite."

The holodeck is the catalyst for a Raymond Chandler-esque episode which both Frakes and Gates McFadden cite as one of their favorite adventures yet. In "The Big Goodbye," written by Tracy Torme, the holodeck malfunctions, trapping our heroes in a dangerous fantasy world.

Nearby on Stage 16, a bulldozer is sitting idle as workers scurry across the huge soundstage in which Styrofoam rocks appear to stretch into the horizon. The set is used for creating alien terrain and also houses an underground area which can be flooded, if necessary.

"We did it the same way we did it twenty years ago," explains supervising producer Robert Justman, one of the veterans from the original *Trek*. "We have a slightly larger stage this time, but it's much the same idea." He adds that there will be a "50/50 mix of planet to ship shows."

The man endowed with the thankless task of creating *Star Trek*'s alien worlds is production designer Herman Zimmerman, who, in conjunction with a varying tinting and lighting scheme, is charged with

transforming Stage 16 every week into a totally new planetary environment. "Production design and art design is problem solving," Zimmerman states. "Problem solving with an intent. I like to say that the art director/production designer is in the unenviable position of making himself invisible. Because if what he or she does is correct, it supports that story; it becomes the environment. If what he does becomes visible to you, then he's probably stepped out of line and you are noticing the technique of the matte painting denoting an alien landscape, rather than believing you are there on an alien landscape."

Back on Stage 10, filming has begun. Captain Picard is attempting to console the wife of a *Starfleet* ambassador whose husband has been taken hostage by terrorists. The set is quiet as the cameras begin to roll.

Outside the cramped soundstage is a small trailer court, housing all the principal cast. Extras lounge around in front of the soundstage door, while Marina Sirtis' make-up is being applied and the Beatles blare loudly from a portable radio. Jonathan Frakes pops out from his trailer in his pink bathrobe to see when he's needed on stage and in costume again, and then retreats back into his trailer, out of the hot California sun. Wil Wheaton is bouncing around the set, even though he won't be appearing in any scenes that day. LeVar Burton is inside his trailer, appearing to be having some very serious conversations with his agent, as Michael Dorn reclines in a patio chair outside his humble *Star Trek* chateau.

Old is indeed new again, even if the next generation of starship Enterprise crewmembers are part of an all-new *Star Trek* that has changed more than just the faces at the helm.

"The way we do the show nowadays is different physically," Robert Justman explains. Unlike the old *Star Trek* series, *The Next Generation* is shot on film, but transferred to one inch video for editing. "We've never seen an inch of positive film." The only shooting in which positive film is screened is for certain effects shooting. Processes such as optical printing are eliminated through the new methods which does not only allow for a higher resolution picture quality, but eliminates the degraded image which results from the various generations film stock would go through before airing.

The show's visual effects are composited digitally as well, so several elements can be combined into one shot more easily than through traditional optical printing methods. "We can take VistaVision film from ILM and 35MM film somewhere else, and marry them all digitally," Justman adds. The episodes, once edited, are beamed by satellite to the independent stations across the country who carry the show.

While the method of production has changed dramatically from the original, other obstacles to recreating the *Trek* universe were less easy to surmount. Among the dilemmas Herman Zimmerman had to face was being faithful to the original *Star Trek* concepts established in the series and the movies, and improving on them. "We still have a double warp drive engine, we still have impulse power, we use the transporter room and have a bridge with the captain in the center," says Zimmerman. "All of those things are generic to what we know and believe *Star Trek* to consist of. While we are upgraded in details and cosmetics, we are alike in kind and that's not so hard to do. If we were reinventing the wheel, that would be hard. Why tamper with success?

"There was a desire to come across with a new Enterprise in a spectacular way. [This] Enterprise is twice the size of the last Enterprise, which was considerably larger than the first television Enterprise. The concept from Mr. Roddenberry was not to deviate, in essence, from the philosophy of the original.

"The new bridge design evolves as does the exterior ship design from two basic concepts. One is it is unnecessary to have aerodynamics because space is a vacuum. It is, by the 24th Century, in Mr. Roddenberry's mind, entirely possible that technology has reached such a state of proficiency that it has become an art form. Point two is that instead of a five year mission, we have a 30 year mission with women, children and families aboard. We want to make the whole environment of the starship more comfortable. It never was a battleship. It's a far cry from an all gray militaristic starship. It is indeed a state of the art, comfortable machine that we're proud to call home."

One of the most important facets of designing the new Enterprise was the bridge, which has undergone such a dramatic evolution since the original television series

through the feature films, and now in the new show. "The bridge is large," Zimmerman remarks. "Perhaps larger than it needs to be, partly because Gene wanted the viewscreen to be very large. It's considerably more advanced looking than the original Enterprise viewscreen, and it lends a great deal of dramatic impact to the shows when you can see the face of Q, for instance, nine feet high in front of Picard, who is standing there a little more than half that height."

The construction of such a large viewing screen demanded that the rest of the bridge be built to a scale which would be compatible with it. The bridge, in fact, is the same width as the original Enterprise bridge – 38 feet – but is two feet longer. The height of the ceiling, which was never visible in the original, is 14 feet. The descending ramps, leading from the rear of the bridge to the helm, lend to the illusion of even greater height.

In order to shoot the sets, including the bridge, in which most of the action occurs, walls are built "wild." "Wild walls" are moveable to allow for camera placement. "In order to put the camera in the right place, you have to build your sets so they can be taken apart in pieces," Zimmerman adds. "You put the camera on one side for the master, then put that wall back. Move the camera, pull another wall out and do coverage. Those are experimental matters – you either know how to do them or you learn how to do it very quickly."

Complicating matters even further is the limited amount of time available between design and execution of all aspects of the *Star Trek*

production, ranging from visual effects to make-up and, of course, set design. "The norm is to get a script two weeks in advance of principal photography, and have two production meetings," explains Zimmerman. "One is a preliminary concept meeting and one, hopefully, a week or three or four days prior to the start of production. We get together in the production meeting and talk out the problems, coming up with new ideas, submit budgets and revise concepts and ideas to fit [those] budgets. We proceed as fast as we can and sometimes will start shooting a picture and not have all the elements in place for a particular scene until the night before."

"It's pretty intense," Rob Legato concurs. "I sometimes have as much as five weeks, and usually less. Ideally, you want to get the script, read it, absorb it, figure out how you're going to play out the sequences, but often in television the scripts don't come out until a couple of days before you shoot it. You have to very quickly come up with a concept and immediately have it built.. It is kind of unheard of to do the amount of work we're doing in the time we're doing it in."

According to Legato, the writers' uninhibited imaginations are providing a bevy of creative ideas which are not necessarily as easily translated into reality. "They're writing it without any constraints in mind. What's a lot more interesting to do is have someone create something that is unbelievable so it has a more charged feeling on the set. The actors are acting to something that's really phenomenal as opposed to writing a dialogue scene where you have to play everything out. Instead, they look at the viewscreen and see something magnificent is on the screen. Well, thank you, I appreciate that."

One of The Next Generation's most engaging dilemmas was retaining the look of the far more expensive feature films in its weekly Trek episodes. Even at an approximate budget of $1.5 million an episode, it is difficult to mirror the look of a $20 million motion picture. "We have to keep on trying," says Justman, who is encouraged by what the show has achieved so far. Wil Wheaton, who's starred in a number of motion pictures including Stand By Me, states, "We're not a three camera sitcom. We go on film and are transferred to video on the same setting as a feature film. It definitely feels like a feature."

Among the directors who have helmed Trek episodes have been Corey Allen, who directed the pilot; Richard Colla, who also directed the three hour premiere of Battlestar Galactica as well as Gene Roddenberry's The Questor Tapes, and Rob Bowman, Trek's most prolific director whose work includes "Where No One Has Gone Before" and "Too Short a Season." The cast is almost unanimous in its praise for the men behind the camera. "We've had some good directors that have been very perceptive," Michael Dorn remarks, rubbing his bony facial appliance which transforms him from mild-mannered actor to Klingon warrior. "They know more about directing than I do and I know more about acting. If they say run out in this scene and break down and cry, I'd say he doesn't do that. The director gives you param-

eters and limits, but you take it and fill it up with as much color as you can."

"I think Roddenberry's gotta be pretty pumped up he turned the networks down," says Jonathan Frakes. "He had such a shitty time with them the first time."

First run syndication has notoriously been a medium for trashy two camera sitcoms and hokey revivals of failed series such as We Got It Made and What's Happening, so it came as a great surprise when Paramount announced they would bypass traditional network deals and a lucrative arrangement with the Fox Network, and syndicate the show on their own. Among the benefits that syndication holds for the show is freedom from network interference, something Gene Roddenberry was only too well acquainted with from his days of doing Star Trek for NBC.

"We did a scene the other day where I call Q a son of a bitch," Frakes notes, "and no one even suggested I do it another way."

Producer Robert Justman admits that while the ratings may suffer because of Trek's unique broadcast method, it was a sacrifice worth taking. "My feeling is that network interference has become more objectionable. I think our ratings would be phenomenal, but we'd have lots of grief."

Brent Spiner agrees and is excited about the opportunities for creative growth syndication allows. "I certainly prefer it. I've never actually met a censor before and I'm not sure I'd like to. I think Gene himself is sort of our censor and he has a certain responsibility to the many fans of Star Trek, and I think he's real sensitive to

that. It's not the same as having some arbiter of taste suddenly decide what is tasteful."

Almost all agree that you'd never see the Edo cavorting semi-nude on ABC. "We're already into shows dealing with certain situations you couldn't do on a network," Michael Dorn believes. "In this day and age of AIDS, networks have a responsibility. They're umbilically tied to their sponsors, but we're not under that type of gun and that's really nice . . . really nice!"

"I think they're going to try and push the limits a little," Frakes says excitedly. "It's interesting, because Roddenberry stories always have little morality plays and so to carry it into the actual production of the show makes the line very thin as to what is appropriate and what's not. I'm curious to see how it's drawn. To have it put in the creator's hands is a very powerful position and I love it. I think he likes it and I hope he handles it appropriately. One wonders if it's appropriate to call someone an S.O.B. at 6 o'clock on a Sunday night."

While the cast acknowledges that the freedom allows for a greater flexibility in addressing contemporary issues, it doesn't mean the new Trek will deal with them in any greater depth than its predecessor. "The old show never did it adequately," Robert Justman says, "but it did it as best it could. What the show says is that mankind will never be perfect, but the thing that makes humanity human is that we're continually attempting to reach perfection. We'll never reach it, but we keep on trying and it's the same thing with the show.

We keep on trying, but we will never be able to do it as well as we would like."

"I think if we were to adequately explore these elements we wouldn't be making a television series, we'd be doing documentaries," says Patrick Stewart. "It's present always, though. There's not been an episode where there has not been a central argument dealing with a moral, psychological or social problem. I think Gene Roddenberry takes very seriously, not solemnly, what has to be done with this series and that each story is taking a view of life and has a point of view."

"A lot of the episodes have been dealing with the need for a vaccine that has infected a planet," adds Frakes, "and that's obviously an important issue now. As well as terrorism and the threat of being overtaken by negative forces."

Despite the sometimes rather forceful attempts by the cast to accentuate the differences between the original *Star Trek* and the new formula, the comparison is one that plagues them like the proverbial carrot on a stick, so it was particularly satisfying when William Shatner allegedly gave his tacit blessing to the endeavor. "One day our cast was eating at the commissary," explains Wil Wheaton, "and Mr. Shatner name up and it was real tense. He said he liked it. When Captain Kirk likes the *Next Generation*, it's a big deal."

"As a friend of mine put it when I accepted the job," Stewart recalls, "how do you think it will feel playing an American icon? It did make me a little uneasy, so I'm happy that people seem to have accepted the

captain as a non-American. The other thing that has pleased me is that people have written and said you are the crew of the Enterprise, and we believe in that crew. They refer to the vivid contrast between the previous captain and myself, not in a competitive way, but in that they are so different there isn't any sense of overlap."

"Some people were afraid of the new *Star Trek* because the old people wouldn't be in it," Justman states. "It was a threat to them. But I don't think that lasted very long. You form new relationships all through life. Sometimes the old relationships are the best, sometimes they're not. But there's room in this work for diversity. People resist change for various reasons. It's just a natural reaction to put a show or an enterprise down out of hand, but it's not very science fiction. The great thing about people interested in science fiction is that they have open minds. They're eager for new ideas. Otherwise, why do anything different? Let's do *Space Patrol*. It was on and people liked it."

Zimmerman agrees that while he has fond recollections of the past *Star Trek*, it does not color his approach to the present and the future design of the show. "I don't think we should be burdened with the past, only instructed by it. We give a nod backwards, but we don't look backwards for inspiration." Similarly, Rob Legato's visual effects work was not drawn from the original's lead. "People don't judge it as a TV show or as special effects. They have a warmer recollection of it, like looking at home movies. You don't look at

them for the photography. It just brings back nice memories."

"We don't want people to forget the old show," asserts LeVar Burton, who plays the blind navigator Geordi LaForge in *The Next Generation*. "We're not trying to supplant in anyone's mind the affection they feel towards the old characters. We just want them to give us the opportunity to be ourselves and judge us based on who we are and not compare us to something that came before us."

Brent Spiner elaborates, "It's the easiest sort of way to approach it. I think that will go away and we'll all be part of the same mold eventually."

Among almost the entire cast and crew, Gene Roddenberry is readily acknowledged as the auteur of *Star Trek*; the man who gave life to the show and oversaw its rebirth. Like Lazarus, Roddenberry supervised a resurrection of sorts which challenged him creatively and emotionally. "It's Gene's vision," Stewart says firmly. "We are caught up and embracing that vision and expanding it, but it belongs to Gene. I feel his hand everywhere and I respect it."

"This show has a style that I don't think any other show has," Frakes speculates. "That style is undefinable, but it exists and comes out of Roddenberry's scripts and thank God he's aboard. He referred to himself the other day as the highest paid rewrite man in Hollywood. He keeps his eyes on every page of every script. It's his show, his vision and we're his players."

Roddenberry's involvement was part of what prompted LeVar Burton to accept the role as Geordi. Burton explains, "I liked the old show an awful lot, and when I heard Gene Roddenberry was also doing this one it said to me that this show was also going to be done right and with taste, dignity and integrity."

Rob Legato puts the unadulterated praise in greater perspective. "It's very interesting. He comes up with some great ideas. They're impossible, but they're great. They just write it and I wet in my pants when I look at it."

Roddenberry has directed his efforts towards refining the stories and the scripts for the series, leaving the massive logistics of keeping the show on schedule and on budget in the capable hands of producers Justman and Rick Berman, who oversee the day to day operations ranging from scheduling to color correction. Justman acknowledges that he shared Roddenberry's emotional reasons for returning to the show nearly twenty years after its cancellation. "When I left *Star Trek* in 1968, it was a disaster. It was a failure as far as the network was concerned and the industry. The only thing that saved *Star Trek* two years in a row were the people who cared about it. By the time the third season rolled around, the handwriting was on the wall and Gene and I both know that it was so. I have a need to return to prove that the show did have value and was successful and could be successful again, and that you can go home again and prove to the people who doubted you that there was value there all along, that this was a worthwhile, if you'll pardon the expression, enterprise."

Not surprisingly, the cast is quite enamored with the ensemble that has been assembled and despite my attempts to discover discord behind the happy family facade, I could not.

"One of the reasons this show didn't take the dive we all feared it would in the back of our minds in comparison to the old show," Frakes says, "is because the characters were so well thought out ahead of time."

Patrick Stewart agrees with Frakes' assessment. "One of the things that makes this show successful is the sense we have of a very distinctive group of individuals working as a cohesive whole."

Dorn laughs in agreement. "This is a very happy set. I think Brent and Jonathan are two of the funniest guys I've ever worked with, and Patrick is a consummate professional with a great sense of humor."

"We have one of the best ensembles in the business," Burton proclaims. "We all respect and admire each other."

"We've always had fun. All the directors have said they've never worked on such a fun set," Marina Sirtis says in her own affable manner. "It's incredible to have actors who get along so well. It's so cliché, but we're all so happy to be here."

"I don't know how they cast this so well," reflects Frakes. "We go out to dinner after 14 hour days. They hired actors who like to act instead of hiring movie stars or models. For virtually all of us, this is the biggest job of our career and we're so happy about that. It's an ensemble and I think it's a good ensemble."

"The company takes on the personality of the leader," Justman says. "There's an old saying and it's a terribly crude expression, that the fish stinks from the head. The old show had that same feeling. We were a family. It's still the same show and it's still the same people doing it with the same personality and the same beliefs. Gene is the great bird of the galaxy and everything comes from him. That's just the way it's been and that's the way it will continue to be."

Denise Crosby, in a brief moment of introspection, reveals what appealed to her about doing *Star Trek.* "There's a lot of personal reasons why one takes a job like this, for me and my career, but also I thought it would be pretty fascinating. It's pop art to me and it's folklore. It's kind of great that way."

One of the other aspects that appealed to the cast was their ability to contribute input during reviews of the scripts prior to filming each episode. "We have a script meeting," reveals Michael Dorn, "and that's when we go through everything. For example, in one scene, Worf, the consummate warrior, is stalking these soldiers and when battle comes, I dodge one bayonet and trip. I said if this guy is the consummate warrior, he doesn't trip on a rock. They go you're right, and change it."

"They do take into consideration how the actors will feel about the scripts," Wil Wheaton says, "which is wonderful. Our characters are like our alter-egos, so I don't want to see the episode where Wesley turns into a brat, because it's not true to his character."

"We discuss what our feelings are and where we have problems," Spiner adds. "I think more than anything else it's a timesaver."

Patrick Stewart reveals that he would not have accepted the offer had he not been granted input into shaping the character. "For years my career has been spent on working on either classic texts with some of the very finest living writers and I have never experienced anything other than a complete openness about the creative process. If I had been denied input into what I say, I would have walked away. I have no interest in being someone else's vision and being totally locked into a third person view of the role."

While trying to downplay comparisons to the original, the new series often offers subtle reminders regarding the inspiration. "The McCoy scene was an extremely sentimental thing to do," Michael Dorn acknowledges of the first episode. "I think they're just trying to be cool about it, and it's sort of a twist because we're saying we're trying to get far away from the old characters . . . but here you go. You could recognize we're trying to say we know where we come from, we know why we're here and we want you to know that we know also, but let us make it on our own merits."

"It was nice," concedes Brent Spiner. "It was really generous to be with us then in the beginning." Frakes concurs. "There are references in the scripts where we go through old data logs and find James Kirk out of respect to the old series. It's been done in very good taste. I don't think there's any way we can or should eliminate the memory of the past."

As far as paying homage to the original inspiration, Wil Wheaton offers his own scripting suggestion.

"I'd like to do 'Mirror, Mirror' again, but who am I to say? I'm only an actor, not a writer damn it." He dismisses the comparisons to the original as groundless when made in the improper context. "If you sequelize a movie, you immediately compare it to the original. With *Alien* and *Aliens*, the only constant was LV-4, the alien and Sigourney Weaver and references were made, of course, to the mission. It was a case where the sequel was equal or better than the original. I think that's what we're doing. We're not trying to discount the original, we are continuing the saga and trekking on."

"We're landlocked on this planet Earth," says Herman Zimmerman. "Probably not very many of us, maybe a few scientists, can appreciate what being in space is. I think the point, however, is philosophically we are talking about our everyday problems. We like stories about ourselves and our problems, and that's what we're interested in. Whether we put them in costumes of the future and generate imaginative settings, we are still dealing with good and evil, love and hate relationships and all of the basic emotions and problems that human beings are running into daily.

"That's one of the things that makes Roddenberry's view of the future so believable. It's a republican view of the future, where life can be easy. You don't have to work at something you don't like. You can find the thing that allows you to contribute and that is what you can do for a living."

Producer Robert Justman attributes the failure of science fiction on television in the past to these concerns and points out *Star Trek's* willingness to grapple with these fundamental questions of existence on and off this planet. "Most science fiction shows were not about people, they were about special effects. They weren't about morality, or [if they were it was] in a very minimal sense. Their people were two-dimensional characters. The shows that are successful deal with the human equation: mankind, the difference between right and wrong. They deal with the things that have intrigued mankind since the dawn of time. Why do you think the Ten Commandments got written? Aesop's Fables? Man is a moral creature who is attempting to achieve a state of grace."

Ultimately, though, the old adage that the more things change, the more they stay the same is borne out. *Star Trek* for all its newfound glitz and '80s maturity, still harkens back to the essential elements which encompassed it in the '60s, and it is still wrestling with the same issues which have intrigued audiences for the last twenty years. "I think the content is much the same as it ever was," says Justman. "While our techniques may be a little slicker [and] the shows may have a better look, I think the show's content is much the same. Just because centuries have passed, we haven't dispensed of the Ten Commandments. They still work.

"I can't say I'm ever satisfied. I'm pleased. I'm never satisfied. The show could be better, but it could be a helluva lot worse. You can't turn out a Picasso every week. Supposedly we're dealing with some kind of art. It's not possible in a collaborative effort to turn out a work of genius once a week. All we can do is attempt to win some and we'll lose others. I think no matter how bad our episodes will be, and some will be really bad, we're trying. You don't make mistakes if you don't try."

A clapboard snaps closed. A voice emanates from the bridge: "We're rolling!" The voice of Captain Picard is growing harder to discern as I leave the soundstage, some extras still mulling around outside. I pause and look back, pondering all of the subculture which the original *Star Trek* has spurred. Thousands of conventions, fan clubs, books, buttons a Saturday morning cartoon, comics, fanzines and the like. Now, only several feet away, the same team which created it all are attempting to recapture the magic which has engaged and challenged the mind of a generation. I can't help but think of the fans who would pay untold fortunes if only to sit in the captain's chair of the Enterprise for a moment. It's quite a sight and quite a cast and crew. Unlike any other set on the Paramount lot, there's something very special going on at Stage 10.

Shaking my head, though, I can't get the sneaking recollection out of mind that has weighed on me my whole visit – the profound remark William Shatner offered on *Saturday Night Live* which is probably the most telling of all: "For God's sake, it's only a TV show!"

PATRICK STEWART
The Man Who Would Be Captain

"I think it is high time that I became involved in some action," Patrick Stewart laughs as he reclines in front of his trailer during a break in shooting the latest episode of *Star Trek: The Next Generation*. "I'm somewhat of a sedentary character and since Riker leads the away teams, he's having all the fun."

Stewart, one of Great Britain's most well respected thespians, has in only several weeks immortalized the character of Captain Jean Luc Picard in the minds of television fans across the country. His other recent works have included *Smiley's People* and *Tinker, Tailor, Soldier, Spy* for the BBC as well as essaying the roles of Gurney Halek in *Dune* and Leondegrance in John Boorman's *Excalibur*. He most recently starred in a London production of *Who's Afraid of Virginia Woolf* for which he was the recipient of the prestigious London Fringe Best Actor Award.

"It's been my lot in life to play a whole list of national leaders, dictators, kings, princes and party bosses, and I've never found that tiresome," he affirms. "For one thing, if you play a king you get to sit down a lot when other people are standing. In this series it tends not to work out that way. I tend to be on my feet all the time."

Pondering the subtext of Picard, Stewart confesses to a fascination with the use of power which is such an essential part of the character's success. "I am truly interested as a human being and as an actor in the use of power; how it is acquired and how it works. I've always been quite a political person and I've always been fascinated with the use of power in politics.

"It was always important to me to try and establish and affirm the quiet, but absolute authority he has on the ship and that seems to be successful. The letters I have received have talked about the authority of the captain, that he is truly a commander and that's important because if you don't have that as an actor playing the role, you're drowning from day one."

While the way in which the characters who Stewart has played in the past have wielded power differently and utilized it for incongruous ends, it is an aspect of the personality which has characterized a large body of his work. In addition, as Stewart readily notes, the structure of *Star Trek* is something he felt at home with as well. "There is truly a classic form to each *Star Trek* story. They have a shape that is exactly in the mold of classic theater. So in that sense and the slightly epic nature of the characters was something that was familiar to me. But at the same time I must be careful not to make that in anyway two-dimensional."

Stewart discards the notion of television as an inferior medium and points to its tremendous impact on society as warranting serious consideration. "It's a medium that has to be taken very, very seriously now. Television, in every area of our lives, is probably the most potent whereas how many people does the theater touch? I'm told we played to over two million people in the Greater Los Angeles area last Sunday night. That's more people that I've played to in a lifetime while acting on the stage."

JONATHAN FRAKES
He's Number One

"I think the costumes look great, but I'm not really crazy about wearing thick spandex," confesses Jonathan Frakes, as he lounges around his trailer in a radiant pink bathrobe. "I like Riker . . . a lot. I've played a lot of sleazy shitheads, so it's nice to play a hero."

Frakes admits to a bit of trepidation over inheriting the mantle of a legendary television series, but it was a challenge he approached with great enthusiasm. "There was alot of skepticism and there was a high potential for failure. There have also been a lot of comparisons with Shatner. I'll take his career, he's quite good. The differences between the two series are so cut and dry, yet the quality has stayed the same."

In the '60s, it was often difficult to draw the distinction between Shatner's on-screen persona and Shatner himself. The same can be said for that of Frakes and his alter-ego, Riker. While Frakes is more relaxed and humorous, he also shares many of the same traits of his celluloid creation and, as a result, is interested in seeing him develop in a manner consistent with his own ideals. "I'd like to see a character have a little more fun, he's really the most stable and straight-laced of the lot. I'd like to go backwards in time to Dixieland, New Orleans and to approach subjects and see what they would be like in the 24th century such as sports and the arts. Now, with the holodeck on the ship, we can go and be anywhere.

"I'm looking forward to developing more of the romance with Troi," he adds, hinting about future romantic entanglements with the attractive Betazoid counselor. "That has sort of been on the backburner lately, but it is an element that needs to be played up. I think it's a good idea to keep that approach/avoidance thing. I think it's titillating to an audience. It certainly worked on *Cheers* and *Moonlighting*. I like that stuff. It's fun."

Among the episodes Frakes cites as his favorite are "The Big Goodbye," an upcoming show which places Riker, Captain Picard, Data and Dr. Crusher in a 1940's Chandler-esque detective yarn while trapped on the holodeck. I spend a lot of time in period costume in that one. I liked in the old *Star Trek* when they beamed down in suits, anything to get out of this costume."

Frakes numbers playing the trombone as one of his most passionate interests along with acting, and ponders whether it is a pursuit he will be able to develop on the show. "I hope I will eventually get to play the trombone . . . somewhere. I could be in a Dixieland Band in *Star Trek* . . . Roddenberry's vision of the future is also so positive that anything is possible."

BRENT SPINER
Data Entry

"Assuming the show goes six years, I think my character is on a journey towards humanity," says Brent Spiner, the Pinnochio of the new *Star Trek* series. "He is a character who is growing because he's amongst humans. I think of him as being very young in terms of how long he's been existing so there's a childlike quality, a naiveté and a wide eyed acceptance of everything going on around him."

Spiner, who has numerous Broadway stage credits to boast of (but doesn't), accepts the comparisons with his illustrious predecessor as the Enterprise's science officer, but draws some important distinctions. "The similarity is in the factual area; information, logic, etc. In every other way, we're complete opposites. I long to be human and he had no interest in even recognizing his own humanity."

Pondering the thought of seeing a replica of himself in the hands of excited little children on Christmas morning (and Chanukah evening) is a thought that stirs mixed emotions in Spiner. "I'm not the most high profile person, but all of that stuff is really part of it all. if I ever feel weird about it, I think Harrison Ford and Alec Guiness had action figures, so if it's good enough for them, it's good enough for me."

Playing an android is an unenviable task for an actor who has to follow in the footsteps of a myriad of spectacular screen android performances. Spiner approached the role from a different perspective. "I sort of just had to start with what was in the script and what was available for me from myself. I didn't see *Making Mr. Right*, because I was afraid I would like what John Malkovich was doing and want to go towards it. My interpretation is as valid as anyone else's as to what an android is going to be like in the 24th century."

Among Spiner's plans for the hiatus are a performance of his one-man play, *The Greenes*, a performance of Lorne Greene reading excerpts from Graham Greene. "I may have Graham Greene doing excerpts from *Bonanza* and in the musical second act Shecki Greene sings Verdi."

Don't expect to see Spiner doing any convention appearances in the near future, though. As the soft-spoken actor readily admits, it's not his cup of tea. "I'm not one for going out into public and saying this is who I really am and destroying this illusion for you that I've been trying to create all year long."

LEVAR BURTON
Giving Sight to Geordi LaForge

LeVar Burton may be fun loving and amiable on the set with his peers, but when it comes down to talking shop about his craft it's time to turn serious. Burton has worked hard to get where he is, he knows it and wants you to know it too. Among his previous works, Burton can boast the hit mini-series *Roots*, the experimental dramatic TV-movie *Emergency Room* and the highly acclaimed children's show, *Reading Rainbow*.

Now he's portraying the blind navigator of the Enterprise, Geordi LaForge, and he's damn happy about it.

"I find that this fits well into my plans and my career," Burton remarks, speaking softly but firmly. "I have always, above all else, wanted to do good work and *Star Trek* is certainly an opportunity to do good work."

His affinity for the character is apparent, although as he readily points out, if he were playing another character he would find all of the

things about that character that he liked. "I like Geordi for a lot of reasons. First of all, his energetic attitude is much more loose than that of a lot of the other characters. He is very loose and speaks his mind. He has a sort of cynical sense of humor and I like that about him. I like the opportunity to play a character who is handicapped, yet that handicap has been turned into a plus for him and there are all the emotional issues that go along with that."

As for the future development of the character, Burton is more reticent and unwilling to put himself in the shoes of the writers. "I've had several conversations with the producers and with Gene, and now that I'm here they really want to make use of me and they're working on it. I'm being patient and letting them do their job and trusting them that their word is as good as their bond. It's a creative process that involves more than just me and what I want for the character. There are certainly many other people who have input in the decision-making in terms of where this character goes. I'm very happy that they respect my opinion and ask for it, but just in terms of the future development of Geordi, it's like throwing pebbles in a pond, it has ripples and repercussions. My job is to come and do my work every day and be patient."

For Burton, unlike many of the other cast members, *Star Trek* is only another facet of a prestigious and continually evolving career which has spanned the last decade. However, it is a job he takes seriously and, in his opinion, demands respect. "I love this job. I love the opportunities to

do these stories with this group of actors, producers and writers and to provide entertainment that also makes you think once in a while. That's what I built a career on and I'm really happy to be able to do it in this framework."

DENISE CROSBY
The Joys of Tasha Yar

Denise Crosby has come a long way since that classic high-camp moment in "Encounter at Farpoint" where she admonishes Q from the floor of his council chamber, "You should get on your knees to Starfleet." Since then, good old Tasha's been abducted by Legonites, launched a fair share of photon torpedoes and recalled visions of the rape gangs which roamed her savage planet. Well, if anything, it's nice to know that not everything is all well and good in the 24th century.

In describing Tasha, Crosby is the first to admit there is a lot more to the character than meets the eye. "The emotional side of Tasha intrigues me as well as her feminine conflicts and being able to establish relationships with people in a trusting way. She's never had that, there's no history of that in her life. There's no family, there's no love."

Among the stories Crosby is particularly interested in seeing occur are those that would involve aspects of human behavior. "I would like to see a kind of romance happen with her where she has that conflict of career and romance. Basically, we're all open to that kind of thing. It's human interest stories, not just the story of babbling aliens."

Crosby is intent on creating a unique character with depth who fans will find appealing, not just one that fulfills Gene Roddenberry's vision of a watered down Jenette Goldstein. "They originally envisioned Tasha as more butch. I think Tasha is reflective of women's roles and what they're trying to achieve at this point. In the '60s, there really weren't too many roles like this. There were things, for instance, like *Julia*, in which Dianne Carroll played a single working mother living on her own, and I think that was revolutionary. If you look back that, it was incredible. It was amazing because women were very much struggling with being pregnant in the workforce and trying to raise kids, as they still are."

Affirming Tasha's distinct multi-facetedness, which ranges from the hands-on security chief to the voluptuous vixen which was unleashed in "The Naked Now" (which was what many fans were probably hoping to see in syndication), Crosby notes, "What I like about this character is she's strong physically and direct and is comfortable with who she is. I envisioned Tasha as what I brought to it. I sort of like the quality there that she could be attractive and sexy and still be able to kick the shit out of anyone."

MICHAEL DORN
For Battle, Come to Him

"This guy is about power and strength," Michael Dorn, the man under the make-up, reveals about the first Klingon Starfleet Academy graduate. "All the other characters have a certain softness, except Tasha, so it's

a compliment. The character is proud of his heritage and proud of his record. This guy's a madman, but he's extremely loyal to his ship and his crew. I use my voice a lot, it's a lot deeper and gone deeper since the shows have gone on."

Reflecting on Klingon heritage, Dorn doesn't find their newfound alliance with the Federation all that unacceptable. "Klingons weren't exactly evil as they were totally aggressive. I approached it with that attitude. They liken it to after World War II and how the Japanese and the Americans worked so closely together, bitter enemies were working together and citizens were in each country. That's taking a page right out of history. Also us and the Russians, you have to have your head in the sand not to believe sooner or later we're going to be friends . . . or, at least, allies."

In preparing to play Worf, Dorn notes that he was not influenced by any of the other classic *Star Trek* Klingon performances. "You knew who they were. You looked at Kruge and said, 'That's Christopher Lloyd,' or Michael Ansara was playing himself — we need no urging to hate humans. That's their thing. With my character, because I'm not well known, I can build it from the ground up. I can make my character totally different and a lot deeper.

"I'd love to have a story where he meets someone from his past," Dorn says, pondering Worf's future adventures. "Either a family member or a love interest – which is always interesting." Of the shows shot so far, Dorn points to "Justice" as one of his favorites. "We were on a Planet of

Lovemakers and there were some great lines that had to do with me and sexuality. I like the ones with a touch of comedy. The fun stuff is what I really enjoy, although the action is always fun. He's always been right in the middles of the battles and fight scenes."

Of all the cast members, next to Wil Wheaton, Dorn is probably the biggest *Star Trek* aficionado, so the opportunity to participate in the saga was particularly exciting. "I said to my agent I want to get on that show somehow. When you get the call, the actor takes over and you have to approach it as just another job. After I got the part, I got all excited. If I hadn't gotten it, I figured I could always guest star."

GATES MCFADDEN
The Doctor is In

Gates McFadden never considered becoming a Pre-Med student when she went to Brandeis University in exciting Waltham, MA in the early 1970s. "I'd rather just slip right into the position at the hospital without the Pre-Med," she jokes. She could have hardly expected to find herself aboard the bridge of the starship Enterprise, tending frozen crewmembers, stricken space travelers and the like, but, of course, that's exactly what she is portraying as Dr. Beverly Crusher, the Enterprise's chief medical officer and mother of the brilliant Wesley Crusher.

"I think it would be interesting to see the women have more relationships," McFadden reveals about her hopes for the future development of the show. "That's an area to explore. I am also fascinated with what medicine is like in the 24th century. Do you do laser surgery? What sort of care does one get? Especially nowadays when you're talking about the depersonalization of medical care and how difficult hospital stays are. Illnesses are changing and people can linger now for years with a debilitating disease. I am interested in delving into issues like that because I find it fascinating."

Having taught and participated in experimental theater for years, the role of a pop icon seems like an unlikely one for McFadden, but it is one she fulfills admirably. "It is an ensemble show and I like the other people who were cast. I felt the producers really wanted me to be a part of it and it was nice to be wanted. I was also impressed with Gene Roddenberry.

"I've had many comments from people who would reinforce the position that we are not just another evening soap," she states vehemently. "There are some philosophical points of view that are presented and that's always going to be part of it."

Some of McFadden's most impressive accomplishments were her involvement with the behind-the-scenes execution of two of Jim Henson's most impressive and ambitious projects, *Labyrinth* and the fantasy segments of *Dreamchild*. A mutual friend had recommended McFadden as a choreographer to Henson, who had already cast her in a small role in his film *The Muppets Take Manhattan*. "I was doing something in Woodstock when he called and said, 'I have this movie *Dreamchild*. Can you fly

over and do it?' I had already done some stuff for him, so I flew over, he briefed me for an hour and took off. He's definitely a baptism by fire guy. I was doing something I had never done in my life – rehearsed for a week, shot a week and was done."

WIL WHEATON
Kid Genius at Large

"It's new to me to play a very smart kid," says Wil Wheaton, the new kid on the *Star Trek* block, literally. "I've always played the nice, down to earth guy, so Wesley is a big change for me."

Wheaton, though, is well aware of the child genius syndrome which can alienate an audience and is anxious to avoid such as Robbie Rist's annoying inept Dr. Z in *Galactica 1980*. "He's precocious, but not intentionally. Our characters are like our alter-egos, so I don't want to see the episode where Wes turns into a brat because it's not true to character. I don't want to see him become the ultimate brain or the stupid little kid. Wes is in the position where he is a teenager with the intellect of an adult. It's not his fault, but he likes it and doesn't try to prevent his intellect from showing. A lot of times it will come across as smart ass, but he doesn't mean it."

The critically acclaimed actor admits to an intense affinity for *Star Trek* and is well aware of the fact he's living out every Trek fan's dream. "This is a big deal for me because I'm a Trekkie. I love the show. It's sort of like the kid who always wanted to be President and is in the White House and gets to meet the President. When

I was a kid I never thought someday I could be in *Star Trek*."

As a fan who's anxious to keep up with all the latest *Trek* memorabilia, Wheaton devours all the latest books, comics and technical manuals. "I justify my purchases of any *Star Trek* items as a business expense. I'm researching my character, thank you very much ... write that off."

Wheaton particularly relishes the thought that *Star Trek V* may be shooting at the same time as *Star Trek: The Next Generation*, assuming the series is renewed for a second season. "I'll get to meet Captain Kirk, Spock, McCoy, Chekov and Uhura." For the moment, though, Wil Wheaton couldn't be happier. "My two passions are surfing and acting. Surfing I can only do at the beach when the waves are okay. Acting I can do every morning and get to work with these wonderful people. It's a learning experience. There's no such thing as the actor who knows everything, because every day you learn something new. I act because I want to. Almost all of the very dedicated actors act because they want to. Everyone on our show is here because they want to be here – they love acting."

MARINA SIRTIS
If I Could Read Your Mind

"I got recognized in the car park ... even with dark glasses on," says Marina Sirtis excitedly. Unlike her on-screen counterpart, Counselor Deanna Troi, Sirtis is a bubbly Brit whose personality bares more of a resemblance to Tracy Ullman than the blushing Betazoid.

Sirtis, who radically transformed her character after the pilot, has undergone the most dramatic character metamorphosis in the series so far. "We felt that the character was a little too intense. There wasn't enough range in Troi. All she seemed to be feeling was a lot of anguish and, as an actress, it would have gotten real boring after two episodes. I watched the pilot with my hand over my eyes, I didn't feel it was working really well.

"If you are telepathic, a psychologist and hugely super intelligent, she would be so understanding, so nice, so forgiving and laid back that she would be the Linda Evans of *Star Trek*. What we want is a little more of the Alexis," Sirtis affirms, alluding to the ABC soap opera *Dynasty*. "I've worked more on developing the human side of her. That's far more interesting to play because she's half human. Human beings are interesting and quirky. The old *Star Trek* episodes which were really fascinating were where Spock's guard dropped or he felt something, not the totally Vulcan thing."

Sirtis is thrilled with being a part of the *Star Trek* phenomena, although she acknowledges her fear of failure in the beginning. "If you look up actress in the dictionary, it says insecurity. This was my Hollywood dream. There's pressure, but it makes me feel really good. The bad part is when you can be knocked down. If it didn't work out, we were going to be destroyed. We're good actors, though, and it's a good show."

One of Sirtis' favorite episodes is "Haven," because of its ironic echoing of a real-life experience she had in her own family. "It's an arranged marriage kind of situation, and being Greek my parents tried to do that to me once. The relationship between me and my mother on the show (Majel Barrett) was so similar to the feelings of me and my mother. I worked harder on that episode than I've ever worked on anything in my life."

Her two most difficult acting challenges are working with props and the dreaded shaking action when the ship is struck by phaser fire or any mysterious force. "We point our phasers and nothing happens. When you see it, this magic blue light comes out. I don't ever have any props, though. They tried to shove some props at me, but I said I'm the mental character, I don't use all that stuff. I don't like using it because if you can drop it or break it, I will drop it or break it.

"I'm not adept at the shaking action either," she laughs. "I thought everybody shook better than me. I can't take it seriously, though. Maybe it's because I'm British. The Americans shake and do it really well and I'm on the floor doubled up with laughter. If my drama teachers could see me now they would die."

Sirtis, whose American Visa was rapidly expiring when she got the role, admits to a passion about her vocation and her role in the ensemble cast of *Star Trek*, despite the 17-hour days and hectic shooting schedules. "I've always said I act for free, they pay me for waiting around."

THE FERENGI
Another Day, Another Dollar

With the Klingons as allies of the Federation and the Romulans banished to somewhere in television never-never land, *Star Trek* needed a new villain. The creators also knew that they didn't want these new antagonists of Starfleet to be simple retreads of any of the rogues the old Enterprise had faced before. Enter the Ferengi.

The Ferengi are nasty and diminutive little creatures who, in the words of Jonathan Frakes, are the ultimate capitalists. "I think that's fascinating," he states. "I don't know if it's played clearly enough. They don't do anything unless they make a profit from it. They're not physically threatening."

"The bad guys this time are not consummately evil," says production designer Herman Zimmerman. "I think Gene is kind of tongue-in-cheek with the Ferengi because he makes them the merchants of the universe, the money lenders and the profiteers."

Designing the Ferengi technology was a more daunting task for Zimmerman and his crew. "We are, as humans, subject to our imagination. We can only put together something new from something old. We can only create something new out of bits and pieces of what we are familiar with. The Ferengi ship was compared to a horseshoe crab in the description from the writers. We endeavored to make it a machine version of that kind of ship, assuming that it was a natural creature's body that the Ferengi, for whatever reason, found pleasing.

"The color was a rust tone on the exterior," he adds, "and a greenish cast to the interior. I think we've got a lot of graphics in the Ferengi ship. The Ferengi keep their bridge very bright because they have poor eyesight. One of the reasons they have such big ears is that they've developed their hearing to compensate for their poor eyesight."

The largest miniature of the Ferengi ship is approximately two and a half feet long. There are three other Ferengi models, which are all used for different aspects of visual effects shooting. One can be fully articulated for use in close-ups. "It's more nimble than the Enterprise," explains visual effects coordinator Rob Legato. "It's smaller, it's more like the difference between a Corvette and a Lincoln Continental. It's a bizarre looking ship, that has to be appear ominous. They're cunning little schmucks who piss everybody off."

The Enterprise is bright and white, cheery and happy," Legato adds. "This is like the people – grim, small and nasty. Parts of it extend. The nose extends out and the armament comes down and folds out from the bottom. It's smooth and it's bird-like. It's not like the Bird of Prey, but it's in that family. It's more organic looking than the *Battlestar Galactica* or *Star Wars* glued ships where they glue various parts of models on top of things."

PART III
WHAT'S WRONG WITH STAR TREK: THE NEXT GENERATION
by Mark A. Altman

Mark A. Altman, currently editor-in-chief of Sci-Fi Universe, *penned an insightful review of the early days of* Star Trek: The Next Generation *in 1987. That review is reprinted below with permission of the author.*

Perhaps the harshest and most unfair way of critiquing the future is by judging it against the past, yet it is probably the only way in which *Star Trek: The Next Generation* can be approached. Judged on its own merits, the successor to the 1966-69 run of *Star Trek* is a slickly produced and intelligent science fiction show. However, despite pleadings to the contrary by members of *The Next Generation* cast, *Star Trek* must be approached as a cohesive whole which has undergone a discernible evolution. Thus the present should not only be compared to the past for nostalgia's sake, but demands to be in order to assess the growth of the saga's premise. It is in this sense that *Star Trek* has failed so far. The newest incarnation of *Trek* in mimicking the structure of the original: teaser, dramatic conflict, and coda has failed to incorporate into it any of the changes in the medium that have occurred in the last twenty years, most notably the multi-story ensemble drama for which MTM is most renowned.

There can be no doubt that in creating a nine-member ensemble, Roddenberry was not only attempting to distinguish his latest effort from the original, but emulate the ensemble dramas which have become a staple of contemporary television. Yet the new *Trek*'s ensemble is a series of stick figures who repeatedly replay the one-line descriptions that have been set down in the Writer's Guide. This fault cannot be attributed to the fine acting ensemble since the show, for the most part, was impeccably cast, but to the writers who have failed to color the one-dimensionality of the protagonists. There are no shades of gray, only black and white. Unlike *Hill Street*'s Dennis Franz, who portrayed Norman Buntz, or *L.A. Law*'s Douglas Brackman, *Trek* has no moral ambiguity to its players. Without greater dramatic conflicts within and between characters, the external and depersonalized conflicts of the Enterprise vs. the universe seems less pressing. Essentially *Trek* has taken a step backwards instead of forward. *Star Trek* cannot and should not attempt to be what it once was (and even less so, try to draw inspiration from the feature films). It must attempt to redefine the concept and expand upon it. Roddenberry's universe is the ideal one in which to explore the contemporary issues of the day and grapple with the moral questions which confront mankind. Unfortunately, *Star Trek* has chosen to manifest these ideas in only the basest of terms, often taking the shape of a mysterious alien force menacing the Enterprise. To see these issues explored within the context of the present cast in confronting their duties is far more effective than introducing a load of hocus pocus which can disable the Enterprise with a single strike and then be just as easily dismissed with a closing speech by Picard. Why should mankind aspire to the stars if every unknown he meets is superior and judgmental? Rather than deal with these epic (and ultimately passive) engagements in a benign and overtly intellectualized manner, it would be far more interesting to see present day conflicts transposed to the 24th century and see how our crew approaches them.

To say that *Star Trek* cannot adequately address questions of social relevance and make it entertaining is ludicrous. *Lou Grant, Hill Street Blues, L.A. Law* and *St. Elsewhere* are all shows that haven't sacrificed the quality of their entertainment while still retaining a social conscience. It strikes me as the height of absurdity to liken the AIDS crisis to the need for a vaccine in "Code of Honor" or to the intoxication of "The Naked Now." If you're going to make the pretense of dealing with morality, then do it. Let's see the Enterprise go to a world where a minority of indigenous aliens are subjugated to a minority of human colonists and see how our crew deals with it. Perhaps Worf would find nothing wrong with the Social Darwinist aspects of apartheid and it would make a clearly interesting contrast to the liberal leanings of Captain Picard.

Syndication was offered as a panacea for removing the constraints of network censorship, and yet the new show has been far more tame in its approach to the world than its predecessor. Showing scantily clad women in "Justice" and calling the deus ex machina of the episode God instead of Vaal isn't really taking advantage of the freedom of self-censorship, it's wasting it. What is the point when "The Apple" dealt with a similar situation and did it better? While a strange sense of deja vu has pervaded many of the episodes, nowhere was it more evident than in "The Naked Now," a homage to "The Naked Time" at best and a trite and shallow imitation at its worst. The plot is a familiar one and is obviously ideal for acquainting us with the new Enterprise crew.

Unfortunately, the deeper emotions which the crew display are not fully realized. Beneath Tasha's Rambo-ette veneer of violence is a smoldering sexuality and embitterment (Viewers can only wonder what this Sigourney Weaver clone looks like in *her* underwear). Yar's strength emanates from the emotional traumas of her youth, yet these qualities are not explored in order that the episodes' alleged humor can be accentuated. Likewise Data, who is presented to us as an android infected by a biolog-

ical disease, which leads me to believe he is more similar to a genetic replicant – to steal a phrase from Philip K. Dick. However, Data refers to his circuitry in an episode, which makes it unclear as to what an android is defined as in the series. It's important to remain true to the facts of your established universe in order for a show requiring such a substantial commitment to the willing suspension of disbelief to retain its credibility.

Riker is clearly a leader in the Kirk mold, yet he possesses none of the darker qualities which made Shatner's early portrayal of the starship captain so intriguing. Kirk's obsession with his ship and self-reliance, coupled with an air of self-importance, helped elevate Shatner's Kirk into the pantheon of pop culture hero. Unfortunately, through Frakes, Riker has yet to display any of the tendencies which would make us believe he's anything but a moderate's version of Ollie North. Perhaps that's an exaggeration, but I feel Riker is one of the series' most interesting characters and warrants further attention from the show's scriptwriters. Certainly the show's best episode "Haven," was a step in the right direction.

One of the aspects of Riker's dossier which is most interesting is his past romance with Ilia, uh, Troi, which is only dealt with in the pilot and bears a striking resemblance to what Roddenberry was trying to achieve in *Star Trek: The Motion Picture* between Will Decker and Ilia. While having each episode end with them bathing in a holodeck hot-tub, like Captain Furillo and Joyce Davenport, would not necessarily be

preferable to their present asexuality, it would be nice to see some romance onboard as well as emotional entanglements and romantic complications, particularly noting the length of their mission. Both Tasha and Troi are obviously very sexually inclined and there's no reason to believe that a devotion to Starfleet should force them to abandon relationships with other members of the Enterprise crew. A romance between Worf and Tasha seems as though it could be particularly interesting, perhaps such a relationship would help establish the narrative continuity which *Star Trek* seems so desperately in need of. The new *Star Trek* readily lends itself to the narrative form utilized so adeptly by shows like *Crime Story*, in which each episode deals with one story but carries its subplots over from week to week.

One of the greatest obstacles inhibiting *Trek* from fulfilling its full potential is Roddenberry's strong hand in the show's continuing development. There can be little doubt that he has succeeded in populating his universe with characters who can be just as interesting, if not more so, as the original players. The problem, though, lies in his utopian and occasionally naive view of the future. *Star Trek* has never been particularly educated in its approach to politics, as evidenced by the way issues were dealt with in the original series, including the Vietnam quagmire for "A Private Little War," which can be seen as supporting American intervention in the conflict, and in the new show in which the Ferengi seem to be a communist's perception of a capitalist taken to comic extremes.

However, the serious conceptual flaws seem to be in Roddenberry's view of human nature. While it is fair to assume that mankind can mature and eventually live in harmony, ultimately reaching out to explore the uncharted reaches of space, it is foolish to assume that such vices as greed, ambition, selfishness and hedonism will simply cease to exist. As a result, it is the fight to prove to ourselves that we are moral creatures that is inherently interesting. There is no need for aliens to act as catalysts for human introspection. If all the evils of the world have been redressed in 300 years, leaving only upstanding and accommodating beings in the universe, then how can a 20th century audience relate to these characters and empathize with their situations? It is impossible to deal with our socially relevant issues in the framework of a society which doesn't have any socially relevant problems.

The first feature film, which was under the auteurship of Roddenberry, failed to engage audiences because the characters' situations were too far removed from their own reality and the interaction between the characters too infrequent and uninteresting (the reverse may also account for the tremendous popular acceptance of Nimoy's fourth installment in the series). The new series seems to have fallen prey to the same failings which made Roddenberry such a brilliant conceptualist, but one whose skills lie other than in the execution. The same Roddenberry philosophy which

led to the Organian Peace Treaty barring conflict between the Klingons and Starfleet has accounted for the annoyingly infrequent fisticuffs and space confrontations which livened up the intellectual content of the first series. No one is saying *Star Trek* should only be social commentary, it shouldn't. It is a vital component though of what makes *Star Trek* unique in the canon of visual science-fiction works. But if the new show is to succeed on the action/adventure level for which the original first garnered its following, there must be more physical as well as emotional conflict. The same criticisms that plagued *Star Trek: The Motion Picture*, that the cast was only a bunch of wooden figures on the bridge staring out into space the whole movie, can easily be made of the new show. There's nothing wrong with Roddenberry's disdain for violence, but perhaps this sentiment would be expressed more effectively if the implications of aggression were made more clear. Nothing is a more haunting indictment of war than the casualties it claims. *Star Trek* is capable of illustrating this occasionally while still retaining the rousing fight scenes which helped make episodes such as "Shore Leave" so enjoyable.

There is a happy medium between the pedantic pacifism of the new series and the gung-ho jingoism of the movies. I have no doubt that Roddenberry is capable of finding this niche. He just should remember

that before he can make us believe in solar Starfish he has to give us credible and fully realized characters who have the same human frailties that we all do. In trying to find the future, Roddenberry has overlooked the present and, perhaps even more importantly, the past. By ignoring the essential ingredients which made *Star Trek* a classic, he is condemning the new show to a life of mediocrity. *Star Trek* was not a good television show because of its structure or because of the starship Enterprise, but because in each episode the viewer invested themselves in the characters and the conflicts they faced. Because Kirk cared about the Enterprise, so did we. To see Picard's 1701-D explode in front of us would be far less disturbing than the threats which imperiled the original ship and the penultimate (if silly) moment in *Star Trek III* in which Kirk destroys the Enterprise.

The original cast were human beings who were dealing with the unique dilemmas the '60s posed. At that time, *Star Trek* was a groundbreaker. Now it is a different era full of complicated problems, including the dangers of space exploration, which was so vividly illustrated by the Challenger disaster. Maybe this is the point with which Roddenberry should make his most fervent rebuttal and reassert *Star Trek*'s lead as a trendsetter and a show which warrants all the attention which has been lavished on it.

PART IV
STAR TREK: THE NEXT GENERATION
Season One Overview

The following section – previously unpublished – was written early in the run of Star Trek: The Next Generation. As a result, some of it may seem dated, but it nonetheless provides an inside look at the early days of the show from the standpoint of creating the first season episodes.

The premiere or pilot of any television show is usually considered more significant than all other episodes of a series, for the simple reason that it lays down the groundwork for the ensuing weekly version. Here, the premise is set up, the primary characters introduced and the audience given the opportunity to determine whether or not these are people they care about, and if their adventures are worth following week after week.

In other words, it's a crap-shoot, and depending on the roll of the dice, the series will either be a winner or a disaster.

Ironically, for all intents and purposes *Star Trek: The Next Generation* had had seventy nine live action, twenty two animated and four feature film pilots, and yet the worry was still there. This *Star Trek* would be featuring an entirely new cast in a show that was similar to, yet different than, the original. Added to this was the fact that the audience for this type of show had changed since the sixties, and one had to wonder what elements from that distinct time period would still work some two decades later. Would the current generation be as socially conscious as its predecessor?

Producer Robert Lewin, who was involved with *The Next Generation* throughout most of its first season, feels that bringing *Star Trek* back to television was a unique challenge.

"I thought starting from ground level was the only way to go," he says. "The old show was not a big hit originally, and became a big hit during the seventies because the ideas being dealt with were advanced. While the show looks primitive now, it has a lot of content. Here, the idea was to provide the same content in a 1987 capsule; within 1987 parameters.

"We were all very, very excited about it," he adds. "The difficulty has been that the public is extremely sophisticated and the ideas that seemed new and revolutionary in the early show are no longer revolutionary. The possibility of getting new and revolutionary ideas in today's marketplace is difficult, so we struggled with that. Also, the basic idea was that the new ship had to be enormous and highly advanced, and in order to do that it needed a larger complement of command people. So we ended up with a very large crew on the bridge, and in trying to deal with the three main elements of the show – ideas, adventure and personalities – it has been a difficult combination to get exactly the best episodes possible out of each idea. Some of the shows are uneven, and some are excellent.

"Part of the problem is due to the fact that the first year of any television series is really a shake-down. I remember when I worked for Quinn Martin and he was struggling with *The Fugitive*. He said he learned how to do the show by *listening to the show*. The show told him what it had to become, and that you could not force your ideas into the show. The show had to tell you, as long as you listened to it. That's what's going on in *Star Trek*. We started out with preconceptions, and some of them were very difficult to execute. It was a stimulating process, though, because we were trying to cover new ground. We discussed themes for stories and in trying to make those themes work in an adventure format, sometimes we could do it and sometimes we couldn't. We began to struggle with trying to create what we thought would be the best approach and found, as we began to work, that the show began to talk to us. 'You can't do this because (a) it's too talky and (b) the characters are not going to be developed enough.' Now we're finding that there are better ways to go. I think that more emphasis will be placed on individual relationships, which will probably be quite different than they are now on the show. But in order to deal with human beings in a framework we can understand now, we have to deal with them on a 'now' basis."

Katharyn Powers, one of the writers behind the third episode of *The Next Generation* titled "Code of Honor," wonders if today's audience will react the same way to *Star Trek* as yesterday's did. "Remember, the show in the '60s caught on very slowly," she relates. "At first, it was your basic 20 percent hardcore science fiction audience, but then after it went into syndication it began to grow and cross over into general audience appreciation. Now, *Star Trek: The Next Generation* has so many more people who are going to be watching and the potential is that much greater. I also think that they're going to try to say something to everybody, but whether everybody will be up to listening or more up to watching the pizzazz, we'll have to wait and see. Today's youth are not burning with curiosity to solve the great questions of the day. Certainly the potential is there to do the same kind of intellectual probing of mankind's position in the universe, and his responsibilities, although I don't know how many people are going to want to hear that right now."

Writer Tracy Torme, most recently Creative Consultant on the series, became involved with *The Next Generation* as a freelance writer shortly after the show's inception.

"I guess one of the most exciting things was watching the show grow from scratch," he recalls, "because

when I was first involved with them, they hadn't cast anything and they really hadn't built any of the sets. It was all still in Gene Roddenberry's head. The exciting thing for me was watching it take place from the ground floor up; seeing the visualization of the characters in the sense that when I first heard about Riker, Picard and the others, I had no idea what they were going to look like or what the ship was going to look like. So I've seen some subtle changes that they've made in the characters in terms of their names, backgrounds and so on. Someday it will be interesting to look back to see where it all started from.

"I think one of the strengths of this series is that it is *not* a clone of the original," he elaborates. "Gene has made a real point of having this show stand on its own two feet, and I think he's gone out of his way to do that. He doesn't want to draw too much at all from the old show. That's a big gamble, and I respect him for taking such a chance. I think the show has been quite updated and the characters are much more for the 1980s than the 1960s."

Richard Krzemien, a writer who had penned a script for the revised *Twilight Zone* as well as the story for "The Last Outpost" episode of *The Next Generation*, believes that Roddenberry's involvement gives this show's revival a better chance at survival than that of *Twilight Zone*, which was forced to go on without the contribution of the late Rod Serling.

"Gene's being executive producer is a good aspect of the show," he enthuses. "In some ways it's evolving from the first three years of the

show where . . . if someone else had been producing the series, there might be an entirely different tone to it. I think that Roddenberry is bringing to it a continuity that it really needs. It's sort of what wasn't there, in some ways, with *The Twilight Zone*. Obviously Rod Serling couldn't produce the series, but there was a certain vision that started that show, and a certain energy and a way of carrying that vision that Serling did best. And he found a couple of people who helped him create it. He had his hand in all the shows, and I think the vision changed drastically when Phil DeGuere took over the series. Whether it was good or bad, other people can decide that, but it wasn't the same show. I think it's a positive aspect to have Roddenberry still around to be able to produce, and that's because it can have a continuity to it. He pretty much sets the direction and it's like a flagship leading the cruisers behind it. I think that's the advantage of having somebody who knows the vision of the show. He demands such high standards, so it's trying to dictate what those standards are twenty years later. How do you top yourself?

"How do you recreate values from 20 years ago, given a certain time and a certain age, and what has kept the series alive for all of this time?" Krzemien asks rhetorically. "This isn't a fluff show like most of the things on television. They were taking chances by looking at the human condition. That's what makes it so hard to write for *The Next Generation*. You can't just come up with an action shot and have somebody run across a field and get shot. You have him running across a field and they ask you *why* he's running across the field. And why is he getting shot? Why does he die? You have to answer all those questions, because if you can't, then it's wrong. If it doesn't make sense in the larger context of the story, then that's wrong too. So it takes a long time to write story ideas for the show."

Despite the enthusiasm of the staff, the question still remained: how would *Star Trek: The Next Generation* kick off its premiere season? The answer came in the form of "Encounter at Farpoint," written by Dorothy Fontana and Gene Roddenberry, which began with the galaxy class starship Enterprise on its maiden voyage to Farpoint Station, where it will pick up First Officer William Riker, Chief Medical Officer Beverly Crusher, her son Wesley, and navigator Geordi LaForge. Enroute, it is boarded by an alien being identifying itself simply as Q, who demands that Captain Jean Luc Picard turn the Enterprise around and head back in the direction from which it came. Q accuses the captain and all of mankind of being a savage, barbaric and war-like species that does not deserve to venture into the far reaches of space. Picard argues this, pointing out that man has reached maturity and that the barbarism the alien speaks of is centuries behind them. Q is absolute in his belief, refusing to listen to Picard's words, although he does admit that it will be intriguing to watch the humans futilely try and prove their case. This ultimately leads to Picard and company being brought to a 21st Century court, wherein Q, who has a penchant for changing costumes, is

now serving as judge. Again, Picard defends his species, with Q eventually determining that the opportunity for Picard to prove himself will occur at Farpoint Station.

Once arriving there, and after new personnel transfer to the Enterprise, Commander William Riker, who now serves as Enterprise's Number One, informs Picard that anything a person could want materializes at the mere thought; that somehow thought is transferred in to energy, and that thought becomes a reality. Before they can give this potential problem much consideration, a much larger spacecraft arrives and begins firing energy beams at the city below, causing massive destruction.

Ultimately we learn that this alien spacecraft is, in actuality, an alien being capable of shape-changing, and that the city below – Farpoint Station, essentially – is also a living creature that is the first one's mate, who has been held as a virtual prisoner, forced by the inhabitants of that world to grant their every wish. Enterprise supplies the city-creature with enough energy to break free, while simultaneously proving mankind's tolerance and understanding of other life forms, reinforcing the point that the human race has every reason to be this far out in space. The creatures depart, as does Q, although *he* doesn't promise that they've seen the last of him [and this is one promise that is most definitely kept].

Overall, this was a very exciting opening for *Star Trek: The Next Generation*, serving as a fine introduction of the new Enterprise crew, while presenting a fascinating antagonist. All of this is only marred by Q's con-

demnations of mankind as a barbaric species, which is rather old hat by now. Still, the two hour pilot manages to capture the best elements of the old show, while paving the way for the new.

A great deal of the credit for the premiere's success must be given to actor John DeLancie, whose abilities so successfully brought Q to life and made him a very real and tangible threat to the Enterprise crew. In fact, to make the whole thing more realistic for *him*, DeLancie created a background history for Q.

"I wanted to know who 'Q' was before we saw him here," relates DeLancie. "There may be a bunch of 'Qs', maybe fifteen of them, who operate way above the human plane. We're really talking Gods here; minds that grasp far more than the human mind is able to. Maybe he's one of the young Qs who's sitting around a table, hardly ever being asked any opinions about anything. He hears that these humans are coming into this sacred sector of the universe that they simply haven't come in to, and the general thought is that they pollute everything they come in contact with. I volunteer, 'Listen, I'll go out and I'll handle them.' 'You think so?' 'Yeah, sure. Can I dress up?' 'You can do anything you want, as long as you clear them; as long as we know that they're not here to disrupt.' 'Great, I'll see you later.'

"Listen," the actor elaborates, "we could sit down and talk about humans being born of Zeus, but I was trying to come up with a thing that permitted . . . he shoots from one to the other to the other, and then he relinquishes quite quickly. When he discovers that humans do indeed have a capacity, he relinquishes. In a wonderful way, he's got kind of an amorality to him. He's not encumbered with an opinion. He just wants to get the facts. He's not here to promote his point of view. He's out there to figure out what you're about, and as long as what you're about is okay, then everything else is okay.

"If it isn't, God help you," DeLancie laughs, adding that he took this line of thinking a bit further, trying his best to analyze exactly what sense of power "Q" held over the Enterprise crew, particularly Picard. "This is all hypothesizing, which is actor talk, but I had thought that it would be interesting that the punishment is an unraveling of Picard; a genetic unraveling of him so that he, in his attempt to make a final mark as he's getting older, or desire to leave something behind . . . his punishment – what he has at risk – is that I can make him disappear, not only from everyone, but from himself. I can turn him, in fact, into a non-entity, so he has something to push against. Not only does he want to be right, but he doesn't want to lose the essence of Picard and all the Picards that were before. We were just talking about the things that enrich any project. You can have the same discussions about Shakespeare and then go out and play it, but it doesn't mean your playing of it is going to be particularly different from the person who played it before you. But if it gives you something to work on, then that's fine.

"That's the fun of a good script. A good script allows you to think. There are lots of scripts that are so bad that they have no possibility of

discussion, whereas you and I can sit down over a drink and talk about all sorts of possibilities about this script because it's well written."

* * *

Television science fiction has often suffered from the fact that its budget has never been strong enough to support the necessary special effects that the scripts usually call for. Exceptions to this have been "V", which was actually a mini-series, so therefore had the time and budget to do the effects right, and the original *Star Trek*, which relied more on powerful scripts and the acting abilities of its cast to make up for its rather low budget F/X. Due to the expense of doing the show, chintzy effects or not, every fourth episode or so had to be a completely shipboard show.

This particular problem raised its head again when Paramount attempted to resurrect the show in the mid 1970s as *Star Trek II*, and once again with the plans for *Star Trek: The Next Generation*. Actually, this budgetary dilemma was more pronounced on the latter, because the audience would no longer sit still for anything less than the best in special effects, no matter how good the scripts and acting were. Everyone involved with the new version of the show was aware of this, and that's why it was decided early on that every other show would have to be a shipboard show. As fans would soon discover, that ratio increased quite a bit throughout the first and second season, with very few shows actually taking place off the Enterprise.

Bearing all of this in mind, Gene

Roddenberry looked back at the original show's "The Naked Time," one of his favorite episodes, and one which, he felt, managed to explore some of the inner layers of the show's main characters. For instance, we learned the turmoil within Mr. Spock that was waged between his Vulcan and human halves, the fact that Captain James T. Kirk was more in love with his ship than he could ever love a woman, and that it was something he actually resented; Lieutenant Kevin Riley fancied himself a starship commander and Lieutenant Sulu was something of a swashbuckler at heart. This was no small feat in a one hour show, and it was something that Roddenberry wanted to use to provide insight into the new characters.

"The same basic story holds true," explains Paul Lynch, who would eventually direct the resulting episode, "The Naked Now", "in that the Enterprise contracts something from another ship and the crew begins to change. Because it's a new cast, they change accordingly. Everybody drops the way they are and lets their inhibitions come out. I'd say that 'The Naked Now' is slightly more adult and a lot more comic than the original. In that show, one of the guys [Sulu] picked up a sword and started running around with it. In this, it's much more of a character change in the way of romance and strangeness leading towards humor. Everybody in the show is affected by it in different ways, but not that dissimilar. For instance, while one person might be affected by becoming more amorous in a serious way, someone else becomes amorous in a lighter sense. It's all quite subtle compared to the original, because the original episode was quite heavy-handed, like most of the original episodes were."

Roddenberry, after studying "The Naked Time," decided to do a sequel (in actuality a remake), and produced thirteen pages of a teleplay entitled "Revelations," which begins with the Enterprise receiving a distress signal from the starship Tsilkovsky; a signal interrupted by a female voice wondering if there are any "pretty boys" aboard the Enterprise. Then, a moment later, an emergency hatch is blown, effectively killing the crew of that starship. Our people beam over, and Geordi LaForge is the first to contract the disease. Once back on the Enterprise, he makes a move on Tasha which he later brushes off as a joke, but contact has been made and the disease spreads. Moments later, she suggests that the two of them work out their moves together in an exercise room. In the meantime, Picard calls a meeting of his key officers to explore the situation aboard the Tsilkovsky, and that's where the Roddenberry material leaves off.

It should be pointed out that much of this script eventually made it to the air, but not without a valiant attempt by Dorothy Fontana to make some sweeping changes and give it a harder edge. Primary among the things she wanted to excise was a preoccupation with sex that these pages suggest. For instance, the initial communiqué from the Tsilkovsky wants to know if there are pretty boys on board the Enterprise. Then Geordi and Tasha get the hots for each other, all of which is a bit disconcerting, detailing nothing about the characters

except for the fact that they're a horny bunch.

Fontana's first draft teleplay had the ship threatened by a collapsing star, while the crew is affected in considerably different ways. Geordi remains the carrier who wishes he had normal eyesight, and bemoans the fact that he doesn't, but the first person he comes into contact with is Wesley, who, like Kevin Riley from "The Naked Time," fancies himself in command of the Enterprise. Then, Tasha is determined to come up with a softer, more feminine look, and comes on to Data, but he politely refutes her advances, pointing out that he cannot help her cope with these emotional needs, although he wishes he could. However, the disease has touched the android, and the result is that he tries his best to behave like a "good human boy" so that he will – believing in the tale of Pinocchio, the legend he identifies with most – become human. Beverly, meanwhile, is frustrated at being the widow of a hero, because she is considered "sacred ground," and for that reason men in general are afraid to approach her as a woman. She has the need for a man, and Picard is the person she turns her attention to, although the captain is resistant to her considerable charms.

As the disease reaches Troi, she finds herself overwhelmed by the emotions of all the people around her, and proclaims that she hates never being alone in her own mind. Riker helps her and is affected, stating that he should proclaim his love for her, instead of denying it. He is also fearful that he will go the route of many potential starship captains,

living life alone without the comfort of a woman.

Elsewhere, Picard is affected, finding himself distraught when he learns that a chunk of the exploding star may be blown out towards them, and the ship is incapable of moving due to engineering problems. Ultimately, he turns to Data, confessing that he fears for the lives of his crew and their families, and that he doesn't know if he could handle anything happening to the children on board. Ultimately, and before any serious damage can be done, Beverly Crusher comes up with a cure to the disease and everyone reverts to normal.

In short, this proposed version of "The Naked Now" is far more effective than its final form would be, this despite the fact that the story is really the same. It's the tone of the piece that is far more effective than Roddenberry's previous and subsequent rewrite of it. This is, as was stated earlier, due to the fact that Fontana's outline is not preoccupied with sex, instead doing exactly what this story was intended to do in the first place: providing insight to the new characters.

For instance, while Geordi and Wesley would be affected in much the way they were here, Tasha does not become a horny bimbo. Instead, she wants to be recognized as a woman instead of as a security officer; she wants to strip away her hard exterior and reveal a softer side. Beverly, while still longing for a man's companionship, points out that as the widow of a Starfleet hero, no man will come near, considering her "sacred ground." This is a wonderful character bit, and it was a shame to lose.

The effect that the disease has on Troi is wonderful, pointing out how difficult it must be for an empath to be surrounded by the confusing minds of humans. Picard's fear of harm coming to the children fits the character perfectly, reinforcing his statement from "Encounter at Farpoint" that he is not a family man, and is uncomfortable around youngsters. Still, he is concerned about them and his fear of forfeiting their lives is a very nice touch, possibly bringing up the point that he considers them, in one way or another, *his* children.

Data's desire to be a real-life "boy" is a natural development for the character, as he has pointed out that he would give up all of his superior abilities to have the chance of being human. Riker's reaction to the disease, however, is probably the best. We learn that he sees himself traveling down the same path as such starship captains as James T. Kirk and Jean Luc Picard, and he is afraid of it. Half of him wants the intimacy of a starship command, while the other half yearns for female companionship. The struggle between the two is an ongoing one, and it will undoubtedly plague him for the rest of his life.

Unfortunately, in the rewritten – and aired – version, Geordi and Wesley are affected in pretty much the same way. Tasha is looking for sex and is willing to come on to a crewman in a corridor or Data. The android, instead of yearning to be human, merely acts goofy and proves that he can do *anything* a man can do. Beverly gets the hots for Picard and the captain, in turn, acts like a teenager with a bad case of puppy love. Riker is essentially unaffected,

and Troi wants to know if he would like to spend "time" with her. Where's the character development? Where's the insight into their thinking? It's gone, as simple as that. There really are no comparisons between the two versions. Fontana's original is far superior and it's really unfortunate that it was not used in the actual episode.

Director Paul Lynch, despite these faults, felt excitement about the episode and the idea of doing a new *Star Trek* television series.

"The main difference," he says, "is that the production has changed over the years. The production design of the ship and the costumes and all of that are much more futuristic 'modern' than the old series. The original show always looked like it cost a dollar ninety eight with four walls painted blue. The engine room, in the old ship, was a painting. The new engine room looks like it belongs in a spaceship in reality. It's wonderful and quite stunning."

Lynch believes that the new *Star Trek* will be every bit as successful as the original, *if* people come to it with an open mind and don't expect a re-tread of the first series. In addition, he's confident that the show has found its own direction, having overcome the Yin/Yang stigma of having to live up to the legend that *Star Trek* has become.

"What they're staying with," explains Lynch, "is the old morality play system of stories, and they've gotten a cast that is absolutely wonderful. Staying with the same kind of stories with a very strong cast, I would assume that the people who love the original *Star Trek* will hopefully come

over to it, and if they will accept the new characters, which is the key thing, then I would think they would accept it on the same basis as they accepted the original.

"I think they're starting with a known audience for a certain kind of show," he concludes, "and they want to give them that kind of show. I think that through the first six or eight episodes you'll see *Star Trek* in a new way that's appealing. This is not Leonard Nimoy or Bill Shatner. It's a different group of people in a different situation in a future beyond that time, getting involved in compelling situations with wonderful special effects. I can't imagine what more an audience could want."

Judging by the success of *The Next Generation*, not much.

* * *

"When I was started writing episodic television," explains Katharyn Powers, who, with co-writer Michael Baron penned the "Code of Honor" episode of *Star Trek: The Next Generation*, "I began on *Kung Fu*. There were many shows 10 to 14 years ago that seemed to have richer characters and more emphasis on story. Looking at the new season, I'm not impressed. I was involved in *Logan's Run*, *Fantastic Journey*, *How the West Was Won*, *Young Pioneers* and *Petrocelli*. These shows were very interesting to write for, and *Star Trek: The Next Generation* was an opportunity, for the first time in years, to address the bigger issues, the human issues; do interesting characters and go out of the realm of the *Falcon Crest/Dallas* soap opera mentality. I'm not that excited about writing for those shows, so the inspiration for 'Code of Honor' was to combine interesting characters with interesting problems, juxtaposed with this wonderful new cast. And even though it's a new cast, they still wanted to have the same kinds of *Star Trek* stories, the same feeling of camaraderie and family. To prepare for the script, we watched many of the old episodes and the movies to immerse ourselves in 'space.'"

"There's a great deal of potential in the characters," interjects Michael Baron. "They're interesting and there are many ways they can react off of each other. It's obvious that what happened with the earlier *Star Trek* was that the characters evolved into a wonderful family. If the same magic happens with the actors in this show, I don't see why it can't be as successful. One thing we noticed in our research is that if you watch the earliest episodes in contrast to the later ones, there's a big difference in the content. It changed a great deal and that will probably happen with *Star Trek: The Next Generation* as well."

The writers became involved when they went to one of the show's many pitch meetings, where they discussed several ideas.

"They liked 'Code of Honor' the best," says Baron. "It underwent many changes, but the idea was to create an alien civilization with an interesting look and a central theme to it. We based them somewhat on the Samurai culture in Japan and made parallels, which was fun to do. I've always been fascinated by Japanese culture and history."

In "Code of Honor," the Enterprise is negotiating with the people of Tellis for a very rare vaccine to a deadly disease. Beamed aboard the Enterprise is Lutan and several of his followers, who wish to make sure that the Federation are an honorable people worthy of a trade agreement. While there, Lutan becomes fascinated by Tasha Yar and then boldy kidnaps her via a transporter beam. Shortly thereafter, Picard finds himself in the position of having to ask Lutan for Tasha back, in order to "preserve honor." This is done at a ceremony wherein Lutan's mate, Yarena (who is also trying to salvage her honor), challenges Tasha to a battle to the death. This combat ultimately does occur, with Tasha proving victorious, and Yarena dying from the poison on the weapons they are using. *But* 24th Century technology manages to bring the woman back from the dead, and in this way both Yarena and our people are able to discern Lutan's true intentions: to retain his mate's property without the woman being around to tell him what to do with it, while possibly ending up with Tasha as his new mate. If not, he'll make do with his new found riches. Of course Yarena is furious and hurt, removing Lutan as her "First One," replacing him by someone who had been a subordinate, but was obviously deeply in love with her. Enterprise gets the needed vaccine and departs this sector of the galaxy.

As was a problem with many of the initial episodes of *The Next Generation*, "Code of Honor" has some striking similarities to the original *Star Trek*, in this case the "Amok Time" episode, in which Spock returns to Vulcan due to the Pon Farr illness that affects his people once every seven years. He gets involved in a battle to the death, and finally learns that he is the victim of a manipulating female who loves another, but has arranged this battle so that she will be able to claim his property. Yet despite these similarities, this episode isn't so bad an effort, although it was obvious that everyone was still searching for a direction that this show could call its own.

As originally conceived by Powers and Baron, the Tellisians were a reptilian race whose philosophy mirrored that of the Samurai Warriors of ancient Japan. The story structure is essentially the same, with the added element that Lutan is slowly poisoning Yarena's uncle, so that this, coupled with the death duel between his mate and Tasha, will allow all of the man's property to fall in to Lutan's hands. So desperate is he, that he orders his followers to kill the Enterprise Away Team immediately after the combat, though they are hesitant for this will result in war with the Federation. Lutan is nonetheless confident, noting that he has become allies with an enemy of Starfleet (which one can only deduce would be the Ferengi).

*   *   *

From the outset of *Star Trek: The Next Generation*, Gene Roddenberry had made it clear that he did not want this version of the show to be a retread of the original. To this end, he did his best in creating characters which were not clones of the first Enterprise crew; he refused to have a Vulcan in a key position on the bridge and had initially resisted the idea of utilizing the Klingons or Romulans, feeling that it was time to create a new threat to the Federation.

As time went on, it seemed that he was as good as his word, although a Klingon (Lieutenant Worf) does serve on the bridge (as there is now peace between the Federation and the Klingon Empire) and the Romulans reappeared in the last episode of season one, "The Neutral Zone," and during the show's second year. The new "threat" mentioned above is the Ferengi, an alien people driven almost completely by the love of material acquisitions. The impression given by certain dialogue in "Encounter at Farpoint" is that the Ferengi are a fearsome people, and one that the Federation had never encountered visually.

Richard Krzemien supplied a story titled "The Last Outpost," which became a teleplay by producer Herbert Wright, chronicling the Federation's first contact with the Ferengi, as the Enterprise pursues one of the alien's flagships in the hopes of regaining a stolen T-9 gold extractor. They lock into orbit around a nearby planet, and both suddenly find themselves trapped . . . unable to escape with ship weapons and life-support systems rapidly failing. With no choice, they beam down to the planet's surface with the intention of working together to solve this mystery, but the Ferengi are quick to act, utilizing their laser/energy whips to incapacitate Riker and his Away Team. The Ferengi move in for the kill, but are interrupted by a cloaked figure known as Portal, the last survivor of the Tkon Empire (which was destroyed by a super nova), who

accuses all of them of being savages (shades of Q!), and decides to judge their worthiness to survive. It is Riker's knowledge and utilization of the philosophy behind *The Art of War* that proves the Federation's maturity to Portal, and his compassion that allows the Ferengi crew to survive.

As originally conceived, the Away Team and the Ferengi still beamed down to the planet and immediately launched into an attack against each other, but were forced to work together to combat savage dog-like creatures and escape from a crystalline chamber. Portal, known here as Dilo, is confused by their actions, admitting that he had intended on destroying them as savages until they started working together for a common cause. In addition, he is later saddened to learn of the demise of his people, particularly because he is a spreader of knowledge and now there is no one to spread his accumulated knowledge. It is Riker's suggestion that this world become a library planet. "Let every nation share the information of a thousand centuries," he says. "Help us learn to lower our defenses; to surrender to wisdom and higher truth."

Frankly, if this version of "The Last Outpost" had been filmed, it would have cost upwards of three times the normal price-tag for an episode of *The Next Generation*. Overall, the episode as aired is an effective one, although the theme of accusing man of being barbaric savages is already proving itself to be an old and tired one. The Ferengi are terrific and highly original villains, and their appearance here only hints at what future episodes might hold.

Richard Krzemien is philosophical about the final episode, obviously grateful for the experience garnered on the show.

"Herb kept as much of my story as he could," admits the writer, "and I think most of it is there. The story evolved from a small one, when I pitched it, to six drafts later when it turned into a stepping stone to introduce the Ferengi, who are essentially the new Klingons. With that element added, it became more of the focus. The main thrust came to be how we could best develop the Ferengi.

"Admittedly," he continues, "it was hard to come up with a payoff for that episode. We had to introduce these people with this major problem, and then you had to come up with an ending that made it worthy of the set-up of the beginning. That was hard right from the start. I think the first half of the show is really dramatic. There's a lot of things happening, and all of those things have to be tied up at the end. You could start off developing a great show, but if you can't tie it up, it just doesn't work."

He does note the many changes between original concept and final script. "In the script they're confronting the Portal," Krzemien explains, "who is something of a cloaked creature. He represents the entrance to the Tkon Empire. Originally that Portal was a small guy named Dilo, who was the caretaker of this planet, and he was meant to be a light, upbeat kind of character who got caught in the fact that he was asleep when his entire group of planets died. This is where the interesting thing about successive drafts comes in. The concept of that still exists, but it's how Dilo is embodied that's changed. That was essentially the main change from my story. That was in the fourth and fifth acts. The first three are basically the same, with the ship getting caught around the planet and getting confused by the fact that they think the Ferengi are doing it, but in fact the planet's really got both of them. Again, it was how do you pay that off on sort of a grand scale? Gene Roddenberry sort of likes to have galactic ideas and themes being dealt with. Having a noble civilization die and yet having its values carried on by its gatekeeper was an interesting concept for him."

* * *

To this writer's mind, one of the finest episodes of The Next Generation's initial season was "Where None Have Gone Before," written by Diane Duane and Michael Reaves. Their story was merely the fourth presented, and yet it would take over a dozen episodes for any other to even come close.

Many writers who penned stories for the first season have complained vehemently about the rewrites done to their material by executive producer Gene Roddenberry and other members of the show's staff, and often times their anger was justified. And yet, despite the fact that Duane and Reaves were not that pleased with the script's final direction, one must say in Roddenberry's defense that a wonderful rewrite was done, in this case by Maurice Hurley. By the same token, this is not a criticism of the original

outline, treatments or scripts by Duane and Reaves, for theirs is just as good. Frankly, this is a situation similar to the one that occurred on the original series' "City on the Edge of Forever." Harlan Ellison had written the treatment and script for that episode, and Roddenberry did an uncredited rewrite. The resulting episode is considered by many to be Star Trek's finest hour, going so far as to win the Hugo Award. This, as well as "Where None Have Gone Before," serves as ample proof that the same idea can go in to separate directions, but end up with one as workable as the other.

"We really lucked out," admits Reaves. "It was our concept and everything, but we were massively rewritten. I will agree that it was the best episode [at that time]. Yes, they had an all powerful alien in it, but at least he was not a cranky child. One of the things we liked about the show as aired, is that there was some honest emotion involved, although not nearly as much as we had. I've only seen a few episodes of the show, but so far it seems very one-note to me. At least this alien had some problems; some things he wanted to accomplish that were viable within the Star Trek universe. Also, one thing they did keep from our story is that this was a problem that was not solved by slowing something up, which I kind of liked. Production wise it was wonderful, and the acting was all very good. It came together much better on the screen than we thought it would when we read the script. We were lucky, because it was out of our hands."

As aired, "Where None Have

Gone Before" deals with a Federation scientist named Kosinksi, and his assistant known simply as the Traveler, who boards the Enterprise with a formula that will considerably enhance the ship's warp speed capability. Plans to utilize his program are put into effect, but a terrible mishap happens and the Enterprise finds itself hundreds of thousands of light-years away from where they should be. Another attempt is made, and they are pushed even further away, achieving a distance that no man has gone before, and where no man will soon ever be. At this location, reality starts to break down, and the crew begins experiencing various hallucinations. For instance, Worf finds a Klingon targ (essentially a wild pig) on the bridge, Tasha momentarily finds herself back on the hell-hole of a world she was found on, Picard encounters his long-dead mother, and other crewmembers find themselves living out either fantasies or nightmares. They must, it rapidly becomes apparent, find a way home before they lose all sense of what is real and what is not.

In the meantime, Wesley has discovered that the Traveler is the one behind the enhancement of the warp engines, and the one inadvertently responsible for their current situation. In the boy, he, in turn, senses a genius – another Beethoven or Einstein – who must be given the opportunity to develop his abilities naturally. Picard, who has taken a momentary break from their predicament to listen to these words, accepts the Traveler's proclamations, and by episode end, after everything has been restored to the way it should be, makes the youth an acting ensign.

As stated earlier, "Where None Have Gone Before" is, quite simply, spectacular, with wonderful special effects, the cast handling themselves masterfully and Rob Bowman's direction of the superb script right on the money. There is, however, one particular complaint. "The Naked Now," not to mention numerous episodes of the old show, already explored the idea of hidden thoughts coming to the surface, and this seems only a variation of the theme. Such repetition is slightly disconcerting, but acceptable in this case.

Also interesting to note is that this is the first time that Wesley Crusher has been treated with the respect that he deserves, and it's good to see this positive direction given to the character. In fact, Duane and Reaves had intended this respect for his mind to be apparent in this story, even without the presence of the Traveler. In their outline, Kosinski is amazed that Riker has gone to Wesley for an opinion, and acted on it. Riker's response is that if he didn't value the boy's opinion, he wouldn't have asked for it. In addition, once that opinion was given, why wouldn't he accept it?

Even earlier than this, in the "Code of Honor" outline by Katharyn Powers and Michael Baron, the writers noted that during a key crisis, "Picard's wisdom and experience are evident in the way he supports the boy — and the calm he imparts to keep the youngster intensely focused without becoming unnerved." This is a much better approach than having the bridge crew tell the boy to shut up everytime he makes a suggestion, particularly after these suggestions manage to save the ship.

As initially conceived, Kosinski himself was responsible for the warp speed enhancement, as well as the accident that ensues. His character was also much more fully developed, with his balancing a career with the raising of a son, who wishes that his father had more time for him. The crew of the Enterprise, conversely, hold the man's accomplishments in awe, believing that, if successful, they will be able to further man's exploration of the galaxy. Picard in particular is impressed, believing that the resulting warp capability may enable them to discern whether or not the universe was created by a divine force or if it occurred accidentally.

As in the aired version, there are two leaps via the new technology, and the Enterprise finds itself in a far distant area of space where reality starts to break down, though to a much more dramatic degree. Riker finds a welt on his arm from a bite he had once gotten from an animal, Picard finds the lifeless body of Jack Crusher on the bridge, but it disappears soon thereafter; Beverly is on the ruined deck of the Stargazer, and standing in front of her is Captain Picard, holding Jack Crusher's body outstretched in his arms.

The only solution to these visions is for the ship to get back to its own galaxy, and ultimately the Enterprise materializes within a monoblock; a cosmic egg, which is supposed to be similar to the one which supposedly exploded and created our universe. Because ship engines have been weakened from the journey, the crew attempts to absorb energy from the monoblock to recharge them. Kosinski believes that since the monobloc

exists outside normal time and space, the ensuing explosion might "kick" them back into their own universe. The attempt is made, and the Enterprise materializes *exactly* where it should be.

It is Picard's feeling that perhaps they had help; that perhaps in that moment of creation, something realized they weren't supposed to be there, and sent them home. Riker counters by musing that perhaps they themselves were the creators. There is no response to that statement, although Data informs them that the Enterprise has been away for exactly six days. Not missing the irony of that, or the universe left behind, Picard suggests that they take the seventh day off.

"There was talk at the time, very briefly, that this would be the pilot episode," says Michael Reaves, "because they needed something outreaching. This story would have taken your basic viewing audience out there and say, 'Wow, this is going to be some show!' Instead, it's *just* television. The ironic thing is that Gene Roddenberry likes stories where the Enterprise meets God. We went one better. We gave him a story where the Enterprise *becomes* God! The upshot of our outline was that they wind up in an unexploded monobloc, and in order to get back to their own space and time, and have to imbalance the monobloc, causing it to explode and a new universe to begin. The irony is that when they're doing a little low budget science fiction show, no one pays any attention. When they're pouring this kind of money into it, everybody has to comment. That's what upsets me, because here was an opportunity that I feel was missed."

* * *

In "Lonely Among Us," the Enterprise is escorting diplomats representing the reptilian Selay race, and the "furry" Anticans, who hate each other with tangible venom. A peace conference at Parliament may be the only way to stop them from going to war against each other.

Meanwhile, the Enterprise passes through what seems to be a harmless energy cloud, and accidentally picks up a sentient being which enters the vessel through ship circuitry. Then, it passes from a console into Lieutenant Worf, from him to Doctor Crusher and then to Captain Picard. As one with the captain, they realize that they have much in common, and as one they beam themselves back into the heart of the energy cloud, where they will explore the universe together. But something goes wrong, and Picard is suddenly "stranded" out there. Utilizing the transporter memory circuits, Riker and Data are able to lock onto the captain's energy pattern, and beam him back aboard. And, so, everyone lives happily ever after, with the exception, perhaps of the Selay ambassador, who has been killed and eaten by the Anticans.

All in all, "Lonely Among Us" is a fairly effective episode with an original premise, if nothing else it was proof that *Star Trek: The Next Generation* was finally beginning to establish its own identity without the stigma of constantly being compared to the original.

Also, the motivation for the alien taking over the bodies of crewmembers, culminating with Captain Picard, is a wonderful one: curiosity. Essentially, it wants to know what makes us tick, and that's a refreshing change from aliens who wants to use human hosts to take over the galaxy, or condemn us for being savages.

Important to note is that the idea of using the Enterprise to transport ambassadors from warring planets to a peace conference was quite similar to the original show's "Journey to Babel." This was done on purpose, as explained by the scriptwriter for both, Dorothy Fontana.

"In 'Lonely Among Us' I pulled from myself," she admits, while agreeing that elements from old shows appeared in many of the early episodes, "in that the mission was to transport these diplomats from here to there. The flow, however, was entirely different. Besides, they were a subplot to be in point a fun kind of thing, as opposed to serious 'drama,' like in 'Babel.' So what I did was pull from myself and switch it around. I feel there's a difference between the two. There's a definite delineation and separation here, both in intent and content."

The episode began as a treatment by Michael Halperin, which begins with Enterprise dilithium crystals suffering a breakdown. The ship has to go to Capella V for repairs, and the journey will take some 72 hours. Enroute, they encounter a flickering energy tree-like structure (a variation of this idea would eventually be utilized in the episode "Datalore"). Worf suggests that they fire a photon torpedo into the cloud, so that sensors can take readings of the energy levels given off. This last point is moot, as ship sensors would be able to gather this information without the need for detonating a torpedo within the cloud. This does, however, come into play (rather contrivedly) when Geordi and a "grunt" are in the midst of repairing the tractor beam emitter via shuttlecraft, when a particle of energy strikes the grunt. He goes crazy, doing his best to fight off Geordi, who attempts to help him.

Once the duo is back on board the Enterprise, Tasha escorts the grunt to sickbay, and an electrical charge passes between them. She is filled with unexplained anger for a short time, but this passes as the alien entity leaves her body. We are told, however, that both she and the grunt remain under its "distant" control, which is an interesting variation from the aired version. There, as detailed above, the Enterprise picks up this life form by passing through the energy cloud, and the "possession" of the crew only occurs to one person at a time.

The entity eventually goes from Tasha to Beverly, and from her to Wesley, who in turn transfers it to Data. On the bridge, it moves on to Worf. Troi eventually realizes that someone or something has been taking over various members of the crew. Later, she confides to Riker that in many people she is sensing *two* personalities, as though something is sharing their minds. However, it's only a short matter of time before Riker is possessed as well. Picard confronts him, and the commander goes into a trance, with the alien speaking through his mouth. We learn that it is desperate to survive, and means no harm to human beings. Unfortunately, it was taken aboard the ship by accident, as a result of the exploding photon torpedo. If it is not returned to its own galaxy, it will die. This is made even worse when they discover that if it dies, so will the sum total of eons of evolved intelligence. According to the treatment, "The Enterprise will have destroyed a higher-level inner universe."

Picard's real dilemma is the fact that the ship is so close to Capella V, and will not have enough power left to make the journey back again. He then decides to use the "slingshot effect" (last utilized in *Star Trek IV: The Voyage Home* as a method of time travel) to return the ship to Capella V to an earlier time with minimal fuel loss. The momentum of their trajectory will provide enough "push" to the alien to send it back to the cloud. The entity explains that it will share its knowledge of humans with the rest of the cloud, and suggests that perhaps they will one day meet again. The slingshot effect is completed, the alien is sent home and the Enterprise arrives at Capella V.

After Michael Halperin handed in this story, he was essentially cut off and the treatment was put on the shelf. When the show ran into a script crunch during its first season, Dorothy Fontana suggested ways to save the story, and hence went about adding the prediscussed elements. The final result is an enjoyable hybrid of both writers' efforts, although by having Picard becoming one with the alien and transporting into the cloud in the pursuit of greater adventure, Fontana added a highly enjoyable humanistic

element to what could have been merely another *Invasion of the Body Snatchers* kind of story.

* * *

"The story is called 'Justice,' and it is a story about the absolutely human answer to what you do when violence in the streets and every place else becomes rampant," explains writer John D.F. Black, who had served as the original *Star Trek*'s first story editor, authored "The Naked Time" and was one of the first people invited aboard *The Next Generation*. "What do you do if you're a colony? What do you do, and how would it look to somebody else when you have responded to it in the only way you and the rest of the people can?

"It has to do with justice," he adds. "For everybody, and how you deal with terrorism and anarchy, if it's rampant. How do you stop it? And once you've stopped it, what happens next? Let's say that what we do is kill everybody who is a terrorist or suspected of being a terrorist. Now the people who have killed everybody, what do they do? We're not simply talking about a person dealing with somebody else. We're talking about a society dealing with some aspect of itself. And this society is made of Earth people who went out there to set up their own democratic society. It's the same thing that happened with the Greek democracy and what corrupted that Greek democracy. So we're dealing with old history, new history and the reality of the future."

John D.F. Black is referring to his original version of "Justice," which differed drastically from the final form

the episode took. As aired, the Enterprise, after depositing an Earth colony, proceeds to the planet Edo [Eden?], which seems to be ideal for shore leave. An Away Team, including Wesley Crusher (who represents the young people aboard the ship), beams down and meets with the head council of this world, who welcomes them with open arms. What we rapidly learn is that this world is something of a paradise, with total peace and completely open about emotions and sexuality. There is no crime, and this is due to a process by which certain areas at certain times are zones in which *any* crime, no matter how big or how small, is punishable by instant execution. Unfortunately, Wesley Crusher steps on some flowers after inadvertently committing the crime of walking on the grass. Now, he is to be terminated, although a certain length of time has been granted because he is alien to this world.

Picard's problem stems back to the Prime Directive, which forbids him from interfering with the natural progression of a planet. Still, how can he allow Wesley to die for such a nonsensical crime? To make matters worse, there is an alien muckity-muck floating in space that is interfering with ship functions, while simultaneously demanding that the Enterprise leave this area of space, taking all humans with them.

The episode as described really doesn't work for a couple of reasons. First, once again we are seeing this show's preoccupation with sex, which is fine when it's done for a reason, but annoying when it seems as gratuitous as it does here. Second, the idea of using a booming alien voice – essentially God – to manipulate the plot has been done time and time again on both the old show and the new. Here it seems to be a tired retread of what's come before.

In Black's original version, the Enterprise has been ordered to investigate the planet Llarof, an experimental Earth colony practicing the pure democracy of the ancient Greek principle of "demos." It's been 80 years since the last contact between the Federation and the colony. An Away Team beams down, and is immediately told by a police officer that they should walk on the right as the law demands, and that they should consider themselves lucky that this isn't "the day." Eventually they decide to contact the planet's government, and learn that 80 years earlier terrorism had run rampant on this world, but by instituting their system of government, they have successfully been able to put a halt to it. Our people are told that at a randomly selected time each day, computers are triggered which locate a quadrant for a specific amount of time that serves as a place where all crimes are punishable by death. These crimes can include, as an example, speeding, and the passengers in the car would be sentenced as co-conspirators and put to death as well.

One of the council members, Trebor, is so proud of this planet, that he suggests the Enterprise use it for shore leave. Tasha is horrified, stating that they will not allow children to be murdered. Trebor tells them not to worry, that the Capital area will not be included in the computer's choosing, as it never is.

Thus far, we've seen an interesting build of a mystery, and it's quite effective. In addition, there is something truly frightening about the leader of a planet who can speak so casually of a justice system in which those guilty of, or thought guilty of, crimes are exterminated in a way that is similar to our stepping on a blade of grass.

The Away Team returns to the Enterprise, where they discuss the situation on the planet and the viability of shore leave. Aspect Experts voice concern over Llarof's prison system, as each building has been constructed to hold somewhere between twelve and nineteen thousand people, and yet there are only twelve in each. Picard thinks Riker should talk to Trebor about this.

In the meantime, shore leave parties do beam down, and the children – under the supervision of Enterprise security officers – are apparently having a great time. Things turn tragic, however, when two children are play fighting, when they accidentally fall down a slope and come between local police chasing criminals. One of the cops, Siwel, raises his weapon. Enterprise security officer Tenson pleads that they are from the starship and are immune, but the cop nonetheless pulls the trigger and kills Tenson. The other officer, Oitap, screams to the shooter that those people were off-limits, and with that he reluctantly kills the offending officer, as the law dictates.

In the aired episode, no one from the Enterprise was actually killed. By doing so, the earlier draft gives a much more tangible sense of the justice system on Llarof. It's one

thing to talk about extermination people for the barest of infractions, but quite another to actually see the process in action. Also, the killing of Siwel by Oitap shows the seriousness by which this system of justice is followed.

Elsewhere, Riker and Picard are discussing the prison situation with Trebor, and is told that the prisoners are exterminated on their "day," and the twelve people in each are actually guards. Then, news of Tenson's death starts spreading, and the Enterprise personnel immediately move to beam back aboard the starship. One man, Reneg, sensing what the Federation stands for, fills Riker in on some of the planet's history, emphasizing that doctors, scientists and the governing body were considered the elite class and were spared from possible executions, and that the system of elections established 80 years earlier was abolished. Immunity began to be handed down from generation to generation as though it were royalty. The people became fearful, and that fear began to rule their lives. No one had the nerve to challenge the government or to demand a return of the elections. Reneg adds that nearly every family has lost at least one member under this system, and that in itself is enough for a revolution. Both Picard and Riker point out that they cannot interfere, and that even listening or counseling him could be seen as an act of interference.

Later, the Aspect Experts state that there is combat going on in all parts of the planet, with the exception of the government area. Picard uses Federation doctrines to his advantage, pointing out that there is a rule where a starship captain can make sure that fair elections are being held where the attempt is made. Therefore, it can be reasoned that Reneg is running for office, so to this end Riker and Tasha beam down as "observers."

With barely any assistance from the Away Team, Reneg is able to launch his planned revolution, and the election process is returned to the planet.

This version of "Justice," for the most part, would have worked as an effective episode of The Next Generation. The theme, as previously discussed, is fascinating, and the idea of immune status being handed down from generation to generation is simply wonderful. However, it's not surprising, considering Gene Roddenberry's determination to stay as far away from the original show as possible, the ending was dropped. Riker and his Away Team serving as "observers" of the situation, who actually play a part – no matter how small – in the revolution, is right out of the old show. Captain Kirk often reinterpreted the Prime Directive to fit his way of thinking, a perfect example of which was "A Taste of Armageddon," in which the Enterprise comes across a pair of planets who have been engaging in a computer war for centuries. The computer targets certain areas, and those people living there would voluntarily walk into disintegration chambers, so that the society itself continues. Kirk took it upon himself to destroy those chambers, thus forcing the two cultures to do away with their war or each other. This was, really, a flagrant

violation of the Prime Directive, and would have been equally erroneous in "Justice."

The primary difference between Black's first and second drafts is that the Enterprise personnel play a much larger role in what happens (with Wesley being one of the children who slide down the slope). It is Reneg's hope that Picard's intervention to save the children will result in a breakdown of the justice system on this world, thus allowing the people to revolt, for it is his belief that the people would do away with this. All of this eventually leads to a trial, wherein the children of the Enterprise are set free thanks for Riker's information concerning Reneg's motives. Reneg, in turn, is executed in front of everyone for treason. All starship personnel return to their vessel, and the Enterprise breaks orbit.

On the bridge, Riker tells Picard that Reneg was probably right in regards to this system of justice, but the captain emphasizes that is not their place to judge; perhaps the people would want to leave things exactly the way they are.

"Perhaps they'd rather risk being legally executed for dropping a piece of paper on the sidewalk," Picard muses, "to live without fear of being raped or robbed or murdered in their sleep. In any case, they have a right to choose their own system of justice."

This version works far better than the first draft does, and it ends on a somewhat downbeat note, which the original Star Trek was able to pull off wonderfully. The courtroom scene serves as a better setting for the conclusion of the episode than an

action-filled revolution would have. The death of Reneg, if filmed, would have been shocking to the audience. This was terrific drama, and the only bit of business missing is Riker's guilt for having the man confess the truth and then being killed for it. One would imagine that the commander would at least feel pity towards the other man.

"I'd been trying to do this story for years and years," explains John D.F. Black. "It's been in my mind and there's been nowhere to hook it. It would have to be a movie or something like Star Trek."

Unfortunately, Black would not take this story any further. As longtime Star Trek fans know, he left his story editing position after thirteen episodes because Gene Roddenberry insisted on rewriting every script. Feeling his position was being compromised, he left the series.

"Gene Roddenberry is Gene Roddenberry again," he explains, cryptically. "He didn't sound any different today talking to me than he sounded when I was sitting with him on the old Star Trek. The same things are on the line. G.R. is still G.R., as he was. He exposes himself as a human being to writers at the same level now as he did before. His own human situation, his history . . . everything. He's no different. He's suddenly Albert Einstein's Theory of Relativity in place."

While Black is hesitant to talk about it, one source close to the show has stated that when the writer questioned some of the changes that were asked of him, he was unceremoniously dropped from the script. That particular writing associate who stated this, has added that it was a grossly unfair action. Apparently the same types of conflicts that had risen before between writers and *Star Trek*'s creator reared their ugly heads again, and history simply repeated itself.

Writer Worley Thorne took on the next two drafts of "Justice," and between him and Gene Roddenberry they crafted the episode as aired, with an incredible preoccupation with the sex lives of the people of Edo, and the intervention of a God-like being. Something was lost in the transition.

* * *

The Ferengi reared their ugly little heads again in "The Battle," which was scripted by producer Herbert Wright from a treatment by the late Larry Forrester.

In this story, Damon Bok, a Ferengi commander, delivers to Captain Picard the remains of his first vessel, the Stargazer, which had engaged in battle with a Ferengi vessel years earlier, the result being that the other ship was destroyed while Picard and his crew were forced to abandon the Stargazer. Picard isn't sure what to make of this, but he accepts the gift, utilizing tractor beams to tow it alongside the Enterprise. Unbeknownst to him, Bok has a hidden agenda, which includes a pair of mind control devices. Ultimately, they cause Picard to go from having severe migraine headaches to having hallucinations about his time aboard the Stargazer, reliving the final battle in his mind. Finally, the captain breaks off the tractor beam, transports over to the Stargazer and prepares to take

on the Enterprise, which he believes to be the Ferengi vessel from years ago.

We learn that Bok's only son was killed in that battle so long ago, and that he has spent his entire life preparing this revenge. The only hope in this situation comes from the unlikely source of the Ferengi first officer, who tells Riker that Bok has been arrested for participating in unprofitable business exercises, and he details the operation of the mind control devices, so that Riker can convince Picard to destroy the one on the Stargazer which is controlling his mind.

As aired, "The Battle" is a delightful episode of the series, and one which is highly original as well. Director Rob Bowman manages quite a bit of suspense, the Wright/Forrester story is excellent, and Patrick Stewart is superb as Picard, particularly during moments when he is interacting with the "ghosts" of his former crew aboard the Stargazer. Considering that he acted alone, and the other images were superimposed later, this was quite an acting feat.

As is often the case, as much as there are changes between first draft outlines and final scripts, there are stories which remain virtually intact. The latter is the case with "The Battle," as the storyline follows the treatment quite closely, albeit in expanded form, and in turn the aired episode is rather similar to Herb Wright's first draft teleplay. One thing to be noted, is that many of the early drafts of *Next Generation* teleplays seem to focus much more on character interaction than the shows themselves. This was no exception, particularly where Picard and Beverly

Crusher are concerned. There are some really nice moments where they begin to explore their true feelings for each other, as well as their mutual past, as her late husband, Jack Crusher, had served under Picard on the Stargazer. In fact the man's death, and the fact that Picard is the one who brought his body home to Beverly and Wesley was supposed to be one of the most important aspects of their relationship. It was dealt with slightly in the premiere episode, "Encounter at Farpoint," and has only been touched upon peripherally in a couple of others. Ironically, an early draft of the fourth episode, "Where None Have Gone Before," dealt with this issue in an illusionary and powerful sense, but the sequence never made it to the air. Later, in "Arsenal of Freedom," they are trapped in a cavern and are struggling to stay alive. An early draft of that episode had them deal with their true feelings for each other, but that too was ultimately dropped.

One important point regarding the Forrester draft is that he felt it was necessary to devote a significant amount of story time to the Ferengi, going aboard their vessel and providing conversations between them. This is significant, because it provides some insight into this race, in some ways mirroring relationships on board the Enterprise, and helps to elevate them above the role of stock villains. The Ferengi were never very popular, mostly because they were played for laughs after being built up to supposedly represent an awesome threat to the Federation. In providing this counter-balance between them and "us," Forrester was establishing a situation much like the original series episode "Balance of Terror," which introduced the Romulans.

* * *

If there was one guest star of *The Next Generation* who leaped off of the television screen, it had to be John DeLancie, who portrayed the enigmatic Q in "Encounter at Farpoint." So popular was he, that he made his second appearance in "Hide and Q."

"Q can be a little 'more' than he was before," explains DeLancie of his character's return. "When he's playful, he's more playful. When he's angry, he's more angry. He's a little more relaxed. The ways in which he tries to get his way are more varied, all the way from the beginning where he's being very much the joker and bombastic, then going from being kind of sly and full of himself and then, interestingly enough, using a very . . . I do a scene where it's very straight. It's almost like two guys having a cigarette, where one is saying to the other guy, 'God, I don't know how much I can really appeal to you to think this through.' It just goes back and forth and back and forth, and then his deciding to 'become' a priest. Having so much fun, and the constant baiting of Picard."

Besides being pleased with the chance to return as Q, DeLancie feels that the entire production had improved in between his episodes.

"I was there the day after the pilot aired and everybody was kind of flushed with the general feeling of having done a good job," the actor recalls. "I think the second show was very good. So they all had a sense

that they were on the right track. It's fun. You have a group that works hard and is successful, and is gaining in success as they begin to see what they have, and everybody is a lot more open. The director of 'Hide and Q', Cliff Bole, is someone to whom I can say, 'Let me try it *this* way.' Everybody's much more relaxed. When you come onto a set where things are not going well, usually the control freaks stop down and it's dense. But it's just the opposite on that show.

"The ship kind of has headway now, and it will gain steam, I believe, as people become more and more confident about what it is that they're doing. But I think that this is light years ahead of most of the crap you see on television. And you have to understand that it's still the same medium, isn't it? And the same restrictions, the same time allotment, and yet they're really beginning to pull things off.

"It's almost like a play," he continues. "I also thought it was really clear and interesting that Q would come back after all this farting around with these guys. He'd come back and say, 'Look, there's something you have that I need.' It almost made me think about reading *The Foundation Trilogy*. The enormous amount of time that they talk about, and the fact that Q is actually capable of seeing that far in advance, and is capable of coming to realize that the human race, if it continues at this sort of intellectual pace, will *overtake* the Q."

As DeLancie has explained it, Q returns to the Enterprise, fully cognizant (as a result of their encounter at Farpoint Station) of the fact that mankind is indeed destined for greatness. To help understand the human equa-

tion a little better, he decides to bestow upon Riker the power of the Q so that the commander and he can become as one. What follows is Riker's having to come to grips with this newfound power, while somehow managing to resist the temptation to use it in ways that would alter the destiny of individuals or the human race itself. What we gradually see happen is the corruption of absolute power, a theme slightly reminiscent to the second *Star Trek* pilot, "Where No Man Has Gone Before," but Riker is brought down to reality by his fellow crewmembers who each, one by one, reject his offer to make their dreams a reality. Again Q has failed in his efforts, and is zapped away by his fellow Qs at the end of the episode.

In the original treatment of this story, Q makes the crew play out these bizarre games because, as Picard notes, the alien is like a child who has no idea how to make friends, so he plays games with them. It is his assumption that Q has a favor to ask, but doesn't know how to do so. The captain is right. We learn that there are a total of three Qs, and the planet they reside on is dying, so they need to relocate. Naturally, Picard reasons, the Q have the power to move themselves, but, as the alien explains it, there are a little over a hundred thousand inhabitants on their world, and they don't know where to go. They need a planet which will supply the same kind of isolation that they have now. Picard says that he will have to discuss this with Starfleet.

While the early portion of the first draft treatment by Maurice Hurley follows fairly closely the aired version, the ending falls apart. Besides the fact that there really is no conclusion, the idea that Q needs the Enterprise's help to move his people is a bit hard to believe. With everything we've seen this alien do, there's no way you could convince anyone that he and the others like him couldn't replenish their world. The final script, written by Gene Roddenberry and C.J. Holland, is far more effective, and his purpose is much more intriguing. In fact, one cast member compared the story to the last temptation of Christ, and that may not be too far from the truth, as Riker is torn between remaining human and something akin to being a God.

One final thought "Hide and Q" leaves the viewer with, is whether or not we would see the return of this unique alien. During the second season he would show up again in "Q Who?", with rumors of yet another return during the third year. DeLancie has his own feelings about Q's return, and where he would like the character to go.

"I take 'em as they come," he smiles. "I'd like to play Q five or six more times. Whether I can or not is another thing, but I think to leave a legacy of Q episodes out there would please me. It's a good group, they've been kind to me and it's fun. As far as the direction, I have no idea. I keep thinking of Q in terms of what it would be like to meet the others Qs. We had a wonderful thought – one of the makeup guys and I – that one day if you would ever pull away Q's face, it would reveal the universe. Or maybe the next time Q comes back, he's lost all that playfulness and he's just fucking angry. I thought of one

story where he goes back and is going to get Picard . . . I mean *truly* get him. The way that he's going to get him is to go back in time and screw up his mother and father. You could do anything you want, but that's provided they want to use Q again, and I'm not in the decision-making process other than being available or not being available.

"If I were writing this," DeLancie elaborates, "I would love to explore the nature of the Q. Where is the Q continuum and what is it? I think that would be kind of like going back to Krypton. It would be kind of fun to go there and say, 'My God, this is where they all live!' These are just actor's thoughts, but another thing we thought of it is what would happen if Q was on five in a row and actually became a member of the Enterprise. Then he has to deal with whatever that means, and dealing with humans on a constant basis would keep him in therapy."

* * *

One of the most confusing aspects of *Star Trek: The Next Generation* has been the relationship between Riker and Troi. In "Encounter at Farpoint" the show quickly establishes that they have something of a past with each other, and the impression is that its a relationship will develop as the series goes on. Ironically, these characters strike an interesting similarity to the romance between Commander Decker and Lieutenant Ilia in *Star Trek: The Motion Picture*, wherein those two people came together, we learned that they had once been involved, and the film culminated with their joining V'Ger to

become one being; a hybrid of man and machine.

In *The Next Generation*, there has been an occasional hint towards continuing the romance between Riker and Troi, but it has more often been forgotten. The "Haven" episode, however, dealt somewhat with Riker's reaction to the fact that Deanna Troi must go through with a pre-arranged wedding ceremony, which will take place aboard the Enterprise between her and her pre-determined mate, Wyatt. In fact, writer Tracy Torme presents a wonderful moment where Deanna forces Riker to acknowledge the fact that a starship is his true love in life, and that the chance of someday captaining a vessel is too great a temptation for him.

As though Deanna's situation is not tough enough, there are two other additional problems. First, her mother, Lwaxana Troi, comes aboard, and she creates complete chaos by insulting virtually the entire crew via her Betazoid telepathic abilities and a complete devotion to honesty (coupled with a healthy ego). Then there is a plague ship which is approaching a paradisical world known as Haven, whose inhabitants do not want potential death to infect their home. Picard is therefore put in the position of keeping these dying people away from Haven, without having to destroy them in the process. In addition, Wyatt, who has presumed he has been telepathically linked with Troi for all these years, discovers that the woman whose features he has painted and sculpted, does not resemble the counselor at all. Ultimately he discovers that this woman is actually aboard the plague ship, which is why their vessel is there in the first place. It is destiny that the couple be united, and to this end Wyatt has himself beamed over.

While not entirely successful, "Haven," at the very least, presents an original story and does provide some character insight regarding Troi and her relationship with Riker.

The original version of this story, titled "A Love Beyond Time and Space," provided many of the story beats, but truly was unusable as written, as the characters had no consistency at all, and there are too many holes in the story. Writer Tracy Torme managed to breathe new life into the story, and made it work the way that it does.

"'Love Beyond Time and Space' was written by a writer who I really don't think understood science fiction," Torme points out. "When they offered it to me, I had mixed emotions. The bad was that I couldn't even get through the outline that had been written, and the good was that I thought it was *so* unusable, that anything I did would be an improvement. It was a no-lose situation for me in a way, so I basically told them that I thought the story would only work as a comedy. I wanted to do a broad comedy about these two families who couldn't really stand each other, but wanted to go through with the wedding.

"My version was more caustic and the comedy had a sharper edge to it," he says, comparing the script to the aired episode. "'Haven' was re-written maybe 20 or 30 percent, and most of the comedy was softened and taken out of the original piece, so the net result was that I didn't particu-

larly like it when it first aired, and it's still one of my least favorite shows that I've been involved with, but for some reason it's popular among fans. I'm grateful for that. Maybe when I see it again in repeats down the road, I'll feel better about it."

* * *

Time travel has often played an integral role in the genesis of *Star Trek*, providing some of its best stories, such as Harlan Ellison's "City on the Edge of Forever" and the feature film, *Star Trek IV: The Voyage Home*. While the premise has not been used yet in *The Next Generation*, the next best thing has presented itself via the ship's holodeck in which a user can recreate any time period on any planet that is stored in the Enterprise computer memory banks.

This device has been used to its best advantage in Tracy Torme's second effort for the show, "The Big Goodbye," in which the aforementioned holodeck is programmed to recreate the fictional world of 1940s detective Dixon Hill, when a computer malfunction traps Captain Picard and several other crewmembers there and they find themselves in very real danger in an artificial reality. This created an interesting task for the episode's director, Joseph Scanlan, in combining this future world with the past, while still sustaining the reality for the audience.

"Had you asked the question the other way . . . in other words, combining the past with the future world, I would say that it's a little difficult, and that is indeed what we had to do," explains Scanlan. "I'm not a fan of the show, so I'm bringing a dif-

ferent perspective. The holodeck, in my opinion, was never totally clear as to its function to the audience, and it's the first time that people, in effect, got trapped in it because of a malfunction of the equipment. They're trapped in the past, and yet it's *not* a time warp. It's very tough, I think, to tell the audience that this is not a time warp when we are deeply involved with a subplot, which really became the main plot, in a holodeck image of San Francisco, where bullets start flying and somebody gets hit and starts to bleed.

"That's pretty tough not to consider a time warp," he adds, "even though it was not. It was just an emotional and visual experience in the holodeck as equipment screwed up. I guess I'm not directly answering the question, because I treated the two pieces as entirely different pieces. I, in actual fact, did all of the 1941 stuff – and there's no other way to do it, frankly – as if Picard is indeed playing Philip Marlowe, or rather the name they gave him: Dixon Hill, and play that for all it was worth as a genuine thing. The only key, the only balance, to keep the audience's memory of being on the ship is the dialogue that Tracy put in. There's a point where Captain Picard says to the doctor, 'We should be getting back to the Enterprise,' and she says, 'We're on the Enterprise.' He replies, 'Of course. It's becoming so real that I forgot.' That kind of thing.

"In this particular episode, there was far less of the futuristic space genre than there is on other episodes, which I made a point to see since the series started. We never looked out the window and saw other spacecraft or hostile whatevers . . . we were strictly on the bridge and down in the emergency area where the holodeck doors weren't functioning properly. In a sense, it was easy because I was able to do a 1940s picture, and going back only occasionally to the real story, which was the ship. But Tracy is the one who really made that happen. His writing, his structure, really made that possible. All I had to do was stay true to whatever period I was in."

As is normally the case with the average episode of the series, there are two stories going on concurrently. While Picard and the others are trapped in the holodeck, Riker is forced to deal with the insect-like Jarada race who need to be greeted in their precise language by the captain so that the Enterprise can enter their area of space. If even the slightest syllable is missed, then they will be insulted and the Enterprise will be forced to go back the way it came. The time for the greeting is approaching, while the "search" continues for those personnel trapped in the holodeck.

Unfortunately, the Jarada never made an appearance in the final episode, although the audience did hear them.

"The budget would have gone sky high, so there was no way to do it," says Joseph Scanlan. "We shot it so that we heard this bug-like buzzing sound. We hear this strange, garbled, almost triple voice as described in the screen direction, but we never see them. Hopefully we were able to sell it that way."

The missing Jarada is the one aspect of the aired version that Tracy Torme is unhappy about.

"They were much more interesting in the script," he emphasizes, "and for budgetary reasons they ended up being a plot point. For instance, they're part of a hive-like race, so when they spoke you heard a man's voice, a woman's voice and a child's voice, all simultaneously. When the show aired, and that wasn't in there – they instead sounded like Alvin and the Chipmunks – I asked [co-executive producer] Rick Berman what had happened. He explained that it was done in post-production and they ignored my notes in the script. So, there are frustrations even in the best of experiences when you're a writer."

And, he emphasizes, the writing of "The Big Goodbye" was a wonderful experience.

"Gene wanted to utilize the Holodeck and had thought of the idea of doing a detective story there," Torme explains. "I have always been a big Raymond Chandler fan, and even more of a *film noir* fan. So, I thought it would really be fun to do something like that, and 'The Big Goodbye,' more than any other script I've ever worked on for feature or TV, just fell into place almost magically for me. When I turned the first draft in, it's the closest I've ever been to being satisfied that I can remember. I just felt very relaxed about it, and believed that it was going to work. Some scripts are a struggle, while others aren't. This one was very definitely not a struggle compared to some of the others, so I have quite an affection for that show."

As well he should, considering that this particular episode went on to win the prestigious Peabody Award.

Interestingly, there had been some talk that the Dixon Hill material would be shot in black and white, but that idea was quickly jettisoned.

"That was the first thing out of my mouth when I read the script and had my first meeting with Rick and Bob," admits Scanlan. "They said no, and Rick added, 'If it wasn't our own characters; if we were observing something back in the forties, we might consider it . . . but if Captain Picard and the other members of the crew 'go back' and turn black and white, and then come back out of the holodeck in color, it loses Gene Roddenberry's original concept of the holodeck.' That concept is that it's an emotional experience that starts visually and takes on an emotional reaction, but you never cease to be aboard the ship. You don't go back to 1941, you go to the holodeck on board the Enterprise. It's a fine line, but one that I obviously didn't feel strongly enough about to argue with. Rick – he's a bright son of a gun – also thought that it was a little obvious; that we shouldn't do it. So we didn't."

Nonetheless, "The Big Goodbye" stands as one of the earliest bright spots in the show's first season, and a show by which others would be measured.

* * *

For some reason, which this writer has not yet been able to discern, just about every science fiction television series that makes it to the air feels as though it's an absolute necessity to do a story in which one of the main characters is split into two versions of him/herself, one good and the other evil.

That's a hell of a premise . . . once.

That's a heck of a premise . . . twice.

That's a boring, cliched premise . . . more than twice.

Yet the idea continues, never quite surpassing the first show to do it, *Star Trek*, whose "The Enemy Within" episode dealt with a transporter malfunction which split Captain Kirk into the aforementioned good/evil twins. The theme was brilliantly handled by all involved, wonderfully acted by William Shatner and has supposedly assisted in the treatment of mentally disturbed people.

Then *Logan's Run* tried its hand at the idea in an episode where Jessica is "copied" into an evil incarnation of herself who is determined to stop Logan from running.

Knightrider gave us an evil version of both the car, Kitt, and its driver, Michael.

"V" gave us the Star-Child being cloned by the evil Diana so that they could unlock the secrets of her DNA in order to develop a vaccine against the deadly toxin developed by mankind to get rid of the Visitors.

Then *Star Trek: The Next Generation* presented a variation of the theme with their episode "Datalore," which, despite the fact it was far superior to every version but the first show's, still seemed a bit repetitious, with an overhead view shot of the two Datas seemingly lifted right from the old show.

In that episode, the Enterprise travels to the world Data was created on, where they find a deactivated version of the android. They bring it to the Enterprise, put it together and activate it. This version, who refers to himself as Lore, seems even smarter than Data, and considerably more human, which ultimately turns out to be a drawback, as it fills the android with a streak of evil and treachery, that leads him to nearly sacrificing the Enterprise to a crystal creature which is credited with destroying Data's world. Ultimately, it comes down to a battle between Data and Lore, in which Data barely manages to prove victorious.

Generally speaking, this is an exciting episode, and one which gives actor Brent Spiner the opportunity to prove his varied talents by portraying two versions of the same character. Director Rob Bowman adds a healthy dose of suspense, and the only drawback are several direct lifts from "The Enemy Within," the most obvious one being the fact that in the original, the evil Captain Kirk was scratched by Janice Rand, and he in turn scratched the noble Kirk to confuse the crew. Here, Lore has a facial twitch, which he gives to Data so as to mislead the rest of the crew, and blur their view of which android is the true Data.

"I would say the show was finally unlocking and moving ahead at that point," says producer Robert Lewin. "We had more freedom to work and the question is: with that kind of freedom, will we be able to get the excitement we want? I think to some degree it can, and that this show can appeal to the same audience that the old one did. But you've got to have tension, adventure and life-threatening situations. That mix is sometimes hard to get, but that's what we were trying to do; to make those characters irresistible."

An earlier version of this story, entitled "Apocalypse Anon", dealt with an Enterprise rescue mission of a doomed planet. A shuttle taken to the world's surface is captained by a Starfleet officer named Minuet, who Riker quickly takes a liking to and just as quickly falls in love with. He is eventually shocked to learn that she is an android, but this does not seem to alter his feelings until she points out their futility.

It's obvious that this draft was an attempt to provide more depth to some of the main characters, which is certainly applaudable. The only problem with the way it's handled is that Riker's irrational love for an android becomes the most important element of the story as opposed to the mission at hand. The character of Minuet, incidentally, would show up again in the episode entitled "11001001," as a holographic image that Riker falls in love with. In that story she is part of the programming supplied by the Binars, and used as a distraction so that Riker will not catch on to the fact the aliens are essentially kidnapping the Enterprise. At least in that situation the relationship works far more effectively than it could have possibly worked here.

* * *

Equal rights for all has always been an important part of the *Star Trek* mix, a point which can be evidenced right from the beginning with the original television series, where, working side by side, were Caucasians, blacks, Orientals, Russians, Scotsmen and aliens. As envisioned by Gene Roddenberry, the 23rd Century is an era that works for everybody, with no one being left out.

While it was certainly refreshing to see this approach continue with *The Next Generation*, an opportunity was missed to explore this theme on an even deeper level in the episode "Angel One." As aired, the story has the Enterprise approach Angel One in search of the crew of a freighter lost several years earlier. Data informs Captain Picard that this world is structured in such a way that females are the dominant gender, with men being considered inferior by comparison.

Riker and an Away Team beam down to the planet's surface and meet with the ruling class, expressing their desire to recover their lost comrades. The women are resistant to this idea, and we eventually learn that the reason for this is that the humans — led by Ramsey — were at first considered a curiosity, and then a threat to the societal structure of Angel One. Coming from Earth, they of course believed in equal rights for males and females, and were rallying support from the other men of this world, which would eventually lead to revolution. As such they have been in hiding, and if the Enterprise can locate them, they are welcome to take them. For, as the leader points out, if they remain they will be executed. Without breaking the Prime Directive, Riker and his Away Team must convince the government of Angel One that even the execution of these men will not extinguish the flames of revolution.

Running concurrently with this story is one in which a respiratory disease rapidly spreads throughout the ship, infecting just about everyone and leaving Beverly Crusher with the task of finding a cure before it's too late. Frankly, this disease business is going a little bit too far already. We've seen diseases spread across the ship in "The Naked Now" and "Where None Have Gone Before," so it's already becoming old hat. In addition, the main plot seems more preoccupied with sex, than with apartheid, which was its original intent.

"'Angel One' was about a reverse role society," explains Herb Wright, "in which women ruled and men are subservient. It's been done a thousand times already, including Gene's *Planet Earth*. So the major issue that we wanted to make sure was straightened was that I didn't want to do Amazon Women that are six feet tall with steel 'D' cups. My feeling was that the hit taken on this should be apartheid, so that the men are treated as though they are the blacks of South Africa. Make it political. Sexual overtones, yes, but political. Well, that didn't last very long. The sexual places it was dragged to were absurd."

As originally conceived by writer Patrick Barry, "Angel One" was very much trying to deal with apartheid. This point is emphasized at the very outset of the proposed story, as Riker, Troi, Tasha, Data and an all woman security team beam down. Naturally Riker is the first to speak to the world's ruler, Victoria, and he is immediately in trouble. Apparently it is against the law on this world for a man to look a woman in the eyes, and the sentence is death for touching a woman, which Riker does when he stops her from striking him. Weapons are leveled at the commander, but Tasha, who recognizes how this system works, uses her phaser to stun Riker, causing him to collapse unconsciously to the ground.

Wow, great opener!

While Data, being a machine, is deemed higher than a man and thus allowed more freedom, Riker is dressed in the attire of the slave class and thrown together with other slaves while Tasha, who has taken over the Away Team in necessity, works on locating the Federation personnel they are seeking. What they eventually discover is that the societal structure on this world is in a state of flux. The male gender have grown tired of their lower class status, and the time is coming for them to revolt. Eventually, the Away Team is able to locate the human leader, Lucas Jones, who is spurring the men into revolution. He is brought before Victoria, attacks her verbally and is killed by her. No sooner has he fallen lifelessly to the ground, than there is an explosion in the distance and then another. His death merely serves as a solidifying base for the other slaves, who make their own vie for freedom.

With this revolution in place — and without the Away Team's instigation — they beam back aboard the Enterprise, where Picard is recovering from the disease discussed earlier, only in this version of the story the captain alone is infected. Picard is concerned that the Prime Directive may have been violated in this instance, but Riker explains that the Enterprise served more as a witness to this uprising than an actual part of it. This seems to satisfy the captain, and the ship is off for its next mission.

All in all, Barry's version of

"Angel One" is a far superior one to that which was aired, giving us a powerful allegory, and an opportunity to explore one of the great crises of humanity currently facing the world.

*   *   *

One of the interesting things that begin to happen with *Star Trek: The Next Generation* by the middle of the first season, was that the attempt was made, at least in some subtle ways, to create a sense of continuity. This is evident in "11001001," in which the Enterprise locks into spacedock for a computer overhaul, and repairs of the holodeck which has "recently" malfunctioned. This malfunction does, of course, refer to the mishap of "The Big Goodbye," in which crewmembers were trapped in one of the false realities created by the Enterprise computers.

This particular episode also serves as a highlight of the first season, and signifies a marked improvement in the quality of the scripts. In this case, the Binars – a race who are as close to living computers as you could find – are the beings working on the Enterprise computers. While this is going on, the majority of the Enterprise crew and their families have left the ship for shore leave activities. Picard has decided to relax and catch up on some reading, and Riker, who is told by the Binars that the holodeck is repaired and enhanced, programs the area's computer to recreate a jazz bar, where he is given the opportunity to play the trombone. In addition, he is instantly captivated by a strikingly beautiful woman named Minuet, who

seems perfectly made for him. Minuet is the name originally given to the android character in the first draft treatment of "Datalore." As Riker gets swept up in the atmosphere of this illusion, the Binars punch some information into the computer and depart the area. Soon thereafter, Picard joins him, and is swept up in the vision as well, simultaneously taking note of the fact that Riker is getting a bit carried away by his fascination with Minuet.

Meanwhile, there seems to be a leak in the antimatter chamber, and Data has no choice but to order those remaining aboard to abandon ship before imminent destruction. Moments later, Data asks the computer for the location of Picard and Riker, but is told that the ship is empty. This is curious to the android, but he does not pursue it further until he and Geordi are beamed onto the starbase. They've arrived, when the apparent damage to the engines repair itself, and the Enterprise breaks away from the space station, before leaping into warp speed.

Picard prepares to leave the holodeck, and as he steps into the corridor he hears the red alert signal. He and Riker quickly discern what has happened and transport themselves to the bridge, where they find the Binars in a death-like state. It turns out that their world was threatened by a super nova, so they downloaded all information from that planet's memory banks, loaded them into the Enterprise's computer – the only computer large enough to hold that vast amount of information – and hijacked the ship. Their home world did survive the nova, however, and

now the only way to insure the lives of the Binars is to "return" the information from the starship, thus reviving the planet's main computer. As there was no real harm done, Picard says everything should be alright, although there will be a hearing.

With everything back in order, Riker returns to the holodeck seeking Minuet, but finds that she is no longer in the computer's programming as she was created by the Binars as a distraction.

Overall, "11001001" is a terrific episode, with an imaginative new alien race and an original premise. Riker's relationship with Minuet, which could have been ridiculous, is actually pulled off effectively. Altogether, this serves as one of the better episodes of the first season.

*   *   *

The idea of aging and mortality is nothing new to the *Star Trek* universe. We've seen the crew of the Enterprise encounter premature aging in the original series episode, "The Deadly Years," and coping with midlife crisis in *Star Trek II: The Wrath of Khan* and mortality in *Star Trek V: The Final Frontier*.

However, the first time that the search for a veritable fountain of youth occurred in *The Next Generation* episode "Too Short a Season," in which Captain Picard is given emergency instructions from Starfleet Command to proceed to hostage situation, where terrorists have demanded that Admiral Mark Jameson come in to negotiate their freedom from Karnas. Enterprise is to serve as the transport vessel.

When we meet Jameson, he's an

85 year old man, bound to a wheelchair by a crippling disease, and he is joined by his wife Anne. Throughout the journey, he is rapidly growing younger, due to an age-reversing drug he had obtained during a recent negotiation, and the primary focus is on his gaining strength, the crew's reaction to all of this, and Anne's terror at watching her husband slip away from her.

Picard wants to know *why* Jameson would risk his own life with this dangerous drug, and why Karnas requested him. We learn from the mid-20s aged Admiral that forty years earlier he had a similar hostage situation to negotiate on Mordan, where Karnas demanded phasers and other Federation technology. Finding himself with little choice in the matter, Jameson agreed, but to maintain a balance of power he supplied other factions on the planet with the same amount of weaponry. Jameson falsified Federation documents to cover up this deed, and now it has come back to haunt him.

Reaching Mordan, an Away Team, which includes Picard, beams down and makes a rescue attempt, but things get botched up when Jameson is stricken with severe pain that racks his entire body. No sooner have they beamed up than Karnas contacts them, stating that if Jameson is not beamed down to the planet within ten minutes, he will kill a hostage. Fifteen minutes later, another will die. Jameson weakly pleads that Picard beam him down, for he knows that Karnas will free the hostages *if he has the admiral*. Moments later, Picard, Beverly Crusher and the young Jameson beam down, but Karnas re-

fuses to accept their claim that he is with them. Jameson collapses once again, with Picard demanding Karnas to recognize that this is indeed Jameson. He refuses, noting that he wants Jameson to see the destruction and scars that his actions from forty years ago caused.

Picard shows Karnas visual proof of Jameson's de-aging, while Anne is beamed down to be with her husband during the last few moments of his life. Jameson manages to show Karnas a scar he received during a private meeting between the two men; the blood scar that sealed their pact. Karnas pulls a weapon to kill the man, but decides not to, believing that the man's current suffering is retribution enough. A moment later, he dies. His need for revenge spent, Karnas states that he will release the hostages.

For the most part, "Too Short a Season" is another fine example of the kind of show that *Star Trek: The Next Generation* should be doing, giving the audience believable characters and a highly enjoyable storyline. As is the case in most classic literature, Jameson ultimately pays the price for his attempts to tamper with nature's process, which is quite unlike the case of the original Michael Michaelian treatment and first draft teleplay.

In that version of the script, Jameson pulled some strings at Starfleet to have Commander Riker promoted to Captain and assigned his own ship, so that Jameson himself could assume the role of Enterprise First Officer. Since Riker is staying on as a consultant during this hostage situation, Jameson finds himself com-

pelled to best the commander whenever and wherever he can, and this includes deliberately excluding Riker from the Away Team by giving the man the wrong rendezvous time.

Karnas is known as Zepec in this version, and his decades old enemy is the High Priest. Picard and Riker use the transporter to arrange a meeting between the two men, and when they recognize the fact that they've been fighting for so long without ever having met each other, they come to the realization that perhaps the time has come for peace. Mission accomplished, and the Enterprise sets off on her way. But what of Jameson?

First off, the de-aging has been somewhat different than in the aired version, with Jameson's aged and youthful personalities continuing to come into conflict with each other; his behavior becoming more erratic and confusion replacing logic. He ultimately ends up 14 years old, and has no memory of his marriage to Anne. The proposed episode ends with Wesley giving the youth a tour of the Enterprise, and the young man's proclamation that he hopes to someday become a captain, like "Mr. Picard."

Frankly, it's best that this was altered. In this version, Jameson somehow actually seems to be rewarded for what he had done 40 years earlier, and the fact that he has cheated his wife of her husband. He is, in effect, given the opportunity to have a second chance at life. Justice is best served in the Dorothy Fontana co-written teleplay.

"The high concept that Michael Michaelian came in with was male menopause," Fontana says, "which is a subject not often touched in television. Michael said, 'Well, I've been going through it lately, and I can really sympathize with the whole idea of wanting to go back to the man that he was, and coming to grips with the man that he is and will be.' It was interesting, but he wanted to do it with reverse aging; someone seeking out that youth for a purpose. Of course using a science fiction gimmick, you can do it in a matter of days. Michael did a treatment and a first draft script, but the key element that always went a little wrong with it was the terrorist angle; why we were going to that planet. The Macguffin. A lot of what I put in at the end was also in Michael's story and drafts, but approached with a different emphasis. Also, instead of it truly being terrorists, it's all a trap, pulling Jameson to the planet. Those were pretty much the changes."

* * *

A primary difference between the Enterprise of the old show and the new, is the fact that the latter has taken entire families on this mission, which will supposedly span some twenty years. When this particular point was originally announced, there was some concern that there would be kiddies running all over the ship, but thankfully this has not come to pass.

Still, "When the Bough Breaks" manages to focus on the children of the Enterprise in a very touching and sentimental way. The ship picks up energy readings, equatable with galactic bread crumbs, that leads them to a mythical world known as Aldair, which Riker compares to the

lost city of Atlantis. Unfortunately, the myth is much grander than the reality, as a pair of Aldairians materialize on the bridge, preach friendship, and then ask Riker, Troi and Beverly to join them on the planet's surface. Once the trio have appeared there, the bombshell is dropped: the people of Aldair are dying, as there are no children. The adults have become sterile, and without aid their race will perish. They wish the Enterprise to leave some children with them, and in return will provide information that mankind will not learn for centuries. Naturally this is not good enough, as humans are extremely protective of their children. Since the answer is no, the Aldairians do what any super powerful aliens would do: they kidnap six of the Enterprise children (including Wesley), and treat them as Gods so they will allow themselves to be assimilated into their culture and continue the race.

Picard makes an attempt to get them back, and in response the aliens propel the Enterprise some three days away and set up a force field. The Aldairian leader proclaims that if another rescue attempt is made, the starship will be pushed so far away that by the time they return, the children will be aged. In the meantime, a couple of the children seem to be adapting, while Wesley and several others are resistant.

The Enterprise returns three days later, and at around the same time Beverly discovers from medical scans that the Aldairians are dying from chromosome damage, so that with or without children, the race is doomed to perish unless she can find a cure. In the meantime, Wesley has spoken to

the children, and convinced them that they have to act completely miserable so that they can be returned home. This comes right down to not eating, so that the message will be driven in.

Picard and Beverly ask to be brought down, and while the planet's shields are down for the transportation process, Riker and Data beam down to the planet's main power source. The captain confronts the Aldairians with the fact that the children want to go home. They protest, but Beverly and Picard argue that they're suffering from radiation poisoning, similar to the type that will affect us – Earth people – without our atmosphere's ozone layer. The aliens are about to zap everyone away, but Riker and Data have taken down the planet's main computer, thus making the equipment inoperative. The children are beamed back to the Enterprise, while Picard and an Away Team help point the Aldairians in the right direction of self-discovery, and are willing to help in any way that they can, right down to replenishing the world's ozone layer. In addition, Beverly is able to reverse the sterilization, and we've got another happy ending.

As stated at the outset of this chapter, "When the Bough Breaks" works so well because it deals with an aspect of the Enterprise crew that has been virtually ignored up until this point. We are also given a lesson in blindly putting faith in technology at the cost of ourselves. Incidentally, this episode has probably been the first to use Wesley to his best advantage since "Where None Have Gone Before."

* * *

Unfortunately, the next episode in the series, "Homesoil," falls short of the high standards established by the previous three episodes. Its biggest failing, in fact, is its plot which seems to be a hybrid of several Star Trek stories which have come before.

First off, it opens with the Enterprise arriving at a world currently being terraformed by a group of scientists who are attempting to utilize Federation technology to bring life where there is lifelessness. The process, and the description of it, sounds like a direct take from the Genesis Project featured in The Wrath of Khan. Then there are elements of the original show's "The Devil in the Dark" episode, in that the scientists in their endeavors are destroying life forms which exist on this planet. In that episode, Federation miners were being killed, and the source turned out to be a moving rock creature known as the Horta, and the reason for its attacks was that the miners were destroying silicone eggs which contained its children, although no one was aware of that fact at the time.

The lifeform of "Homesoil" is a crystalline, intelligent being that is brought aboard the Enterprise and placed in the medical lab in a containment jar. Before long it splits into two entities, which manage to communicate to the crew, referring to them as "ugly bags of mostly water," and it continues to grow, angry as well that the scientists have been destroying its kind. After this intelligence manages to take over computer controls of the ship and it looks like all will be lost, a level of understanding is reached and the crystal-beings are transported back down to the planet, but not before it has the opportunity to call us barbaric savages, emphasizing that it will be three centuries before the Federation can return to this world.

Sorry, but it's awfully tiresome to constantly be called barbaric (hell, Q did the same thing in "Encounter at Farpoint"), and this plot had been used far too many times already.

Things improved somewhat with "Coming of Age," which gave us an interesting pair of stories. The first was Wesley's attempts to get in to Starfleet Academy, and the various tests he must undergo to gain entrance. These include technical exams, practical exams and the dreaded psych-test, in which all applicants must face their greatest fear. It's a close call, but, naturally, Wesley misses getting in by the barest of fractions, which is not surprising, for if he had been accepted, the character would have had to leave the show. One thing that should be pointed out about this story is that it is another opportunity to show that in the right creative hands, Wesley can be more than an annoying teenager who always manages to save the ship. Wil Wheaton handles the part in such a way that you're actually rooting for the character by the end of the segment. Things were destined to improve for both the actor and character, particularly during the second season where the character was treated as a regular as opposed to a boy genius, who happened to be on the bridge.

The other story deals with Admiral Quinn and his assistant Remick, who have beamed aboard the Enterprise to conduct an inquiry into Picard's command abilities. Remick goes about conducting indepth interviews with the various bridge personnel, asking pertinent questions which relate to a variety of past adventures, including the death of Jack Crusher and such episodes as "The Naked Now," "Where None Have Gone Before," "Justice" and "The Battle." After Picard has taken all of this that he can, and Remick has not been able to prove any wrongdoing on the captain's part, he confronts Quinn and is told that there is supposedly a conspiracy in Starfleet which threatens the very foundation of what the Federation stands for. He needs someone he can trust in a position of power, and he wants Picard to take command of Starfleet Academy. Picard wants an explanation of the conspiracy Quinn refers to, but there is none forthcoming, as the admiral eventually dismisses it as paranoia. Ultimately Picard refuses the potential promotion, emphasizing that his place is aboard the Enterprise. Quinn accepts this and departs with Remick.

While the investigation serves little purpose at this point, it is nice to see a sense of continuity between this and a variety of earlier episodes. Take note of the fact that Quinn's concern regarding a conspiracy would return in the first season episode of the same name.

* * *

"I like to give Worf twists all the time," proclaims actor Michael Dorn, "and he has developed from a character who just grunts and growls a lot with a sarcastic one-liner kind of attitude to one who has turned out to be very complex."

Helping Dorn achieve this goal was the episode "Heart of Glory."

"I consider 'Heart of Glory' to be an information episode," he explains, "because it gave you everything you wanted to know about what happened with the Klingons. Why did they become allies? Why is Worf there? How did he get there? That type of thing. It was very good, although I felt it could have been taken a little further. What I wanted was an epic battle in the end, but it was a good show for me, because it showed them that people are as interested in Worf as they are in the other characters." That "interest" is not surprising, particularly when one considers that Star Trek's Mr. Spock was probably the most popular character, due mostly to his alien nature, and it would seem that that has a lot to do with Worf's popularity. The Enterprise answers a distress signal from a Klingon ship supposedly attacked by a Ferengi vessel. Data analyzes debris, and announces that the destruction does not appear to be the result of the Ferengi, although the Romulans are a distinct possibility. An Away Team transports over to a drifting freighter craft, and Geordi's visor detects structural weakness. A search for survivors continues, until they come across three Klingons, one of whom is seriously injured, and then everyone beams back aboard the Enterprise just before the freighter collapses.

In sickbay, one of the Klingons claim that the Ferengi attacked, but Worf points out that the weapons were not of Ferengi design. The Klin-

gons seem to have an answer for every possible question. Picard dismisses them, and Worf escorts them to an eating area, where the Klingons immediately launch into a gentle, taunting assault on Worf, wondering how he can so comfortable working with humans. Their conversation is interrupted by a communiqué from the captain, stating that the third Klingon is dying in sickbay, and there's nothing that Crusher can do to prevent it.

Later, after life has left the warrior's body, the two remaining Klingons continue their questioning of Worf, doing their best to incite his warrior blood and subtly implying that he should join a struggle against humans; pointing out that he should be among his own kind. Eventually – perhaps in an attempt to sway Worf – they tell him that they are the ones who destroyed the Klingon ship, because these rebels were going to be brought back to the Klingon home world due to their rebellious ways, and refusal to accept the peace between their people and the Federation.

A Klingon battle cruiser approaches the Enterprise, informing Picard that the Klingons on board are criminals, and should be transported over to the cruiser when they are in range. A security team is sent to the lower decks to bring the Klingons to the bridge, and Worf finds himself quite literally in the middle of the two factions. Ultimately he does not stop security as they lead the duo away to a holding area. It is a short matter of time, however, before they utilize hidden weapons to escape, killing one security guard, while one of the

Klingons is killed in turn. The survivor makes his way to the engine room, where he proclaims that he will speak only to his countryman, Worf!

Worf goes to engineering, where he finds the Klingon aiming a weapon at the anti-matter chamber, threatening to destroy it if he is not set free. At the same time, he tries to sway Worf to his way of thinking, but Worf makes it clear that his loyalty is to Starfleet, as he fires his phaser, which unintentionally causes the other Klingon's death, leaving Worf alone to ponder his own heritage and identity.

Quite simply, this is an absolutely marvelous episode. Director Rob Bowman, who deserves a lot of credit for the skill he's brought to his Next Generation episodes, manages to convey a tremendous amount of suspense in what is the relatively confined space of the Enterprise. The script presents a tremendous opportunity to take an inside look at the make-up of the Klingons, moving them beyond the status of black hats, and Michael Dorn is given a chance to prove what all of us suspected all along: he is a truly gifted actor, and Worf is one hell of a character whose potential has not yet been tapped.

Thankfully this would be corrected later on.

* * *

Coming off of the success of "Heart and Glory," Star Trek: The Next Generation hit audiences with a one-two punch in the form of "Arsenal of Freedom" and "Symbiosis," a pair of stories which, like their immediate predecessor, demonstrated what this series should and could do, giving us exciting and thought-provoking stories coupled with great characterizations, and all delivered in an entertainment package.

"Arsenal of Freedom" provides a chilling and riveting storyline, involving the ultimate salesman: a computerized Peddler representing all that remains of a planet whose entire population consisted of arms dealers. Arms negotiations were their greatest strengths, but somehow their technology overtook their wisdom to utilize it, and they were destroyed, leaving only the automated weapons systems and the computerized Peddler behind.

The planet is Minos, and this is where the Enterprise has arrived in search of information regarding, or survivors of, the U.S.S. Drake, which mysteriously disappeared. An Away Team transports down to the planet's surface, and is immediately attacked by one of the automated weapons. This is disposed of quickly enough via a single phaser blast, but it is only a short matter of time before a second unit appears, and it takes the combination of two phasers to destroy it. What the team quickly realizes is that each time a unit is destroyed, the main computer assesses the situation and devises a replacement that can adapt to its opponent. Things go from bad to worse when Riker is suddenly held in a stasis-field. It takes concentrated phaser fire to free him.

Picard, who has been monitoring events on the surface, beams down with Beverly Crusher to see what aid they can render, while leaving Geordi in command of the Enterprise. No sooner have they arrived, than they fall into a deep cavern housing computer equipment.

Unfortunately, Beverly Crusher is seriously injured, and the captain has to do everything in his power to keep her alive.

Meanwhile, in space, the Enterprise is forced to raise shields to protect itself from a planetary weapon system, which could conceivably destroy the vessel. Geordi has the saucer section separate and head towards the nearest starbase, while he and the crew remaining use everything at their disposal to destroy this automated enemy so that they can beam the Away Team, Picard and Crusher back on board.

Essentially, there are three stories going on: the Away Team's efforts to stay alive on the planet's surface, Picard and Beverly trapped underground and Geordi's situation aboard the Enterprise. Much of this situation is abated when Picard is greeted by the Peddler, who is terribly excited about showing off the technology he has for sale. When the captain states that he has been convinced, that he will indeed purchase these weapon systems, the Peddler joyfully shuts the system down, thus eliminating those units on the planet's surface. Geordi, through clever maneuvering which includes bouncing the Enterprise on the planet's atmosphere, manages to make the planetary unit vulnerable to phaser attack and, then, destruction.

As stated above, this was a terrific episode, and seemingly an extrapolation of modern-day mercenaries and arms dealers. Per usual, there is at least one complaint: initially the idea was that having Beverly and Picard trapped together underground would give them the opportunity to explore their true feelings for each other, but for one reason or another this was eventually dropped in favor of a more platonic/concerned friend situation.

"Symbiosis" was also an exciting episode, in that it addressed a pertinent issue in a way that *Star Trek* has always excelled at. While studying solar flare activity, the Enterprise comes across an alien freighter in serious trouble. They ultimately beam four people and some cargo (which was transported in lieu of two additional crewmembers) aboard, before the shuttle is caught in the sun's gravitational pull and destroyed. Amazingly, the two Aurelians are more concerned about their cargo than they are about their lost comrades. Also, the two Brekkans continually emphasize that the "merchandise" (i.e. the cargo) is not theirs as of yet, and the fact that payment was destroyed with the Aurelian freighter is of no concern to them.

After some time, we learn that the Aurelians' home planet is suffering from a plague that only the Brekkans have a cure for; a cure known as Felicium. After careful analysis, Beverly discovers that there isn't actually a plague. Rather, the Aurelians are addicted to Felicium, and *that* is the illness they suffer from when not given their dosage; they are plagued by withdrawal symptoms. It is the doctor's suggestion that she introduce an artificial substitute that will gradually relieve them of their dependency. Picard tells her that this is impossible, as it would be a violation of the Prime Directive. These people, he reasons, have had this symbiotic relationship in place for years, and who are they to force *Federation* beliefs on them?

Picard and Beverly inform the Brekkans of their knowledge of the situation between the two races, but the Brekkans are thrilled to learn that the Enterprise will not interfere at all because of their own doctrines. Picard still manages to come out on top, however, when he rescinds a previous offer to supply the Aurelians with coils that their other freighters are in desperate need of. By doing so he will eventually cause a breakdown of the system between the Aurelians and the Brekkans, resulting in the former's inevitable discovery that the plague does not actually exist. By *not* acting, the captain is forcing a change, without violating the Prime Directive.

This was certainly an intellectual approach to a heinous problem currently facing our society, and with the exception of a "just say no" conversation between Tasha and Wesley (though one can understand it's inclusion for the sake of children in the audience), there are absolutely no complaints about the episode. High praise should be given to everyone involved, and one can only hope that future episodes will continue to actually talk about something of significance to today's audience.

* * *

Typecasting has been one of the greatest problems facing the cast members of the original *Star Trek*, and it has undeniably affected their careers for the past twenty years. Perhaps this wouldn't be so terrible a fate, except, as many of them have rightfully pointed out, for the fact that they feel their contributions to actual episodes were limited to such lines

as "hailing frequencies open," "Standard orbit, Captain," "Aye, sir," and the like. These are certainly not the kind of acting challenges that attract the attention of casting agents, thus resulting in the aforementioned typecasting.

Naturally, the cast of *The Next Generation* shared similar fears, with the original cast's fates obviously being held in front of them for comparison. Yet while most of them have been pleased with the material they've had to work with, Denise Crosby felt portraying Tasha Yar was not all it had been cracked up to be. There simply was not enough time to give everybody equal opportunities, thus the supporting characters had little more than supporting parts. She confronted series creator Gene Roddenberry with these feelings, and was told point blank that Tasha Yar simply would not have that much more to do in the future, so she asked for, and was granted, release from the series.

Now, Crosby's character *could* have merely been transferred to another vessel. Instead, the actress's departure was deemed the perfect opportunity to emphasize the danger that faces the crew of the Enterprise at every turn, and so it was mutually decided that the starship's security officer should meet her demise, and the script chosen was Joseph Stefano's "Skin of Evil."

A space shuttle transporting Deanna Troi and a pilot to a rendezvous spot for pickup by the Enterprise, runs into mechanical interference and is forced to crashland on a planet. By the time the starship arrives, the worst is feared. Scanners

indicate the shuttle to be covered by debris that the transporter cannot penetrate, so an Away Team must transport down and make a rescue attempt. Shortly after materializing, however, they have trouble getting to the shuttle due to what can only be described as an oil slick that blocks their path at every attempt to pass. The slick rises into a somewhat solid form, and one of the first things it does is strike out at the woman, sending her reeling lifelessly to the ground. The Away Team immediately beams back to the ship, and Beverly does her best to bring Tasha "back," but to no avail. As she describes it, the slick sapped the life right out of her. Because of the possibility that Troi is alive, they beam back down to the surface, and confront the slick once again.

It rapidly becomes apparent that this being is pure evil, taunting the Away Team in vicious and childish ways, and constantly reinforcing the idea that they are fragile things he can destroy if he chooses to. All they want to do is recover their comrades from the shuttle, but even this will not be allowed by the compassionless creature. Picard eventually beams down and confronts the creature, learning that it is the result of a race of people who managed to bring everything dark and evil from within to the surface and were able to cast it out of their bodies, thus creating this being of unadulterated evil. It wants out of this place, and will allow the captain to get Deanna and the pilot *if* the Enterprise provides transport. Picard agrees in principal, and finds himself within the shuttle.

Meanwhile, Worf and Wesley

devise a plan to simultaneously beam the Away Team and those people in the shuttle up at the same time, noting that when the creature uses its abilities, the power source blocking the transporter beam weakens. The plan naturally works, and everyone returns to the Enterprise, which breaks orbit and leaves the creature behind for all eternity. Picard's log states that he will contact Starfleet Command and have them put this world off limits to all other vessels. The episode concludes with a funeral for Tasha Yar, and a holographic message that she left behind for her comrades in case she should die while on duty.

While this episode works fairly well, and Tasha's death is handled wonderfully, the biggest problem facing it is the creature itself, which looks like nothing more than a man in a rubber suit covered with oil. This, in turn, takes away a great deal from the overall impact the show has.

"When you read the script," explains director Joseph Scanlan, "it has a wonderful intellectual quality to it, forgetting the complications of creating the creature. This entity had such an ironic quality. I thought his dialogue was extremely interesting and found his one on one with Picard to be the ultimate face off. I was very enthusiastic about doing it.

"When I was talking to the producers," he continues, "I said, 'If we don't make this monster believable, we are in deep water, because this could be a most wonderful concept, but he's a very sympathetic character.' It was important that we not have the audience feel sorry for him when it's over, but I would guess that if you and I took a poll, half the audience

would feel great empathy for him. The poor guy is there in this little puddle and that's that. I think the producers really wanted him to be so evil that you'd say, 'Leave him there. F—k him,' but of course it never happened that way. There was no way to avoid empathy for him, which led to the irony of the situation. He killed Tasha, he damn near killed Riker, and I still wasn't mad at him. Look at what his people had done. How could you *not* feel sorry for him?

"If we had a four million dollar budget and were doing *Alien*, I think we had the potential for a very intelligent piece of work. But to do it in seven days is very tough. My first cut was just barely adequate, and it took input from the producers to make it better. I had always wanted a Roddy McDowall-type of venomous evil coming out of the mouth of the guy, but the producers leaned more towards what you got, which was the throaty presence, but always somewhat ominous. The bottom line is that it became a caricature, I think, and as a result, as close as it came to being a good show, it was not a good show. Unless you sell the audience on the black blob, you're dead. You've got this blob of oil to deal with. Sometimes all it's doing is vibrating down there, sometimes it's waist high, sometimes he's out. You *know* there's an actor there, which is the long and short of it. Of all the shows they did, 'Skin of Evil' was probably only on the top rung of the second half. It was like 45 percent out of 100 percent. There were some shows that were bad because they weren't conceived properly. This show, conceptually, could have been wonderful, and the

only reason it wasn't, and it was nobody's fault, were the pressures of time and budget."

It's unfortunate, but the next episode of the series, "We'll Always Have Paris," was something of a disappointment in comparison to what viewers had seen over the past few weeks. The plot deals with the time/gravity experiments of Doctor Paul Manheim, which has resulted in a rip in the dimensional fabric that is causing the present and the future to intermingle at certain moments, resulting in time distortions which could expand to a galactic level if the planetoid where the experiment is still taking place is not gone to, and the equipment shut down. Combined with this is Manheim's wife, Jenice, a former love of Picard's, who is aboard the Enterprise because her husband seems to be dying. As the man eventually explains it, it's as though his mind and soul are sharing two dimensions at one time. It comes down to Data using the doctor's information to shut down the experiment, while attempting to cope with the fact that he is among three versions of himself from different time continuums, all of whom are trying to decide which Data should actually carry through with the shutdown, as it calls for a precise timing with the next time displacement.

It is tough to pinpoint the exact reasons that this show doesn't work. Perhaps it has something to do with the fact that you never quite believe the relationship between Picard and guest star Michelle Philips as Jenice. Also, the time displacement story, while featuring some interesting elements, does not come across as clearly as it should. Why, for instance, should other dimensional copies of the main characters appear, but only for a moment? Logically, they should remain, thus resulting in numerous copies of our people (which undoubtedly would have made the episode even more convoluted). "We'll Always Have Paris" should be chalked off as a fascinating idea that just didn't come together.

* * *

"I wrote 'Conspiracy' with the idea of doing something different; something with an unhappy ending, a harder edge, elements of horror," states writer Tracy Torme. "I thought that even if people hated it, the show would be back to normal the next week. I wrote it intentionally to be different, *hoping* that it would cause controversy."

Torme got his wish, with "Conspiracy" serving as a standout episode of *Star Trek: The Next Generation*. Picking up on threads laid out in "Coming of Age," Picard is contacted by Captain Walter Keel of the starship Horatio, who has Picard meet him and several other starship captains on a remote planet, where – after testing his memory – they inform him of a conspiracy within the Federation that threatens to tear the organization apart. These words almost duplicate to the letter the warning given to the captain by Admiral Quinn in the aforementioned "Coming of Age." Picard has a difficult time believing their words, but is convinced when the Horatio is mysteriously destroyed.

Later, Data is told to investigate all recent Starfleet communiqués, and learns that there definitely does seem to be an attempt to solidify certain sectors of Federation space. Picard now recognizes the potential threat, and orders the Enterprise to Earth, where he will confront the head of Starfleet Command to get some answers. Upon arrival, Picard and Riker are told to beam down to Earth in twenty minutes, while Admiral Quinn states that he would like to be brought up. Picard sees this as a hopeful sign, that Quinn is still on their side, but unbeknownst to them he has brought with him a briefcase containing a scorpion-like creature.

On the Enterprise, Picard asks Quinn about the conspiracy theory he had relayed to the captain, but the man brushes it off as the captain reading far too much into his words. The captain and first officer separate from Quinn for a moment, with the former stating that somehow this man is *not* the real Quinn. He wants Riker to stay aboard to keep an eye on the man, while Picard beams down to Starfleet for his meeting. There he greets the Federation council and Commander Remick, also from "Coming of Age."

Riker goes to the observation lounge, where Quinn is waiting, and is told that in the man's briefcase is a unique life form. Riker doesn't want to take a look at it, but Quinn insists, rather forcefully, throwing the commander around the room as though he were a rag doll (which isn't too bad for a man apparently in his sixties). Riker contacts security before he is rendered unconscious. A moment later, Worf and Geordi arrive, and are quickly disposed of as well.

Before Quinn can depart, Beverly arrives and starts firing a phaser at the man. Shockingly, it takes several bursts before the man is rendered unconscious.

In sickbay, Beverly performs an examination, and states that the man before her is indeed Quinn, but obviously there is something different about him. Then, attached to the man's neck, she finds a small, quivering object that resembles a worm of some sort. When contacted by the captain, she tells him of this parasite and the distinctive mark on victim's necks. Phasers must be set on kill for them to have any effect.

Picard joins the council for dinner, and finds a bowl full of worms. Nauseated, the captain stares at the others devouring the live creatures, while they explain they are aware of why he is there. While they don't answer many questions, they do state that conquest is foremost on their mind, and humans are such easy targets. He moves to leave the room, when Riker walks in, stating that it will only be a short matter of time before Picard is one of "them." One of the council members checks the commander's neck, and sees the tail of a parasite. Everyone sits at the table and prepare to eat, but just as Riker is about to devour a handful of worms, he whips out his phaser and fires at one of the council members, then another. As they fall to the ground, the scorpion-like parasites crawl out of their mouths and make their way down the corridor. Riker, who has obviously been pretending, and Picard follow one of the creatures into another room, where they see it enter Remick's mouth. With little choice in the matter, the duo open fire with phasers, ripping the man's chest open, causing his head to explode and revealing a mother creature, which they next destroy, which has the effect of curing everyone who had been possessed.

The episode ends with many questions, and the unsettling announcement by Data that Remick had sent a homing beacon to an unexplored sector of the galaxy, which will perhaps allow the parasite race to travel back to Earth someday and make another attempt at conquest.

Interesting to note is that in the first draft teleplay, the parasites did not enter Remick. Instead, Picard and Riker went into the outer room, where they found a giant creature – actually thousands of the smaller creatures grouped together as one – sending out the homing beacon, before they destroy it with their combined phaser fire.

Needless to say, even in its aired form, "Conspiracy" is one hell of a *Star Trek* episode, and different from any that had come before or has been aired since. Combining the show's premise with a healthy dose of *Invasion of the Body Snatchers*, Tracy Torme gave audiences a chilling example of what the series was capable of.

"'Conspiracy' began as a show they had called 'The Assassins,' which had gone through a few drafts and was really not close to anything they wanted to do," explains Torme. "I agreed to take it over, with the condition that I could really turn it upside down and basically create a new story. Originally, I had made it a *Seven Days in May* kind of story with a

coup inside Starfleet by various officers who felt that the Prime Directive was too restrictive, resulting in the Federation getting too soft. They believed that peace with the Klingons had made us complacent and somewhere down the line there would be a threat we would be unprepared for. The coup's leaders were all Picard's friends. I really liked that story, because it had nothing alien in it at all. It was about paranoia. Gene rejected it. He liked it, but didn't want to open that can of worms.

"So I knew the story had to change," he elaborates. "Then, I realized that this was the next to last show of the season, and I really felt that although the series had improved a great deal, we were still too comfortable and weren't pushing the limits of what we *could* do. Thanks especially to [then producer] Robert Justman and Rick Berman, who really got behind it, 'Conspiracy' managed to keep 95% of its original hard edge, and because of that, it is a special show for me. I'm proud of *Star Trek* for being willing to take a chance. Die-hard fans who want a nice, neat and comfortable universe at all times, might be a little upset, but that's okay."

Unfortunately, things became a little too neat beginning with the next episode and part of the second season. In addition, there has been no mention of the parasites since, which is truly a pity, considering the impact that this episode had.

* * *

In March of 1988, Hollywood was hit with a major strike by the Writer's Guild of America, which had

a crippling effect on, primarily, the television industry. As a result, there was a mad scramble by the studios to complete their quota of episodes for the season.

The result of such a scramble can be seen in *The Next Generation*'s season finale, "The Neutral Zone," which appears to be a hybrid of two scripts which just do not come together at all. First off, the Enterprise finds an ancient spacecraft from Earth that contains several cryogenic freeze units housing human beings. They are brought aboard the starship, and Beverly states that each of them had been dying of something, and were put into deep-freeze until a cure could be found for their illness. Somehow they broke Earth orbit, and have been drifting ever since. Beverly cures these people of their ailments, and then the task becomes one of assimilating them into the 24th Century, which is not an easy thing considering that this group is supposed to be representative of the kind of people that live on Earth today.

In the meantime, the Enterprise is investigating the destruction of several Federation outposts near the Neutral Zone, and they suspect the Romulans. During a tension-filled (and terrific) final five minutes of the episode, a Romulan vessel appears, its commander stating that they had nothing to do with the destruction of the outposts, as they have been busy with "problems" of their own (which one can assume would be the parasite threat from "Conspiracy"). Their final words are chilling: "We are here to serve notice, Captain. We're back!"

Frankly, those last five minutes

should have been the episode's teaser, with a Enterprise/Romulans tale following the commercial break. Instead, we have a tired and silly retread of the original show's "Space Seed," that serves little more purpose than to provide some awful comic relief. Certainly not an auspicious way to conclude the season.

* * *

As Bob Lewin stated near the outset of this section, every television series goes through a shakedown period where the cast and crew struggle to find out the show's particular strengths and weaknesses.

In the case of *Star Trek: The Next Generation*, it's safe to say that every episode was at least competently made, and quite a few *attempted* something new and dynamic in terms of story and character development, but very few actually made the grade. Of 24 aired episodes during the first season, only a little more than a fifth of them could be considered dynamite, while a little more than that can be deemed very good efforts, with the rest ranging from only mediocre to fair. While this may not seem to be a terrible overall ratio, the number of successes is rather disappointing, and one must ponder the reasons for this.

Is it just that good, solid scripts aren't available? This doesn't seem likely, as many unproduced stories and earlier drafts of produced episodes were far superior to the aired versions. Special effects and set design? No, the effects and basic sets of *The Next Generation* are, quite frankly,

gorgeous, surpassing anything done in the field to date, thanks mostly to the fact that Industrial Light and Magic are handling the former, and the set designers have made the Enterprise appear to be a functional spacecraft. Combined, these elements present a very realistic view of what the 24th Century may look like.

Then, what is the problem? Perhaps it all stems from the attitude, "if it ain't broke, don't fix it."

The original *Star Trek* was a survivor. Like the fictional hero Rocky Balboa, the series managed to go the distance, for three seasons struggling to remain on the air against seemingly overwhelming odds, including network censorship, poor time slots and low ratings. The series was put into a position where it was *forced* to survive, or it would perish. The choice was as simple as that, and for that reason those laboring in front of and behind the cameras did their damnedest to make the show *different* from anything else on the air. The scripts were literate, the ensemble a more realistic "family" of characters than had been presented in quite some time, and the audience constantly felt that *Star Trek* was trying harder than anyone else to deliver quality television.

Star Trek: The Next Generation, conversely, has got it too easy. It exudes a certain confidence that says the cast and crew *know* that the show is going to be a ratings success and will have a fairly long run. For the most part, there doesn't seem to be any challenge to produce scripts or delve into ideas which are different than what's come before, and the

show brings with it a certain sense of familiarity.

Writer Tracy Torme, who has gone from Story Editor to Creative Consultant on the series, sums up *The Next Generation*'s problems.

"It would be nice if people started taking more chances with television, because we're *barely* scratching the surface of its potential," he says. "The medium does very well covering sports and news, but when it comes to drama, it was better 20 or 30 years ago. Everyone is looking for formula, and that really gets boring after a while. The opportunities are there, if you're allowed to take advantage of them, to really do something different that will shake people up a little bit, but hardly anyone is doing that."

Including, he notes, *Star Trek*. "The format of the show opens many of those doors, but then it's up to *Star Trek* to be bold enough to *do* something unusual, challenging or artistically stimulating," Torme points out. "But having the opportunity doesn't mean that you're going to fulfill it. There was a conservative approach taken, that has carried on to this day, of not rocking the boat too much; not taking too many chances. My position on this has been pretty well known. I'm the one person who tries to push to do unusual, unexpected or, hopefully, progressive things on the show, but there always seems to be resistance. It always seems to be a struggle to do something that's groundbreaking. Again, that's because the show is such a success that the attitude has become, 'Why take risks?' "

Jonathan Frakes as Commander William T. Riker, first officer of the Enterprise who was originally designed to serve as *TNG*'s version of an early Captain Kirk. (Copyright © Gene Trindle/Shooting Star)

Brent Spiner as Data, the Enterprise's android science officer, whose quest throughout the series was to become more human.
(Copyright © Gene Trindle/Shooting Star)

Previous page: An early gathering of part of the *Star Trek: The Next Generation* crew: Brent Spiner, Levar Burton, Marina Sirtis, Jonathan Frakes and Patrick Stewart.
(Copyright © Gene Trindle/Shooting Star)

Marina Sirtis as the Enterprise's counselor, the empathic Deanna Troi, part Betazoid, who can sense what others are feeling.
(Copyright © Crosby/Shooting Star)

From left: Jonathon Frake (Commander William T. Riker), Gates McFadden (Dr. Beverly Crusher) and Patrick Stewart (Captain Jean Luc Picard).
(Copyright © Gene Trindle/Shooting Star)

The ambassadors of a reptilian race as seen in the episode "Lonely Among Us."
(Copyright © George Rose)

Denise Crosby as security chief Tasha Yar, a character who didn't last the full first season due to the actress' disappointment at the limited amount of material she was given to play. Tasha died in the episode "Skin of Evil", though she would return in a time-altered universe as presented in season three's "Yesterday's Enterprise".
(Copyright © Gene Trindle/Shooting Star)

Wil Wheaton as Ensign Wesley Crusher, a character fans either loved or hated – there was no in between. Here he is seen in the episode "Justice", where the ensign is sentenced to death for breaking a simple law on an alien planet.
(Copyright © Crosby/Shooting Star)

Brent Spiner's Data was based on a character from an earlier Gene Roddenberry television pilot, *The Questor Tapes*. Data would eventually gain emotions in the feature film, *Star Trek: Generations*. (Copyright © Gene Trindle/Shooting Star)

Striking a pose for the camera are, from left, Denise Crosby (Tasha Yar), Jonathan Frakes (Will Riker) and Marina Sirtis (Deanna Troi).
(Copyright © George Rose)

Previous pages:
Michael Dorn as Lt. Worf, the first Klingon to serve in Starfleet.
(Copyright © Gene Trindle/Shooting Star)

Patrick Stewart as Captain Jean Luc Picard. The actor was originally considered by producer Robert Justman for the role of Data.
(Copyright © Gene Trindle/Shooting Star)

PART V
STAR TREK: THE NEXT GENERATION
From Script to Screen

The following section is a detailed look at the development of some of the earliest episodes of Star Trek: The Next Generation, *from initial story treatments through final episodes. Through this method, the reader will actually witness the metamorphosis of the story, where it was enhanced in the process and where it was hurt.*

"ENCOUNTER AT FARPOINT"

Despite being saddled with some of the difficulties confronting the first *Star Trek* feature, *The Next Generation* got off to an exciting start with Dorothy Fontana's "Encounter at Farpoint," which was co-written by Gene Roddenberry. On paper the script is a mixed bag, with Fontana's sections proving to be highly innovative with an intellectual premise, while Roddenberry's section comes across as a retread of "The Squire of Gothos" and several other episodes of the old show. Thankfully the cast, including guest star John DeLancie, and director Corey Allen made it work.

The show's initial outline, "Meeting at Farpoint," which was written by Dorothy Fontana and dated December 5, 1986, was vastly different from the teleplay which would eventually develop. It begins with the Enterprise completing another mission, with Captain Julien Picard praising First Officer Kyle Summers and Security Chief Macha Hernandez for a job well done. This mission has served as a crowning achievement for Summers, who will be assuming command of a Federation science cruiser. The trans-

fer of First Officers is scheduled to take place at Farpoint Station, a staging planet which is to be used for refueling, the resupply of vessels, the transfer of passengers and personnel, and so on.

The Enterprise and the Starseeker lock into orbit around the planet, preparing to transfer personnel from one vessel to the other. Coming over from the Starseeker, among others, is Lt. Commander William Ryker, who will be replacing Summers as First Officer; Lt. Commander Data, Dr. Beverly Crusher and her 15 year old *daughter*, Leslie. All of these people hold varied feelings regarding duty on the Enterprise, with some of them highly anticipatory and others rather nervous. As the treatment notes, "on the shuttle between ships, there are barbed comments made about 'the android,' which Ryker not only fields but turns back on the commentators. It is clear that his relationship with Data is an old one, and a great loyalty exists between them."

No sooner has the personnel transfer taken place than the regular characters meet one another and immediately fall into place. A feeling of instant comraderie develops, but is interrupted by the announcement

that another spacecraft is approaching Farpoint Station. This vessel sends out one communiqué: "give up; transfer your personnel to the planet surface, or die." The other ship is revealed on the starship viewscreens as a spacegoing gun platform, with all its weaponry aimed directly at the pair of starships and Farpoint. The captain of the Starseeker, who is described as being somewhat bold and perhaps a little too daring, attempts to utilize photon torpedoes, but before he is able to do so his ship is destroyed. Picard, having watched the destruction on his viewscreen, deduces that the gun platform has more fire power than even the Enterprise. Seeing no alternative, he orders his crew to comply. His plan is to have the crew learn the enemy's weaknesses, so that they can be exploited as soon as possible. It is admittedly difficult for the crew to play this waiting game, but Picard *is* the captain.

Once the Enterprise crew has been transferred to the planet's surface, a representative of the enemy appears. They learn that their opponents are the Annoi, a race of simians who have developed the technology to carry out any threats they make. The goal of the Annoi is to gather a mineral called balmine, which exists in great amounts on Farpoint. It is an insignificant mineral to the inhabitants of the planet. Every member of the Enterprise crew and of Farpoint Station are forced to mine the material, and transport the ore to the gun platform. The Enterprise herself is being controlled by a small Annoi crew aided by a group of humans. Together they are able to keep the starship in orbit.

Learning that their guards are part of a caste system that even they don't like, Picard's people attempt to bribe them. Meanwhile, Troi notes that she is feeling someone crying, but Ryker merely attributes it to someone who's having a difficult time dealing with the situation. Both he and Macha would like nothing better than to launch an attack on the gun platform. Picard listens to them, and points out that he's all for it – if every angle is covered.

Considering that the balmine is transported to the platform in a shuttle whose crew complement is made up of a pilot, armed Annoi guard and six prisoners, they could conceivably "take out" the gun platform with explosives they've hoarded. The monkey wrench in Ryker and Macha's plan is that they're not sure of the exact layout of the gunship. Leslie Crusher, who has served as a "runner," whose purpose is to serve as a contact between the gun platform bridge and the ore receiving area, has memorized the layout of the entire gun platform. While the other members of the Enterprise are dubious, at best, Beverly convinces Picard that her daughter has a very special mind, and that it's easy to believe that the girl

has indeed already memorized the layout of the ship. Picard is willing to take a chance.

The prison team, consisting of Ryker, Macha, Troi, Data and two others, board the shuttle, almost effortlessly gain control of it and bring the smaller vessel into the cargo lock where the ore is unloaded. Data notes with curiosity that a great deal of ore has already been brought up to the platform, and yet there seems to be little in sight. He finds it unlikely that it can be utilized so quickly.

Armed with their explosives, the Away Team attempts to find the engine room of the gun platform, but can't. This ship is not equipped with engines. Suddenly Troi is staggered by an incredible amount of emotional pain as random thoughts enter her mind. It will be impossible for them to destroy the gun platform, she explains. It is a sentient being.

Ultimately we learn that the "base of the gun platform and its motive power is the creature – and not willingly." Apparently this alien being wandered into Annoi territory in weakened condition, and the simians quickly discovered that it needed balmine for nourishment. Although there were large quantities of the mineral on their planet, they thought this would be a perfect opportunity to expand their Empire. They constructed a gun platform around the creature while it was still weak, effectively trapping it. The Annoi would be willing to feed it balmine (albeit just enough to keep it alive) if it would allow itself to be exploited as a weapon.

Just as Troi details this story, the Annoi disarm them, and they are thrown into a detention area.

While Picard is worrying about the Away Team on the planet's surface, Troi is still communicating with the creature on the gun platform. She ultimately learns that the creature is a gentle one that despises what it is being forced to do. Ryker tells Troi to communicate that it can land in a deserted area on the planet so that the guns will not serve as a tool to be used against either the Enterprise or the planet. After that, if the creature refuses to move, the Annoi will be helpless and almost harmless. Agreeing with this course of action, the creature follows through, impacting so roughly on the ground that the detention area is cracked open, thus releasing the team and allowing them, with the aid of the prisoners, to overwhelm the Annoi. Picard, with the assistance of others, recaptures the Enterprise, while the rest help to free the creature. The Annoi, it is stated, will be dealt with by the Federation.

The Enterprise, its crew having been given its shakedown mission, departs for its next adventure.

[NOTE: The first thought that comes to mind upon reading "Meeting at Farpoint" is that it's considerably more action oriented than the premiere episode, or subsequent series, would eventually be. Bearing in mind that when announcing Star Trek: The Next Generation, Gene Roddenberry had stated that the series would be much less focused on the military aspects of starship life than either the original series or the feature films, one can see where the softening of the adventure came from in later drafts. This was truly a throwback to "Where No Man Has Gone Before," in which the *audience was given an intellectually stimulating premise wrapped up in an action/adventure format.*

The Annoi, which in the first draft teleplay would be changed to the Annae and used as the name of the people living at Farpoint Station, would have apparently been Dorothy Fontana's tribute to the popular Planet of the Apes *film series, and one can only hope that they would have gotten Roddy McDowall to portray the leader of that simian race.*

We would never actually meet Mark Summers, or have another starship destroyed by an alien threat. It's also interesting that Beverly's offspring was a daughter in the original conception of the show. Also, this draft establishes a long friendship between Ryker and Data, which sounds extremely Kirk/Spock -like. By the time the "Farpoint" story was put on film, they never would have met prior to this mission.

All in all, this would have been a wonderful beginning for The Next Generation, *but there were many more changes in store before the cameras could roll.]*

The first draft of "Encounter at Farpoint," written by Fontana and dated February 17, 1987, begins with the starship Belvidere in orbit around a planet that serves as home for Farpoint Station. The Annae city is situated next to the luxurious spaceport/station, while all around both is a seemingly inhospitable landscape.

Commander William Ryker is meeting with the Annae administrator, Elzever, and complimenting the man on the luxury of the station, while at the same time trying to determine exactly how they had been able to construct it so quickly and efficiently. Elzever is annoyingly coy in his responses, and before ending the meeting he notes that when the Enterprise approaches the planet, their orbital monitors will pick up and transmit the image to the surface.

In the Annae shopping mall, Dr. Beverly Crusher and her fifteen-year-old son, Wes, are making the rounds, discussing Enterprise captain, *Julien* (eventually Jean-Luc) Picard. Wes wants to know what the man is like, but it's obvious that Beverly really doesn't wish to discuss it, stating only that he and Wes' father, Jack, had served on the Stargazer together.

Elsewhere in the station, Lt. Geordi LaForge and Ensign Sawyer Markham are watching monitor screens, looking for any indication that the Enterprise is approaching. Ryker meets them for the first time and they briefly discuss the fact that they've all been assigned to the grandest starship in the Fleet. Noticing Geordi's eye prosthesis, he questions the lieutenant and is told in response that he was born without optic nerves, and that the "visor" allows him to see better than a human can. Their conversation is interrupted when they notice the image of the Enterprise approaching on the monitor screen.

[NOTE: These introductory scenes are similar, and yet strikingly different from those that were ultimately utilized in the final version of the episode. The sequence between Ryker and Elzever (who would eventually become Riker and Groppler Zorn, respectively) is extremely close, with the only bit to come in later drafts being the moment where we get a feeling that Farpoint Station is not what it appears to be, when a bowl of apples mysteriously appears.

Also, it's obvious that Wes does not know the facts behind the relationship between his father and Julien (eventually Jean-Luc) Picard, apparently learning for the first time that the two men served together on the Stargazer. In the aired version, Wes tells Commander Riker that Picard is the one who brought his father's body back home to them.

Ensign Markham doesn't make it to the final draft, and Geordi never discusses his prosthetic eye device with Riker as he does here. Most of his dialogue in this scene would eventually be transferred to one with Dr. Crusher.]

Once those people who have been transferred from the Belvidere to the Enterprise have beamed up from the planet, Picard addresses them in the conference lounge, where we learn that whole families will be making the journey on the starship during the course of its 20 year mission. The captain does his best to come across as friendly as he can, informing these people that tours of the Enterprise can be arranged for civilian personnel who may never have been aboard a starship before.

Afterwards, Picard meets with Ryker in the captain's ready room, where they get right to the point: the situation at Farpoint Station. Ryker explains that somehow the Annae technology is so advanced that it seems just a step removed from being miraculous. Picard states that that's precisely the reason that Starfleet has ordered the Enterprise to investigate. Only a year and a half ago there was just the one city on the planet's surface. Elzever, it would seem, upon realizing the full scope of being a Federation ally, thought that constructing the station would impress Starfleet. Their mission, he goes on, is to find out the secret of Farpoint Station, and, if successful, to get the Annae to construct other such stations throughout Federation territory. Additionally, he mentions that it might be a good idea for Ryker to meet his number two, Lieutenant Commander Data, and security chief Macha Hernandez. He suggests the latter first, as Data will undoubtedly be some time escorting the "Admiral."

Walking through a corridor of the ship is the Oriental-looking Data, accompanied by the elderly (137 year old) Admiral McCoy (formerly chief medical officer of the Enterprise under the command of James T. Kirk – a living legend). Data contacts the transporter room, which doesn't sit too well with McCoy.

"Hold it right there, boy," he grumbles. "You can just cancel that transporter talk right now. Only reason I let 'em promote me to Admiral was so's I could commandeer a shuttle when I wanted it . . . And I want one now. Never did hold with flashin' my atoms across space and gluin' 'em back together on the other end. Damned machines can make mistakes."

Data disagrees with this, pointing out that a machine might malfunction, but a mistake is beyond its capability, unless, of course, its basic program is at fault. McCoy is incredulous, and a bit surprised to find

that Data is not a Vulcan, but is, rather, an android.

"Musta been built by Vulcans then," he snaps. Their conversation continues, with the doctor noting that the starship has got a good name, and that if treated like a lady, she'll always bring them home again.

Ryker arrives at the ship gymnasium, where he finds Hernandez working out with her people. They discuss the physical fitness of the team, and she adds that Enterprise security has won Fleet championships three years consecutively. They continue their introductory chat.

Meanwhile, Dr. Crusher is being given a tour of the sickbay facilities by her assistant, Dr. Asenzi. Just as he mentions that he has arranged for an informal staff meeting for the evening, Picard enters. Asenzi exits, leaving the two of them alone, and the first moment is a bit uncomfortable. In the ensuing conversation we learn that twelve years earlier Picard had been the one that had brought Jack's body back to her. In addition, Picard admits some feeling of guilt regarding the man's death.

"I let him lead the Away team down to that planet," he says softly. "I shouldn't have let him go."

"Jack was stubborn," she counters. "Maybe too brave for his own good. He was only doing what all captains did then – leading the contact teams, placing their lives at risk, instead of taking responsibility for their ships."

Picard offers her the opportunity to transfer from the Enterprise if working with him will prove too painful, but she refuses.

[NOTE: The sequence in the

conference room serves as a reminder that the Enterprise is transporting entire families through space, and that the duration of their mission is 20 years. This particular mission, to investigate Farpoint Station, is much as the initial mission of the Enterprise in the televised form.

As in the final version, the scene between Data and Admiral McCoy is marvelous, and it's a bit surprising to see that it was included so early in the writing of the story. Bones is even grumpier than ever, and his Southern twang is more distinct, much as was the situation when he aged prematurely in the episode, "The Deadly Years." The line about accepting his promotion to Admiral so that he could occasionally commandeer a shuttle is a nice, and humorous, touch. Interestingly, Data was originally conceived as an Oriental.

Macha Hernandez, who would eventually become Tasha Yar, was originally based on the Jenette Goldstein character from Aliens. In fact, the producers even tried to hire the actress, but she was tied up with other projects. When casting Denise Crosby in the role, they obviously softened the character a bit, but it's good to see her in action here, leading her people through their paces.

In the aired version, Dr. Crusher has no assistant. In addition, the dialogue between her and Picard gives even more detail about their background than we would eventually get. For instance, we learn that Picard served under Jack Crusher on the Stargazer (which would be refuted in the later episode, "The Battle," in which it was once Picard's *command), and we get a comment on what is considered a mistake of the original series: the fact that a captain continually beams down into hostile environments, risking himself and therefore his ship. Naturally this was corrected when this new series was designed, as Riker would lead the majority of Away Teams, leaving Picard behind on the Enterprise.]*

Returning to the bridge, Picard tells Ryker that he's beaming down to meet with Elzever. Lieutenant Deanna Troi, who's described as being one quarter Betazoid, enters the bridge as well, and she is introduced to Ryker. It's obvious that they already know each other, and even more so when she projects her thoughts into his mind, referring to him as her *imzadi*. The captain explains that he's bringing her down to the planet with him so that she can gather as much information on Elzever as possible. Ryker wonders aloud if that's any way to treat an ally. Picard responds that Starfleet isn't at all sure that the Annae are allies, which is why Farpoint is being investigated in the first place.

On the planet's surface, the duo meet with Elzever, with Picard asking him various questions about the station, wondering if Starfleet could purchase the construction material used, or if Annae workers could build such stations round the galaxy. Elzever is not at all responsive to these questions, stating that the Annae will not build any stations beside the one on this planet, and that if the Federation cannot accept this, then perhaps the Annae should deal with the Ferengi Alliance. Seeing no where else to go with the conversation, and not enjoying the inherent threat in Elzever's words, Picard and Troi leave the office. The Annae is obviously disturbed by this confrontation.

Alone in the corridor, Troi tells the captain that she could feel someone crying out with hopelessness, but that it was *not* from Elzever. He, she adds, was "lying through his teeth."

Data returns to the bridge, apologizing for having taken so long, and adding that the Admiral had offered to make him a mint julep, but that he doesn't drink. Ryker smiles, saying that the captain knew that he would be indisposed for a while. Ryker says that for some reason he expected Data to be an alien, to which he replies, "I almost qualify, sir. I am an android created and programmed by a race alien to your own. It's all in your point of view, isn't it?"

Ryker admits that he's a bit uncomfortable working with a machine, but Data points out the illogic in that statement: isn't the Enterprise itself a machine? And doesn't he interact with the vessel? It's a point Ryker can't exactly argue with.

On the ship's holodeck, Wes, Mike and Adam are running through a jungle monsoon simulation, allowing themselves to be covered in mud and water. They're about to initiate a snowstorm, when Wes notices the time, utters an "Oh, tribbles," and announces that he has to depart. Going to sickbay, Wes details for his mother everything he's discovered on the ship, and concludes the conversation by asking if Beverly can arrange a visit to the bridge for him. She's hesitant to even bring up the subject to Picard, who has a standing order against children on the bridge, but her expression seems to say that she'll do her best.

On the bridge, Picard, Ryker, Troi, Macha and Data are discussing the situation at Farpoint Station. Macha points out that if the Annae are serious about offering the station to the Ferengi Alliance, it could pose a serious threat to the Federation. Considering this, Picard, still unsatisfied by what he has . . . or rather, has not . . . learned about the station, announces that it would be a perfect time for shore leave. Crewmembers and their families will beam down to Farpoint Station, while Ryker goes undercover to learn all that he can about this strange place. He suggests that Data, Troi and Macha serve on the Away Team, with Ryker adding Geordi to the list.

After they've departed, Beverly arrives on the bridge and asks Picard for a personal favor: to allow her son to take a quick look around the bridge. The captain replies in the negative, pointing out that the bridge is no place for a child.

"He's a responsible teenager, Julien," she says firmly, "and he's Jack's son. He rates just a little more from you than most boys."

At Farpoint Station, Geordi uses his particular abilities to examine the various structures around them, finding nothing out of the ordinary. Macha discovers service tunnels and suggests that they be their method of travel, as they will be able to move more freely and everything that works above the ground is controlled from beneath it. Troi states that she once again feels despair and unhappiness, as she did earlier.

Back on the Enterprise bridge, Wesley has been allowed admittance and is taking everything in with awe. Picard, doing his best to be benevolent, allows the youth to sit in the command chair and instructs him on the use of the various control panels in the arm rests. Wes displays incredible intelligence and knowledge, surprising just about everyone on the bridge. At that moment, Ryker contacts the captain to let him know that they haven't been able to find anything out of the ordinary, but that the search will continue. His plan is to split up the Away Team so that they can cover more ground.

Picard closes communication, when the ship's computer announces that another ship is approaching Farpoint; a ship unlike any they have encountered before. Down on the planet, Elzever is panicking upon hearing news of the other ship, demanding to know what it is and what it wants. No one has an answer for him. Contacting the Enterprise, he asks Picard if it would be possible for him to force the intruder to identify itself. Enterprise tries hailing frequencies, but to no avail.

In a service tunnel, a glow passes over Troi and Macha, with the former noting that it felt like someone had tapped into her brain and asked her a question. In space, the other vessel fires a phaser-like weapon that destroys a building, and disintegrates several of the Annae. Several more blasts follow.

Picard orders all of the Enterprise people back to their transporter points immediately so that they can be brought back up before things get any more dangerous for them. On the planet, the Away Team is gathering up Enterprise personnel.

Once the Away Team is back on the bridge, Troi nearly collapses from pain, reacting to a mental scream that she detected. The bridge consoles suddenly darken, with Data announcing that all of their sensors have gone inoperative. Scanners, on the other hand, are still operational. They try hailing frequencies to the other ship. A picture does form, with a bridge that looks very much like the Enterprise bridge, but in the command chair is a "fearsome-looking humanoid." It looks directly into the viewscreen, and then the image vanishes. Troi tries to reach it with her mind, but finds her attempts forced back at her by what is undoubtedly a superior intelligence. Discussing the situation a bit further, Troi states that the only deaths attributable to the other vessel are those of the Annae . . . no one from the Enterprise has been harmed. Picard deduces that this could be the key to what Elzever was lying about. He tells Ryker that he wants the Annae on board the Enterprise as soon as possible.

Macha and Ryker materialize in Elzever's office, and tell him that he's coming with them. All the man does is beg them to make the other vessel go away, while at the same time claiming that he doesn't know who they are or what they want. Just as the trio beams up, an energy beam strikes the exact place where Elzever had been standing just an instant earlier.

Back on the bridge, Picard demands that Elzever tell him who the people are on the other vessel. Again the Annae says he has no idea. What is described as a "very different transporter effect" moves swiftly over the bridge personnel, before locking onto Elzever, who disappears. Picard deduces that the man has got to be on the other ship. Troi again nearly collapses with pain; a pain coming from Farpoint Station itself.

Picard orders the Enterprise to break orbit and maneuver itself between the other vessel and Farpoint Station. Shields are raised to their maximum. Troi is asked to probe the other ship again to see if they can help Elzever, but unfortunately the alien intelligence "pushes" her away. The only thing she is able to discern is that the alien vessel seems to be projecting an intense amount of rage and hatred which is directed only at the Annae. In addition, she says, it feels as though someone on the ship is reaching out to someone on the station.

The Enterprise reaches a position between the vessel and the planet, with the other ship doing its best to maneuver clear of the starship. Picard, having hailing frequencies opened, explains that they will not retaliate if the alien vessel strikes them with their weapon systems, but by the same token they will not stand by and allow any other Annae to be destroyed. There is no response, with the ship merely trying once again to get around the Enterprise. Macha, growing concerned over the threat to the Annae, requests and receives permission to beam a security detail down to the planet for evacuation. Ryker, too, is given permission to take an Away Team over to the other ship to see if they can gather some answers and rescue Elzever. Troi, Data and LaForge make up his team.

The alien ship begins to move directly towards the Enterprise, but Picard refuses to move the starship, pointing out that "If they impact on us, they won't get off lightly either." At the last possible moment, it veers off, sparing the starship and, most likely, itself from destruction. Once again the Enterprise intercepts its energy beams from striking the planet.

On the alien ship, Geordi points out that the walls of the vessel are made up of an almost organic material. Data, utilizing a tricorder, verifies this assessment. Eventually they find Elzever, suspended in some sort of force field device, and obviously in great pain. Phasers prove useless on the screen. With no alternative, they continue on, attempting to find out who is "driving this buggy." They come across the same alien figure they had seen on the viewscreen earlier, and project the image back to the Enterprise. Data is surprised to find that the figure does not read as a lifeform, but the *wall behind it does*. In fact, the entire ship is giving off the readings of a lifeform. Troi tries to open contact, serving as a mediator between the alien and Elzever. Fortunately the creature perceives her as pure and honest, and is willing to allow this.

On the planet's surface, Hernandez discovers the walls of Farpoint Station to be alive. Back on the alien ship, Troi tells Elzever that the Annae are being destroyed because they have been hurting the alien's mate; that the mate has been enslaved on the planet and is dying because of the energy that has been fed to it. Ultimately it turns out that Farpoint

Station itself is the alien creature, which was dying on the planet. The Annae gave it just enough energy to keep it alive, but, upon discovering its vast transmutation abilities, they held it captive, forcing it to grant them their every desire, and creating this fabulous space station which would be used to impress the Federation. Troi adds that the alien only wants its mate back, and that if delivered, the death and destruction of the Annae would cease. Naturally this is the course of action that follows.

As the two alien beings are united and sent off into deep space, Elzever stares sadly at the viewscreen, noting that they had hoped the station would be their link to outside worlds; a method to allow the Annae to grow and flourish. They now have to work out the future for themselves.

Picard does not see things so bleakly. "You might find it a more rewarding future," he says. "The Federation *is* still interested in Farpoint. With your work and Federation assistance, it can be a very valuable staging station for us. What do you think?"

"I believe my people would be very willing to try," says Elzever.

[NOTE: First off, Deanna Troi is described here as being 1/4 Betazoid, but she would ultimately be 1/2 alien. Also, the Ryker/Troi prior romance is rather cumbersome, harkening back to the Decker/Ilia romance of Star Trek: The Motion Picture. *It doesn't really serve to add anything, and since it has been all but ignored through the course of the first season of the show, it's a wonder that anybody ever included it in the premiere episode at all.*

In this draft Picard and Troi meet with Elzever, but in the final one Riker would join them. The conversation, though, is essentially the same, culminating with Zorn (Elzever) making his Ferengi threat. We also learn that Data was constructed by an alien race, which is, once again, the Questor connection of the character which was discussed earlier.

An interesting addition here is that we get a quick glimpse of the alien captain, before we are "forced out." Nothing of this sort made it to the final episode. The sequence does have some similarity to 2010, when a probe enters the Jupiter atmosphere, catches a quick glimpse of life, and is then jettisoned to deep space.

Here Elzever is snatched by the alien vessel from the Enterprise bridge as opposed to his office, and the Enterprise itself plays a much more active role in trying to save the Annae city from the energy blasts.

The final version of this script would have Zorn freed from the force field "cell" by phaser fire. Another thing that would ultimately be deleted is Troi's telepathic link with the creature, and her serving as mediator. This dramatic device is quite similar to Spock's mind-meld, and one can only assume that it was dropped for this reason. Once you establish a character having this kind of power/tool, then it's awfully tough not to keep going back to it again and again. A good choice by whoever made it.

The actual conclusion of this draft is a bit more upbeat than the aired form, because Picard states that the Federation would still be interested in working with the Annae, thus providing a bit of hope for the *race. In the aired version, there's no mention of continuing to work together.]*

As the second draft commences, Ryker is a bit miffed that no one will tell him exactly how Farpoint Station is able to bring forth his every desire. He gets out of the shower and, while wearing only a "futuristic towel" he enters the outer room to see a Bandi (formerly Annae) woman gathering his breakfast tray. Noting that he has not eaten his eggs, the woman states that the meal must have been unsatisfactory to him. Ryker counters that he probably would have been better off just ordering some fruit. She leaves. Ryker, who has just walked out of the room, walks back in and is astonished to find a basket of fresh fruit – exactly what he had mentioned to her.

Later he meets with Zorn (formerly Elzever) and once again tries to get some answers about the magic of this place. As a test he mentions one painter he likes over another, and when he turns around, he sees that the paintings in Zorn's office have changed to accommodate his wishes. Zorn pays this no mind. They end their meeting, and once he is alone, Zorn looks into the air and says, "You've been told not to do that. Why can't. you understand? It will arouse their suspicions, and I won't have that."

As in the previous draft, Ryker meets Beverly, Wes, Geordi and Markham in the station mall, only this time there is no mention of Jack Crusher.

Shortly thereafter the announcement is made that the Enterprise command module has reached orbit around the planet. Ryker wants to know about the battle section, and is merely told that there is no sign of it. The Klingon, Lt. Worf, contacts Ryker and angrily explains that the Enterprise had been intercepted by an alien vessel and boarded. While the aliens didn't give any formal names, they apparently believe that they have the right to put the Enterprise crew on trial "for existing at all." He was ordered to get the civilians away as quickly as possible, hence the ship separation.

Ryker arrives on the bridge, and is shortly thereafter contacted by Picard who says they should be arriving at 1700 hours. Once the battle section does, Ryker is beamed over where he meets Tanya Yar (formerly Macha Hernandez), who says that Captain Picard would like to see him immediately. Once the two men introduce themselves to one another, Picard explains that the Enterprise, and all of humanity, may be under sentence of "never being allowed to fare out of our own star system again. The question is – how do we prove we're worthy? And will we know we're being tried? In any event, it appears that Farpoint Station will be our testing ground."

At that moment Ryker is given his first assignment as Enterprise First Officer: to link up the two sections of the starship, which he pulls off without a hitch. After that he meets with Picard in his ready room, and the next several scenes, for all intents and purposes, play exactly as they did in the first draft teleplay. One exception is that once the alien vessel begins firing on the Bandi city, Crusher is told to beam down a medical team to help the wounded. Outside of that, the story is primarily the same.

The next, and all subsequent drafts, include the enigmatic character of Q, the being from a different space and time continuum, who has been sent into our dimension to stop the spread of human contamination. His first appearance is on the bridge of the Enterprise, where he tells Picard that the ship should be turned around before it is most definitely destroyed. He and his fellow Qs consider humanity nothing more than a race of savages who are so intent on destroying each other that they do not deserve the honor of going further into space. The captain argues in defense of his race, and the bridge crew ultimately finds itself in a 21st Century courtroom, where Q, adorned in the uniform of a judge of the time, is about to pass sentence on them. Again, Picard attempts to point out that the humanity the alien discusses has become a part of the past; man has reached maturity, and for that reason is exploring further into space. The captain is successful to some degree, as Q agrees that the crew of his ship should indeed be tested in an attempt to prove what they claim. This test will take place at Farpoint Station.

Essentially the story plays out the same as it does in the second draft (with the exception, naturally, of dialogue), down to the last few minutes where Q reappears on the bridge, and encourages the crew to destroy the hostile alien vessel. This, Picard realizes, is the test, and it is Q's interference that proves not is all as it would appear to be. The truth of the situation reveals itself as they learn the craft is actually a living being, and the Enterprise aids in the freeing of its mate. Humanity has proven its point, a fact that Q does not take lightly. He departs, as he had promised to do, but does not promise that he will not return.

And thus, the first adventure of *Star Trek: The Next Generation* comes to an end, and its premiere episode is quite a sight to behold. The special effects are absolutely beautiful, the cast is wonderful and the story, thanks in no small degree to the acting talents of guest star John DeLancie as Q, comes to life in a way that it does not on paper. The overall effect is that this episode proved itself to be much more than a watered down version of the original *Star Trek*, emphasizing that it is the theme and ideals of the show that count more than any other factor.

"THE NAKED NOW"

In Gene Roddenberry's "Revelations," we open on a collapsing sun, with the space vessel Tsilkovsky in orbit. A voice from that vessel is sending out a distress call to the Enterprise, pleading for assistance and explaining that they are trapped in orbit. This communiqué is interrupted by a female voice saying, "So move your fanny, Enterprise honey. Have you any pretty boys aboard for us?" An argument between the two voices begins.

The Enterprise approaches the smaller ship, with Riker asking the crew to turn on its image transceiver so they can learn the nature of their emergency. This plea is ignored, and, with Picard's approval, the first officer gathers an Away Team consisting of Data and Geordi. Tasha Yar (still referred to here as Macha Hernandez) asks to join them, but Picard replies that he will only risk three members of his crew until they know the nature of the Tsilkovsky's emergency. Troi attempts to pick up thought patterns from the crew of that ship, and learns that there is a feeling of intoxication among them . . . or maybe even insanity.

In the transporter room, the Away Team hears a communiqué from the other ship, where someone is telling someone else to get away from the escape hatch. There is a sudden explosion of air, and then silence. The transporter chief explains that all life support from the bridge is gone. Riker orders the man to transport them to a safe corridor, and this is done.

The Tsilkovsky is gripped by the Enterprise tractor beam, while the Away Team continues to explore the ship. they eventually find the dead bodies of the crew, many of them actually frozen while taking showers with their clothes on. Riker vaguely remembers hearing of another situation where people had showered with their clothes on, but can't place the memory. Geordi, meanwhile, touches a corpse, and congealing drops of moisture attract themselves to his hand. This immediately starts to itch. The Away Team transports back over to the Enterprise.

Back "home," Geordi is affected by the disease, as he attempts to "jump" Tasha, and then brushes it off as a joke. But physical contact has been made. A channel is opened with Beverly Crusher, and she arrives, but by the time she does, the disease has affected Tasha, who tells her that it was a false alarm. Once the doctor has departed, Tasha suggests that she and Geordi go to an exercise room where they can continue their "moves" against each other.

Picard calls a meeting of his key officers to explore the situation aboard the other ship. And that's where the Roddenberry material leaves off.

[NOTE: Much of this script eventually made it to the air, but not without a valiant attempt by Dorothy Fontana to make some sweeping changes and give it a harder edge. Primary among the things she wanted to excise was a preoccupation with sex that the Roddenberry pages suggest. For instance, the initial communiqué from the Tsilkovsky wants to know if there are pretty boys on board the Enterprise. Then, Geordi develops the hots for Tasha, and she, in turn, feels the same for him, and the two depart for recreational activities. All of this is a bit disconcerting, detailing nothing about the characters except for the fact that they're a horny bunch.]

As stated above, Dorothy Fontana took over this story, producing her first draft outline on April 27, 1987. Entitled "The Naked Now," it begins much the same way as "Revelations" did, with the Enterprise racing through space to reach the Tsilkovsky. They hear a female's voice, but this time she is pleading for help. Apparently she's locked herself in the ship's transporter room, and the Enterprise crew serves as audio-witnesses to the sound of phasers, set on kill, being fired. Her voice is cut off and replaced by one stating that the starship should stay away from them, unless they have been sent on the wings of angels. The sinners on board the Tsilkovsky will repent, or they will all be taken to hell. The voice considers this for a moment and states that he's decided to take them to hell in any case. The last sound they hear is an emergency hatch being blown. All transmissions cease.

Reaching the other ship, Picard orders an Away Team, consisting of Riker, Data, Geordi and security officers, to beam over. Once there they find, via a viewscreen, the remains of those bodies that exploded on the bridge when the hatch was blown, splattered all over the consoles. Life support systems in other areas of the ship have been set to 40 degrees below zero, thus effectively freezing to death crewmembers in those places.

Elsewhere, Geordi hears the sound of a running shower. Investigating, he finds the corpse of a woman who was taking a shower while fully clothed. The same congealing moisture attaches itself to his hand and itches immediately. The Away Team beams back to the Enterprise. Geordi is eventually ordered to the bridge, but chooses to ignore this, going, instead, to visit Wesley. The youth explains that he has come up with a way that will "soup up" the capabilities of the ship's engines. Geordi seems genuinely impressed and says that he can't wait to see the final results. Suddenly he grows remorseful at having used the word "see." Patting Wesley's cheek, he leaves the room.

Back on the bridge, Data is pointing out that when the collapsing star "blows off" matter, the Enterprise had better be far out of its way. While Picard orders the ship further away, he ponders Geordi's location. We learn that LaForge is in the ship's lounge, filled with "pain and rage." Tasha sees him there and approaches, offering help. He starts to cry, and actually swings out at her. Tasha renders him unconscious in self defense, and calls for security. Later, in sickbay, Beverly examines him, but can't find anything wrong. Tasha leaves, wiping away perspiration. The disease has reached her.

Stationed at the library computer, Riker locates where he had heard of some one taking a shower fully clothed: the original Enterprise, captained by James T. Kirk. Everything is in the records, including the cure. Picard instantly attempts to reach Beverly, but is a bit surprised by her response. He goes to sickbay.

Tasha arrives at Troi's office, seeking advice on different types of clothes she can wear to change her image. Troi is a bit surprised by this, and senses feelings of "uncertainty and helplessness." Touching Tasha's hand reassuringly, she asks what she can do to help. Tasha decides to find what she can on her own from the ship's stores.

Picard arrives at sickbay, finding the two security officers who had brought Geordi in, laughing hysterically. Making his way to Beverly's office, she immediately details for him how tough it is to be the widow of a hero. She is considered "sacred ground," and for that reason men in general are afraid to approach her as a woman. And at this moment she *needs* a man. Picard doesn't really know what to say, so he changes the subject, pointing out that Riker has apparently found a cure to the disease they all risk contracting. Putting her feelings aside, Beverly concentrates on the matter at hand, and begins studying the information that Picard has pulled up on the computer screen. Believing her claim that she'll go right to work, he leaves sickbay, but sooner has he done so than she begins to cry anew.

In engineering, the chief and her assistant are a bit surprised by the captain's order for them to report to the bridge. They do so, and once they're gone, Wesley slips into the room. The duo eventually learn that Picard never gave such an order. At that exact moment, Wesley's voice is heard over the communication system, claiming that he is captain and the warp engines "are going to sit up and do tricks."

Riker and the chief engineer proceed to engineering to remove Wesley, while at the same time Data is receiving reports which cause him to question the mental state of much of the crew. The captain attempts to reach Tasha, but is unable to do so. Data is sent to investigate. He locates Tasha in her cabin, and is surprised to find her "in a pale blue diaphanous gown, with her hair loosely arranged, and especially attractive make-up." While approaching him, she states that this is the way she wants men to see her, and that her tough exterior shell has been built up around her as a protective device against the cruelty of her early life. She touches him, but Data points out that he cannot help her cope with these human emotional needs, although he certainly wishes that he could.

Picard is informed by the chief engineer that Wesley has put himself in complete control of the ship's warp engines, while at the same time effectively sealing off the entrance to engineering from the inside.

Going to Troi's office, Riker finds her curled in a fetal position, screaming out in agony. He grabs hold of her and tried to provide comfort, while she reveals that she's in pain from feeling the emotions of all the people around her, and she hates never being alone in her own mind. Riker carries her to sickbay. Once there, he finds Beverly, who has been holding on to her mental facilities, administering to one of the effected crewmembers what should be the antidote. She pauses a moment, and is horrified to find that it does not work. Apparently this disease is a different strain from the one that affected Kirk's Enterprise. Elsewhere, personnel are attempting to phaser their way into Engineering, while Wesley continues to tinker with the warp engines.

Data returns to the bridge just as Picard is ordering the Enterprise out of orbit. The ship is sluggish, and will not respond. The android touches the captain's hand and asks if he's very good, "can he become a real human boy?"

Beverly, disease not withstanding, is working on finding a cure. She finally learns that the organism has been altered somehow, quickly changing sugars in the bloodstream to alcohol, which results in extremely high levels of intoxication. Understanding this, she is now able to isolate the disease and will, hopefully, find a cure.

Riker, now infected, tells Troi that he should not be trying to avoid her, but, instead, should grab her and proclaim his love. Deeply buried in him is the fear that he will go the route of many potential starship captains, living life alone without the comfort of a woman. "Sometimes he feels the ship is lying in wait to possess him," details Fontana's treatment. "And God knows, he *lets himself* be drawn on. He has to stop somewhere, find the love of a woman of his own, before he is lost forever."

Picard, also falling under the influence of the disease, is distraught when he learns that a chunk of the sun may be blown out towards them, and the ship is unable to move. He looks to Data for support, but finds him sitting on the horseshoe railing of the bridge, behaving like a "good" boy, swinging his legs and singing a child's song. Matters go from bad to worse when the chief engineer contacts the captain, explaining that they've gotten through to Engineering, but Wesley's experiments have misaligned the dilithium crystals. Ship's computers reveal that it will only be fourteen minutes before the Enterprise is struck from the sun, and there is no way for the crystals to be realigned in time. The captain goes to engineering, with Data skipping along behind him. The analogy to Pinocchio and Gepetto is made.

In the turbolift, Picard, now suffering from the disease's full influence, confesses to Data that he fears for the lives of his crew and their families. In all honesty, he doesn't know whether or not he could handle the burden of anything happening to the children on board.

Beverly finally discovers the cure in sickbay. She administers it to herself and Riker, and the two of them almost instantly pull themselves together. Discovering that the captain is headed for the engineering section, Riker grabs a spray injector of antidote and proceeds there. Learning the situation with the warp engines, Picard tries to hold himself together long enough to figure something out. Wesley, angry that he's been taken away from his experiments, condescendingly points out that all they have to do is short circuit the normal restart procedures. This makes sense to the captain, who immediately acts on the suggestion. With no alternative, they proceed with this plan.

The captain and Data are cured of the disease, and they, along with Riker, return to the bridge. At the last possible moment the warp drive engages and they escape from the vicinity just as a chunk of the star destroys the Tsilkovsky, taking the disease along with it.

In a short matter of time, everyone on board the Enterprise has returned to normal. Picard states that they will conduct a memorial service for the crewmembers of the Tsilkovsky, before departing for their next assignment.

In short, this proposed version of "The Naked Now" was far more effective than its final form, this despite the fact that the story is really the same. It's the tone of the piece that is far more effective than Gene Roddenberry's previous, and subsequent, rewrite of it. This is, as was stated earlier, due to the fact that Fontana's outline is not preoccupied with sex, instead doing exactly what this story was intended to do: providing insight to the new characters.

For instance, while Geordi and Wesley are ultimately affected much the way they were here, Tasha does not become a horny bimbo. Instead, she wants to be recognized as a woman instead of as a security officer; she wants to strip away her hard exterior and reveal a softer side. Beverly, while still longing for a man's companionship, points out that as the widow of a Starfleet hero, no man will come near, considering her "sacred ground." This is a wonderful character bit, and it was a shame to lose.

The effect that the disease has on Troi is wonderful, pointing out how difficult it must be for an empath to be surrounded by the confusing minds of humans. Picard's fear of harm coming to the children fits the character perfectly, reinforcing his statement from "Encounter at Farpoint" that he is *not* a family man, and is uncomfortable around youngsters. Still, he is concerned about them, and his fear of forfeiting their lives is a very nice touch.

Data's desire to be a real-life boy is a natural development for the character, as he has pointed out that he would give up all of his superior abilities to have the chance of being human. Riker's reaction to the disease, however, is probably the best. We learn that he sees himself traveling down the same path as such previous starship captains as Kirk and Picard, and he is afraid of it. Half of him wants the intimacy of a starship command, while the other half yearns for female companionship. The struggle between the two is an ongoing thing, and one that will undoubtedly plague him for the rest of his life.

Now compare this to the effect that the disease had on the crew in the Roddenberry-rewritten version. Geordi and Wesley are pretty much the same. Tasha is looking for sex, and is willing to come on to a crewman in a corridor, or Data. The android, instead of yearning to be human, merely acts goofy and proves that he can do anything that a man can do. Beverly gets hot for Picard and the captain, in turn, acts like a teenager with a bad case of puppy life. Riker is essentially uneffected, as is Troi. Where's the character development? Where's the insight into their thinking? It's gone, that's where.

There really are no comparisons between the two versions. Fontana's original is far superior, and it's really unfortunate that it was not used in the actual episode.

"CODE OF HONOR"

"Code of Honor" is a perfect example of a *Star Trek* script that went through a tremendous amount of change before it made it to the air, while at the same time keeping the basic core of its story. The original outline, penned by Katharyn Powers and Michael Baron, seemed to have been written for a series more along the lines of the original show, and not the demilitarized *Next Generation*.

Their outline, dated March 6, 1987, begins with a page worth of notes concerning the planet Tellis. The inhabitants are reptilian in nature and, according to these notes, the "Tellisians are a people of great contrast. Because of the geological instability of their islands, death has always been an imminent factor in their lives. To insure survival, Tellisians became a fruitful race which led to dense populations inhabiting very limited landscape. These factors combined to form a culture which needed a way to resolve death, to live peacefully together and, ultimately, to expand its frontiers into space — to colonize."

The race developed their own Warrior Class, known as the Kadim, whose development closely mirrors that of the Samurai of Japan. Theirs is a race of closely knit loyalty, pride and a distinct sense of honor. Also noted is that "a warrior undertakes a life of rigid training to perfection and understands that his way is always to death. Knowing this, he lives each moment to the fullest, savoring the perfection of a single raindrop as much as a victory in battle."

The story itself begins on a Shore Leave planet, which is orbited by several ships, including those of the Federation and Tellis. Tasha (still referred to as Macha at this early date) is taking part in an exhibition bout demonstrating combat training. She and the sixteen year old son of the Prefect step into the ring. At the same time, Picard is introduced to Lutan, the captain of the Tellisian vessel. The two men exchange pleasantries, and devote their attention to the bout taking place before them. It's obvious that Lutan is quite taken by Tasha.

Yar is victorious, and is soon teased by both Riker and Picard regarding the sexiness of her look in the rather revealing uniform she's wearing. She excuses herself to change back into more formal attire. Stepping into a dressing room, she is grabbed by a pair of Tellisian crewmen. The boy she had "performed" with moments earlier opens the door at the sound of a struggle and is shocked to see the Tellisians and Tasha disappear in a transporter beam. He goes to inform Picard.

The captain, needless to say, is quite put off by the situation and attempts communication with the Tellisian ship, but there is no response. The Enterprise begins a pursuit, as the crew tries to come up with a plan to get Tasha back. Computer records detail that Lutan is considered to be ambitious as well as dangerous. In addition, Lutan's grandfather had once been involved in a confrontation with the Enterprise under the command of Captain James T. Kirk, with the latter proving victorious. Data, noting the Tellisian's code of honor among themselves, suggests that Tasha may have been abducted in an attempt to regain face. Picard doesn't agree, believing this to be kidnapping, plain and simple, and a criminal act as well. Deanna Troi, who has been studying the captain, senses his thoughts and realizes that they share something in common with everyone else on the bridge: each of them wishes that it was they who had been kidnapped rather than Tasha, because of her terrifying childhood.

Later, in his castle on Tellis, Lutan finds that he must double security around Tasha for she is, quite simply, kicking ass. He nonetheless attempts to be hospitable to her, but his offers fall on deaf ears. Tasha cannot accept his statement that this act will bring honor to his people for the act committed against them by the other Enterprise.

Riker, Data, Troi and Geordi beam down to the planet's surface, and are met by Lutan's wife, Queen Yarena. She immediately informs them that now that honor has been regained, Tasha will be returned to them. There is a banquet being prepared, at which Lutan will return her. She leaves them alone, and Riker instantly contacts Picard, filling him in on the situation and suggesting that perhaps Data's theory was correct.

At the banquet, Lutan proclaims to his people that he has settled an old debt between their people and the Federation, and he offers Riker vast riches. We ultimately learn that it is his intention to actually *buy* Tasha. Riker is outraged, demanding her return and claiming anything else an act of war. Lutan says that this is an act of love, not war. This goes over like a ton of bricks, particularly between Tasha and Yarena. Riker orders the Enterprise to beam them up, but there is no response. They are captured by Lutan's guards.

Picard is astounded to learn that not only has the ship lost contact with the Away Team, but the island itself. Somehow, it's gone. Back at the banquet hall, Lutan and Yarena are alone and she feels betrayed. She pleads that he not dishonor her in this way, but his response is only cruelty.

In the castle dungeon, the Away Team tries to come up with a way to break out. There they meet a Tellisian loyal named Hinun, who has been sentenced to death for his discovery that Lutan has slowly been poisoning Yarena's uncle, the highest ranking war lord of the castle. Seeing the humans as possible salvation, he tells them that the only other thing standing in Lutan's way is Yarena. The rights to all the land and property on Tellis belong to women, and the only way for males to gain control of them is by marriage. Should the Queen meet her demise, all that she owns would revert to Lutan, provided that it's proved her death was not by his hands, either directly or indirectly. Why, the Away Team wonders, would Lutan want to get rid of one wife just to take another?

In the guest quarters of the castle, Lutan comes to Tasha, doing his best to be charming and romantic. She has no interest in him and no qualms in demonstrating this fact, but her rebuttal actually inflames his desire. Finally, seeing that he's not getting anywhere with her, Lutan states that the lives of her friends depend on her submitting to him.

Tasha, realizing that he means what he says, lowers her defenses, reluctantly allowing Lutan to begin to make love to her. He embraces her just as the door opens and Yarena walks in. Furious, she challenges Tasha to the ritual combat of wives.

Back in the dungeon of the castle, Geordi's prosthetic device locates a weakness in one of the metal bars of their cell. Utilizing his extraordinary strength, Data tears it out of its place, and they are free a moment later, bringing Hinun with them. Guards prove no match for the group, as they render them unconscious once they learn Tasha's location. Trying to improve their odds, Riker has Troi and Data accompany Hinun to the Queen's uncle, as the latter has explained that the war lords are more likely to follow the leadership of the old man than Lutan. Riker and Geordi, meanwhile, will try to free Tasha, while at the same time disabling whatever has been jamming transmission to the Enterprise.

Riker and Geordi fairly easily dispatch the guards standing outside Tasha's room. She explains that the Tellisians have developed a force field that has affected communication to the ship. She believes she can get them to the control center. Enroute, they meet Yarena, and Tasha immediately takes the opportunity to proclaim her innocence; to explain that she has no interest in Lutan. The Queen doesn't believe her and contacts the guards. Helping the prisoners to escape would shame her family and Lutan would hate her. She honestly believes that her fight with Tasha will win him back.

While in the midst of preparing

for the combat, Lutan is told that Data, Troi and Hinun are still missing. The King curses himself for not having had the latter executed. The only solution he can see is for his men to kill Yarena's uncle now, and then, after the combat ritual, he wants them to kill Tasha and the other members of the Enterprise. His people are shocked, pointing out that such an act would create a situation of war between them and the Federation. The ruler points out that he has made allies with enemies of the UFP, and that a war would help raise him and his followers to a greater level of power.

After Tasha is dressed for combat, she rejoins the Away Team (with the exception of Troi and Data, who are attempting to locate the uncle) and is asked by Riker to throw the match. His reasoning is that if Yarena is victorious, this will save her honor, and convince Lutan that there's no reason to keep them there. She would love to do so, but this battle is to the death.

Hunin leads Troi and Data through secret passages of the castle to the room of the uncle. According to the outline, "[The Uncle] knows his illness has been perpetrated by Lutan. He is weak, but determined, with their help, to stop the ritual, save his niece and deal with the usurper."

In the banquet hall, Riker tells Tasha that although he knows she would willingly sacrifice her life for the others, this "event" is not the proper time to do so. He wants her to fight as best she can, and keep the ritual going as long as possible. The fight begins; a struggle fought more with art and precision than strength. Riker is concerned that Tasha will not be able to handle herself in this form of battle.

On the Enterprise, Captain Picard has determined that he could fire phasers into the Tellisian force field surrounding the planet, but the nature of its energy could, conceivably, create a nuclear reaction. He is using Wesley Crusher's brilliant scientific mind to alter the ship's phasers in such a way as to penetrate the force field. Noted is that "Picard's wisdom and experience are evident in the way he supports the boy – and the calm he imparts to keep the youngster intensely focused without becoming unnerved."

[NOTE: Although we'll be comparing this outline to the aired version in a short time, it's interesting to note the above statement that Picard's wisdom and experience allow him to believe in Wesley. This is ironic when considering that for the first half dozen episodes or so, Wesley is constantly told to shut up or get off the bridge. This is in itself ironic, because he has proved himself over and over again. It might have been more logical to have the character develop in such a way that by the third or fourth episode Picard and his highly trained personnel would face the fact that this kid is brilliant.]

During the combat, Tasha, surprisingly, does get the upper hand and is a moment from delivering the death blow to Yarena. She hesitates, though, causing Lutan to order Riker and Geordi killed if Tasha does not carry through the ritual. Riker shouts to the people of Tellis that Tasha has fought honorably, and it is Lutan who behaves like a thief and a murderer. At that exact moment, Yarena's uncle, along with Data, Hunin and Troi, enter the room, and the truth behind Lutan's actions is exposed for all the people to hear. "As with all tyrants in history," Powers and Baron write, "Lutan calls for honor in the name of treachery and deceit."

Lutan is placed under arrest, and as this happens, Riker informs the uncle that the Federation can provide the kind of aid that his people obviously have need of. He listens to these words, and considers the possibility of opening relations with that organization.

[NOTE: The differences between this version and the final one are many. For instance, the Enterprise has beamed Lutan and his subordinates aboard in the hopes of achieving a medicinal cure for a very serious virus infecting many Federation planets. Lutan's people, as is the case here, believe very strongly in honor and are offended quite easily. Tasha is still kidnapped, but this time Picard must come down and ask for her return, as this would be the honorable thing to do. He does so, but at that point Lutan announces that he has fallen in love with Tasha and cannot possibly let her leave. Subtle threats are thrown back and forth with Lutan stating, "Then there will be no treaty, no medicine and no Lt. Yar."

Yarena still challenges Tasha to a battle to the death, and is actually killed in the struggle, but brought back to life by Beverly Crusher. During this time they learn that Lutan's love for Tasha has been a ruse to get the women to kill each other so that all of his wife's riches would be his to do with as he pleased. As it all turns out, both women live, and Lutan is reduced to Yarena's "second." The Enterprise gets its vaccine and security officer back, and is off to the next assignment.

Undoubtedly due to budgetary restrictions, Lutan's castle was dropped as were the elaborate sets. In fact, the Tellisians themselves went from a reptilian race to a black one.

As stated at the outset of this section, the original version of "Code of Honor" was considerably more action-oriented. That was dropped when it became obvious that the format of this Star Trek would be somewhat different than the original. As aired, the episode works fairly well, with only the slightest trace of similarity to the "Amok Time" episode of the old show.]

"THE LAST OUTPOST"

The Ferengi made their initial physical appearance in Richard Krzemien's "The Last Outpost," an outline that eventually became a teleplay scripted by one of the show's producers, Herb Wright.

The outline, dated May 1, 1987, begins with the Enterprise in pursuit of a Ferengi war ship that attacked a mining colony on Gamma 12 and stole the T-4, a creation that has the ability to locate and remove "even trace amounts of precious metals through miles of rock."

As the chase continues, the considerably smaller Ferengi ship moves into an asteroid belt to avoid the Enterprise. The enemy ship eventually takes refuge on the other side of a small planet. The Enterprise follows and is about to open hailing frequencies when a Ferengi battle cruiser, which is described as being three times the size of the Federation starship, rises behind them and begins its own pursuit. Shields are raised as the larger ship fires. Before any potential damage can be done, all three ships amazingly come to a complete stop. Picard tries to get his ship out of there, but apparently they are being held by a powerful Ferengi tractor beam. Phasers are about to be fired when the word comes that somehow all computer memory banks pertaining to ship defenses have been erased, then the biology section and, finally, history report similar events. Shields are raised to maximum, giving them, according to the computer, approximately two hours before they are vulnerable again. The captain

wants phasers armed, but Data reminds him that they will have to lower defenses to use them, and, if the drain has affected the tactical computers, they could very well destroy themselves. Communication is attempted with the Ferengi, but there is only silence in return.

In a staff meeting, Tasha suggests that they do their best to fight, pointing out that it may have been a mistake for whole families to be assigned to a starship. Picard differs, stating that they will not argue that past decision, and that he will do everything in his power to spare the families, even if that means surrender.

A communiqué of surrender is issued to the Ferengi vessel. Moments later, a near-blinding light appears on the viewscreen as does the image of Picard's equal in rank, Taar. According to the outline, "Ferengis have poor vision, so they operate in an environment of intense light. Before Picard can discuss his conditions of surrender, Taar interjects that they cannot understand how this tiny Federation vessel has managed to hold two Ferengi ships at bay the way it has. They will return the T-4 and offer the lives of the ship's officers, as is the norm for the Ferengi in terms of honor, so that the rest of the crew can be spared. Understandably, this throws Picard a bit off balance, but he recovers quickly. He says he will think about it and closes communication. Data immediately points out that the danger still exists, only its source has now become a mystery.

Geordi discovers that the planet itself is absorbing energy from the three ships. At that time, Data theorizes that they may be in the Tkonion

Empire, an area destroyed some 200,000 years earlier by a supernova. "To enter the empire," Krzemien writes, "one has to stop at a guardian planet. In order to enter one had to offer something in trade. Failure to trade meant death. But what the tariff was, what they had to trade in order to get in to the empire, is unknown." Riker begins to wonder if members of the Tkonion Empire might still be alive on the planet below them.

The Ferengi contact the Enterprise in the next moment. Taar is angry, and perhaps embarrassed. At the same time, he compliments Picard on his "poker face." They, too, have learned that it is the planet that's responsible for their plight, and not the Federation vessel. Letek, the captain of the smaller ship, contacts Picard next, and the two of them decide that a joint landing party might best service all vessels involved. If the landing parties are successful, Letek says, the Enterprise will get back its T-4 device.

Meanwhile, on the planet's surface, an underground crystalline structure takes the form of a being named Dilo, who is watching a holographic image of the Enterprise and Ferengi vessels.

Due to the strange energy emitted by the planet, the Away Team arrives at different points after beaming down, but all have survived and regroup. Riker immediately attempts to contact the ship. This is to no avail, and we see a series of crystals which seem to grow as they absorb the energy emitted by the device. Back on the Enterprise, Picard has communication signals placed on full strength so that they will be able to keep the Away Team informed of what's happening, even if they can't communicate back. The captain is also told that it will only be a short matter of time before the continuing power drain on the ship will affect life support systems.

On the planet's surface, Riker has picked up one of the strange crystals, and as he faintly picks up Picard's voice, the crystal in his hand begins to grow. When communication ceases, it too stops. Data theorizes that the crystals are akin to electro-magnetic sponges, and would appear to be a part of a civilization that no longer exists. Geordi points out an electromagnetic "waterfall" shooting heavenward, which they assume is the tractor beam holding the three vessels in orbit. Just as they are about to depart for it, they are attacked by three Ferengi. Letek aims a weapon at Riker, pointing out that it was easy to find the humans because of their distinct odor. Tasha attempts to make a move and a Ferengi fires, but the beam miraculously goes around her. Not asking any questions, she fires her phaser, but it, too, misses the target. The crystals surrounding them absorb the energy emitted. A fight quickly ensues, with the Away Team proving victorious.

Riker is annoyed to discover that the T-4 is not in the vicinity, as was promised. Letek says that they have hidden it, but, by the same token, they have a right to it since the miners were working on their planet. Tasha says that the Federation had no idea who the planet belonged to. This does not interest the Ferengi. Riker and Letek reach an alliance and hope to discover some answers.

En-route they are attacked by a creature that looks like a hybrid of an earth dog and Ferengi uvex [an un-describable creature]. One of the Ferengi pushes Tasha out of the way before they learn that the beast is only an illusion. When the Ferengi stands up, everyone sees that he has cut his arm open and the wound is oozing green blood. Then, to every-one's horror, the wound begins to crystallize. Letek insists that Beverly help him, but she points out that she doesn't have any medical equipment with her to examine the wound pro-perly before treating it. Looking at it carefully, she does, however, com-pare it to a viral infection and uses a simple antiviral compound to stop its spread.

In his cave, Dilo is watching a holographic image of the two landing parties. After a moment or so, he touches a row of crystals.

The landing parties are on a plateau and are promptly attacked by a pack of the dog-like creatures they met earlier. Their moves are savage, but the humans and Ferengi help each other to survive. Finally they convince themselves that this is only an illusion, and the animals dis-appear. Suddenly they find themselves in a crystalline cell. It is Data's opinion that what they've been through may be some kind of test, and if that's the case, then it's quite possible that the Ferengi are illusions as well. They, in turn, back away from the humans, considering the possibi-lity that they are not real. At that moment, Riker picks up Picard's voice on his communicator, explaining that the holographic image of Dilo has appeared and explained that "they

stand in the doorway, but are denied access." Although they have not passed the test laid out before them, Dilo explained that he is a bit con-fused by the results and is not quite ready to destroy them. The confusion lies in the fact that at first the Ferengi and humans wanted to kill each other, but then they started to work together. Dilo must figure out the contradiction of these actions. To answer the question, he must consult the seat of knowledge.

Data, upon hearing this, comes to the conclusion that this world is the last surviving planet of the Tko-nion Empire and that Dilo is undoubtedly the last surviving gate keeper, whose task was only to allow the most deserving access to the empire. It is Letek who suggests that perhaps Dilo is not aware of the des-truction of the Tkonions. Riker is now trying to figure out what the necessary tariff might be.

Their conversation is interrupted when Letek falls to the ground, ob-viously in great pain. Examining him, Beverly discovers a cut on his wrist which, on this strange planet, is killing him. She removes her hypospray and its last injection and is about to use it on him, when the Ferengi surprises everyone by telling her to use it for their escape. After a moment's hes-itation, she uses the injection on the walls, which are similar to the crystal infections, and the wall crumbles.

They move outside, where they once again take note of the energy waterfall they saw earlier. Riker deduces that this is the one source of energy that is actually leaving the planet, so therefore it would be logical to assume that communication will be possible at that spot. Once they arrive there, they are surprised to find Dilo. It is here that he is attempting to contact the seat of knowledge, but to no avail. Riker contacts Picard and requests that the shields be lowered so that the computers can be scanned by the planet in its never-ending search for knowledge. Reluctantly Picard agrees, and even more reluctantly, Letek gives a similar order to his ship.

Dilo is saddened, having just this moment learned of the death of his people. What a waste, he says, of all the knowledge that exists on this planet. Riker suggests that if Dilo truly believes in the value of information, and the spreading of that information, then it should be shared with others. Dilo, he points out, could be the caretaker of this great library planet.

"Let every nation share the information of a thousand centuries," says Riker. "Help us learn to lower our defenses; to surrender to wisdom and higher truth."

These words have the required effect on Dilo, who agrees with him.

Once Riker has returned to the Enterprise, he informs Picard that Letek has agreed to help create this great library planet, to which both the Federation and the Ferengi Alliance will have equal access. "No culture will acquire more information than it has wisdom to use," he says.

[NOTE: The odds are strong that if "The Last Outpost" were shot as written, it would have cost upwards of three times the normal price-tag for an episode of The Next Generation. While the story would remain essentially the same, there would still be quite a few changes between this initial outline and the final script.

For instance, while the Enterprise is still in pursuit of a Ferengi vessel for the recovery of its device, there is no Ferengi battle cruiser that joins in the chase. The whole idea of the crystalline structures is dropped, as are the dog-beasts. The Ferengi themselves also go through a great deal of change, physically speaking. Here they come across as about the size of the average man, and are people of very strong character, as exemplified by Letek's command that Beverly use the last anti-viral shot on the walls of their cell as opposed to him. In the aired version, and in subsequent episodes using the race, they come across as tiny people who are more humorous and, in some cases, annoying than honorable.

Dilo would go through a great change, as the Gate Keeper of the Tkonion Empire is a much more powerful figure in the televised form. He is all-powerful – actually he initially comes across as a take-off of the all-powerful Oz – and not someone to be trifled with. He finds both the humans and Ferengi interesting, but ultimately realizes the great nobility of the former, and expresses nothing but disdain for the latter. In fact, he even offers to destroy them if Riker so desires. "But then they would have learned nothing," replies the commander. One can assume that this was still the case, as the Ferengi would eventually offer no evidence of change.

All in all, "The Last Outpost" was an enjoyable episode, although, once again, there did seem to be some similarities to an original series show – in this case "Errand of Mercy" – but writers Krzemien and Wright, as well as director Russ Mayberry and the cast, do a nice job of elevating the show.]

"WHERE NONE HAVE GONE BEFORE"

The outline for this episode by Diane Duane and Michael Reaves, dated February 17, 1987, begins with the Enterprise preparing to test a new subspace drive, created by Peter Kosinski, who's on board with his son. The theory behind this creation is that it will allow a ship to travel directly *through* a wormhole [and for an example of a wormhole, it's recommended that you check out a video cassette of *Star Trek: The Motion Picture*], thus traveling hundreds of lightyears instantly. Riker, in particular, is truly excited about the device, believing that it will open up the entire galaxy for exploration. The captain concurs, musing that, if successful, it could someday help determine whether or not the universe was created by a divine force, or if it occurred by "accident."

Kosinkski is proud of what could be his greatest achievement, but his son is obviously upset about something, brushing off the subspace drive as not very important. The device is engaged, and the Enterprise enters a wormhole and exits "a few lightyears from the galactic core, a multi-colored tight-packed aggregation of millions of stars, so close together that you can't see the darkness of space between them. It's like being in a sea of luminous jewels."

A feeling of celebration makes its way across the bridge, but the good news instantly becomes bad when it's announced that none of the ship's consoles are functioning properly. Data studies the situation, and quickly informs the captain that the

gravitation of the star mass has thrown all ship's sensors completely off the scale. There is no way for them to plot a course back to Federation territory. Picard tells Kosinski that he's going to have to plot a new course through subspace, but from their current starting point. The former's son, Karl, tries to talk to him, but Kosinski is too busy. This sets Karl's anger off.

[NOTE: Throughout most of this outline, Karl vies for Peter's attention with little success. His parents are divorced and he feels like he should have stayed back on Earth with his mother. He resents that his father is always too busy to spend time with him, and his seething anger grows to the point where he wanders off in the Enterprise, not caring where he ends up. This is the one part of the story that seems somewhat pedestrian and doesn't really lend anything to the outline. It's cliché ridden, and there's no sense in boring the reader with those types of exchanges.]

Kosinski sets to work, but Riker announces a new problem: a wall of radiation, resulting from the shock-wave of an exploding star, is heading right towards the Enterprise. It will reach the starship in ten minutes, "[going] through our shields like a laser through butter."

The only way to save them is for Kosinski to initiate the subspace drive again without setting a new course. This is done, and they narrowly avoid destruction. Once they come out of the wormhole, the crew is even more shaken than they were during the first trip. Riker, in particular, seems to have been affected, but when asked about it by the captain, he compares it to a nightmare that is hedging around the

outskirts of his memory, but refuses to make itself clear. Then his arm is in pain, and when he rolls up his sleeve he can see teeth marks on his arm. Unfortunately there's no time to follow through on this to find out exactly what had happened.

Studying the viewscreen, the crew learns that they have travelled to intergalactic space, and are looking down upon a galaxy. Picard wants Kisinski to plot a course home, but is told that since the last jump was a random one, he's got to know where they are before a journey home can be computed. Riker gives the order for a search to begin for recognizable pulsars which will provide some indication of where they are.

Meanwhile, Beverly Crusher contacts the bridge and informs the captain that there are numerous patients with bruises and contusions, but no memory of how they occurred.

Data interjects that the effects of the last journey are lasting longer than they did on the prior one. In addition, Deanna Troi explains that the mental "background noise" she usually experiences (which is attributed to the minds of millions of sentient creatures) has apparently become inaudible.

Kosinski is asked to come to sickbay, where he receives an injection of potassium, as the journeys seem to be draining that mineral from the bodies of the crewmembers. Everyone is affected, with the sole exception of Data. Not long thereafter, cases of hallucinations and paranoia break out among several people. Picard states that if the new drive is doing this to his people, then they will be forced to unhook it and travel back to their own territory via warp drive, which will take years.

Once Picard and Kosinski return to the bridge, Riker informs them that there are *no* recognizable pulsars. Apparently they have reached another galaxy altogether, and there's no way to determine exactly which universe they are in.

The disease noted earlier intensifies throughout the ship. Hallucinations are occurring which are so real that there are physical reactions to them. For instance, the outline notes someone reliving a fight in which he received a bloody nose will suddenly have his nose start to bleed. On the bridge, Picard is horrified to find the lifeless body of Jack Crusher, and then it's gone. He tells Beverly about this, and while doing so all of the feelings from so long ago come back to the surface. Again looking at the teeth impressions on his arm, Riker recalls an incident where he was bitten by a Draconian sandcat.

Seeing no alternative, and not relishing the idea of spending the rest of their lives aboard a starship with nowhere to go, they attempt subspace travel again. During the journey, the hallucinations intensify. Beverly is suddenly on the ruined deck of the Stargazer, and standing in front of her is Captain Picard, his arms holding the lifeless form of Jack Crusher. Everyone else on the Enterprise goes through their own hallucinations. When this latest trip is completed, they are horrified to see nothing but darkness on the viewscreen. They've got to a place where nothing exists. Eventually the ship detects the slightest

trace of "life," and, utilizing the main viewer on maximum magnification, they see a "fuzzy blot," which is said to be the universe itself – "as seen from the *outside.*"

The crew, again with the exception of Data, is in an extremely weakened condition. Potassium is running out, and Beverly isn't sure what she should be doing next.

Kosinski goes to engineering to check on the subspace drive mechanism, which is described as being powered by a quantum black hole. While the ship is handling this with no problem, the matter-antimatter nacelles are deactivating due to the altering realities they've been traveling in. It is his opinion that they can make one more trip in subspace. If there is another beyond that, it will wipe out all ship power, including life support.

They make the final jump, with the fear of the black hole powering the device crushing the starship. While in wormhole the ship begins to shake and shudder and the hallucinations begin anew.

After the trip has concluded, the starship arrives in the midst of "a blazing inferno of light and shifting colors." Shields are the only things keeping them from being destroyed. Kosinski determines that they have reappeared within a monobloc: a cosmic egg, which is supposed to be similar to the one which some believed exploded and created our universe. Troi comes up to Picard and tells her that she has once again begun to feel the background intelligence discussed earlier. Beverly reports over 200 cases of delirium, with more people developing it as time goes on.

The situation is growing desperate. Riker comes up with the idea of the ship attempting to drain energy from the monobloc to recharge the engines to try again. Kosinski says that they could probably do this, although he points out that such activity could possibly cause the monobloc to explode, thus creating a new universe. In addition, he believes that since the monobloc exists outside normal time and space, the ensuing explosion might "kick" them back into their own universe.

Picard gives the okay for the siphoning of energy. The Enterprise makes the jump, and the monobloc explodes behind them. In their wake, just as Kosinski had predicted, arises a new universe.

Finally, the Enterprise arrives back in Federation territory, the crew sick beyond words, but relatively alright. While grateful for arriving home, they find it peculiar that they returned exactly where they should be.

"Maybe we had help," muses Picard. "Maybe, in that moment of creation, someone or something realized we weren't supposed to be there and sent us home."

"Or," Riker counters, "maybe *we* were the creators."

There is no response to that statement. Data informs the duo that they have been away for exactly six days. Not missing the irony of that, as well as that of the new universe left behind, Picard adds, "I think we should take the seventh day off."

[NOTE: A highly imaginative story, with an absolutely wonderful conclusion. Probably one of the biggest changes that would eventually

be made, besides the basic idea of the monobloc and the creation of a new universe, is that Koslinski comes across as such a nice guy. He's a highly respected scientist, and his achievements place him in a position where Picard and Riker trust him, despite the sheer fantastic nature of his creation.

The basic nature of the hallucinations works quite differently here, particularly in that the bodies of the crew react to their visions in physical ways. In the aired versions, the illusions were brief intrusions on reality, but here they seemed to have considerably more impact on the characters.

As our discussion of "Where None Have Gone Before" continues, we'll see that there were many more changes in store for the script.]

As the final draft outline, dated March 24, 1987, begins, we learn that Peter Kosinski was once Picard's roommate at the Academy, so there is a specific closeness between them once the man beams aboard.

Riker debates the subspace device with the man somewhat, admitting that he feels a bit awkward entrusting the Enterprise to these experiments. Data, on the other hand, is anxious for the tests to get underway.

The device is installed, and the Enterprise continues its mission to take readings on a dying red star which is a short time away from collapsing into a black hole. Unfortunately, their calculations are off, and when the "compression" occurs sooner than expected, the Enterprise is rapidly drawn towards it. Kosinski manages to activate his creation, but because it is based on a

black hole particle, and the ship is being drawn towards a black hole, rather than increase capabilities by seven percent, it results in something more along the lines of seven *hundred thousand* percent.

When they come out of the jump, they find themselves within the clusters which surround the Milky Way itself. They learn that the ship is hundreds of lightyears from home.

Kosinski points out that the black hole used in the warpdrive booster may have been damaged, and if it has, they must come up with a way to duplicate the collapsing star's energy surge to get them home again. The man goes to engineering, and Picard accompanies him so that the two can catch up on what's been happening in each other's lives. The captain is informed that Kosinski's unborn son had died of a disease not even curable by 24th Century science. He seems somewhat distant as he discusses it, and yet Picard can sense his friend's severe pain. To make matters worse, Kosinski's wife left him when she discovered that he was a carrier of the same disease. Feeling that he's opened himself up too much, he excuses himself and goes back to work. Preparations are made and a second jump initiated.

The result, as was the case in the earlier draft, is that they are propelled even further away from home, and everyone begins seeing things that aren't there, they find themselves disoriented, and the laws of "cause and effect" appear to be non-operative here ... wherever here is. Kosinski himself, resting a bit in his cabin, is visited by a young boy who identifies himself as the man's dead son. Know-

ing it's an illusion, Kosinski doesn't say anything to anybody else. Pulling himself out of this, he theorizes that since reality breaks down in a black hole, the warp booster might be "leaking," so as long as the device is aboard, this bizarre breakdown of reality will last. Unfortunately they can't get rid of it, though, because it's the only thing that could possibly get them home.

As the hallucinations continue, Picard enters his quarters and imagines that Beverly Crusher is there, wearing a "sexy nightdress." But when she turns around, she has no face. He cannot figure out what this means. Contacting Beverly to reassure himself, he learns that she had a hallucination in which her husband's body was brought onto the bridge of the Stargazer, but the face on the body turned into Picard's.

The captain goes to Troi to discuss the situation, and is told that the crew is suffering from *projective* hallucinations. In other words, rather than projecting their own fears, they are experiencing those that other people have. Considering this, Picard realizes that he and Beverly "had interesting questions about how they really feel about each other."

Shortly thereafter, Kosinski is ready to perform the next jump. He is visited again by the son he never had, and, not being able to handle it, he flees from his cabin. The boy tries to follow him, and proves himself to be real as other crewmembers respond to him.

Once more the jump is made, and this time it's the most disastrous yet. Instruments have stopped functioning, physical changes occur within the structure of the ship and the hallucinations are back with a vengeance. Tasha (here referred to as Tanya) imagines that she's back on the hellworld that was home for the first portion of her life. Kosinski deduces that it will take one more warp jump for them to make it home.

Meanwhile, the child who is supposedly the man's unborn son, is continuing the search for his father. Eventually he meets up with Wesley, and together they go off to find Kosinski. In mid-stride the child disappears, leaving a stunned Wesley Crusher in his wake. On the bridge, Kosinski is suddenly screaming that he has to find his son, even though everyone is aware that he is childless. Picard has no choice but to have the man restrained, which leaves one burning question: if Kosinski can't get them home, who can?

Later, Beverly comes to the bridge to report further breakdowns within the crew, and Wesley arrives at virtually the same time. They discuss the fact that Kosinski has no son, but Wesley says that he's seen the child. Troi is stunned by this, pointing out that this is the first evidence of a shared vision. Kosinski is freed and allowed back up to the bridge, and no sooner has he arrived before his "son" does. They try to question him, but the eleven year old has no memory prior to this day. All he knows is that he was searching for his father and has now found him. The child then starts to fade again, but Kosinski hugs him and says, "I won't lose you again. You're real and you're staying with me." The boy becomes solid again, which leads Troi to the conclusion that once they accept something as real, it becomes real. All

they have to do is believe in it. This, they decide, will enable them to get home.

Kosinski points out that if they make it, then his son will undoubtedly disappear again. Picard replies that it's the boy against the lives of everyone on board the Enterprise. Kosinski recognizes the road he has to take.

They try to make another jump, but instead of them traveling, a miniature version of the Enterprise appears, hovering in mid-air. It is Data's opinion that this Enterprise is mirroring their own. They realize that the miniature starship is also equipped with a black hole device, and if the two are combined, perhaps one of them will wink out of existence, while the other will appear back in Federation territory. Of course no one can determine which Enterprise will do what.

After carefully maneuvering the miniature ship to engineering, the two black holes merge, and the real Enterprise reappears at the departure point. Everything is back to normal with one exception: Kosinski's son still exists.

After the scientist and the boy are dropped off on the planet Hamal, Data muses as to why the child remained real. Perhaps this strange emotion called love is stronger than reality itself.

[NOTE: This version of the outline does not work nearly as well as the original. Quite frankly, it seems to be much more convoluted than is necessary and, as a result, becomes a bit confusing and illogical in certain areas. One thing that would continue as the story developed, was the idea

that thought has a great deal to do with space, time and reality.

In addition, Kosinski's son would never make it to the air, and one does have to question the logic of the child remaining a real thing once the Enterprise has returned to its own universe. Speaking of the scientist, in this version he's made even more likeable by the fact he was Picard's former roommate at the Academy. It's amazing that he becomes such a pompous ass in the final script.]

The first draft teleplay of "Where None Have Gone Before," dated April 17, 1987, followed the same storyline as the final draft outline. The hallucinations were a bit more serious and the physical damage to the Enterprise more severe, but for all intents and purposes, the story beats were exactly the same. The second draft teleplay, dated June 22, 1987, is much closer to the version that would ultimately make it to the air, though somewhat inferior to it. It's impossible to discern whether this effort was by Duane and Reaves, or if it was Roddenberry's first attempt at tackling the subject.

This version begins with Picard's log, which informs us that Captain Amula of the starship Resolute has offered the services of an alien traveler who has proved himself adept at improving warp drive efficiency. The captain is discussing the situation with Amula via the Enterprise viewscreen, and is informed that the Traveler had originally been recommended by Captain Jans of the Valiant, who got him from the Constitution. Picard questions the man as to what the Traveler wants in return, and is told that all the extraterrestrial is looking for is a ride. He merely wants to travel throughout the galaxy, and be transported to other ships whenever possible. In return for transport, he is pleased to offer his abilities to improve the ship's warp capabilities.

Riker is a bit suspicious when he hears that the Resolute's speed has been improved by three percent, and he wants to know how the Traveler can perform this action. Amula honestly doesn't know, which is why the Federation has assigned Paul Kosinski to accompany him so as to learn his theories. Picard still hasn't decided whether or not he wants to take the chance of allowing someone outside his vessel to experiment with the engines. Kosinski "vouches" for the Traveler, which does nothing to alleviate Picard's concerns, and Data points out that if there were a problem, it would have surfaced on the three vessels that the Traveler had already been on. The captain turns to Riker, to get his opinion. Number One says that it's worth a try, but he wants to supervise every aspect of the operation. Picard concurs.

Kosinski and the Traveler beam over to the Enterprise, and Picard begins to question the latter regarding his abilities. The Traveler explains that he exchanges his knowledge for passage, but if the captain does not want him to improve the warp drive, then he won't. Riker eventually leads the two to the engineering section. Once they've departed, Troi tells the captain that in Kosinski she detected a strong sense of self doubt and a need for personal gain, while in the Traveler she felt nothing at all, as though the alien were not even there.

In engineering, the Traveler, identifying himself as Hamalki, meets Wesley Crusher, and something of a friendship is immediately sparked between the two. Also, in the ensuing conversation between Riker and Kosinski, we hear the antagonism of their words, with the commander wanting to understand every detail of the operation before allowing *anyone* to toy with the engines, while the latter is so arrogant in his own self-importance that he attempts to treat Riker like a child, too simple to understand the principles behind the equations involved. Once the Traveler has spelled out all the necessary equations, Riker, exercising great trust in Wesley's mind, asks him for his opinion. The boy suggests that the experiments take place. Riker considers this and alerts Captain Picard that they're ready.

"On the word of this boy," Kosinski says dumbfoundedly. "What if he had rejected it?"

"If I didn't value his opinion," Riker retorts, "I wouldn't have asked him for it. Once given, why would I not accept it?"

[NOTE: Already we can see quite a few changes between this version of the story and the outlines discussed earlier. For starters, Kosinski has gone from being Picard's old Academy roommate to someone the captain has never met.

In addition, rather than being filled with a profound sadness at having lost his family, he comes across as cocky and not very likeable, as well as not very productive. For instance, now he has absolutely nothing to do with the warp drive experiments, these falling into the hands of the

new character, Hamalki — The Traveler. Incidentally, by the time this character made it to the final version, he would be acting as Kosinski's assistant (even though he was still the one responsible for the warp experiments) and he explained that his real name would be unpronounceable by humans.

Also, we are once again witness to the fact that Wesley's mind is treated with respect, and he is not looked upon by the whole crew as a mere child. This is refreshing when compared to the aired version of some of the early episodes, where everyone is either telling the boy to shut up, to get off the bridge or ignoring his warnings, this despite the fact he has already saved the ship numerous times. In addition, the final version of "Where None Have Gone Before" has the Traveler recognizing the intelligence of Wesley, and, believing him to be another Mozart or Einstein, he convinces Picard that the boy should be encouraged to develop his mind. On the basis of this, Wesley is made an acting-ensign at the conclusion of the episode.]

The Traveler goes to work, with Riker noting that it doesn't look as though the alien is doing anything different than they would normally do. Wesley replies that he's not. He's just doing it *better*. Hamalki hears this and looks up at the boy for just an instant, but that instant is long enough for a miscalculation. The Enterprise makes its first jump. By the time the ship stops, it has gone 380,000 lightyears in mere minutes. Picard calls a meeting in the observation deck. There, the Traveler apologizes and explains that he had allowed himself to be distracted. Kosinski is thrilled that they've made it to a place where it will take mankind eons to reach, but nobody else seems to be that impressed. They're more concerned with getting back home again.

Once again, Kosinski pleads that they study the formula that got them there rather than the area itself. "This part of the galaxy, or any other part of the galaxy, will be as accessible as your day cabin. Please. Let's understand it, learn it. Then you can come back here any time, for as long as you want."

Riker agrees with this, which sways Picard. The Traveler goes back to work. Asking Wes to concentrate with him, he goes to work, and during the moment before the next jump, sections of the alien seem to fade in and out of existence. By the time the next journey concludes, the Enterprise has gone a total of 1,840,000 light years from the core of its own galaxy. Astounded, the captain goes to engineering. No sooner has he done so, than Lt. Worf [finally added to the proceedings] takes note of a Klingon dog on the bridge. He smiles for the first time that anyone can remember and approaches the animal. Picard meanwhile is in the turbolift, and when the doors open he nearly steps into the endless void of space. He gets back into the lift, and when the doors open next, he finds himself at engineering, just where he should be.

Beverly is in sickbay, and she's examining the now unconscious Traveler, who seems to be suffering from fatigue and exhaustion. Meanwhile, on the bridge, Tasha imagines that she is back on the hell planet she grew up on, being pursued by rape gangs. Then, just as quickly as it began, it ends, with Tasha finding herself back on the bridge. Picard steps in and without even questioning where it came from, orders "that dog" off the bridge.

The captain approaches Data and Troi, explains that what they think seems to become real, and wonders if there is any scientific theory which may explain it. He is told that there is not. Picard gives Riker command of the bridge as he departs. The commander acknowledges this, and a moment later imagines he's in a gymnasium in the midst of a game. He scoops up the ball being used, and it suddenly turns into sand. As he finds himself back on the bridge, Riker is amazed to find sand pouring out of his hand and onto the deck.

Picard, having need of thinking the situation out, has gone to the observation deck. Once there, he meets his mother, a woman who has been long dead. They get involved in conversation, until he finally forces himself out of this illusion. The Enterprise is put on red alert, and as reflex takes over, the crew snap themselves out of their fantasies. He informs them that they must somehow control their thoughts before they will be unable to tell the difference between dream and reality. Going to sickbay, and bringing Troi along with him, Picard orders the Traveler brought around, this despite Beverly's warnings that it could kill him. Hamalki survives, and explains that, essentially, thought has got them where they are. "The energy of thought," says the Traveler softly, "properly focused, is very powerful. I am like a lens which focuses that

power." He admits that he has made some errors, where he had only wanted to be an observer. Picard wants to know if he can get them back, but Kosinski interjects that they cannot leave because no one else will ever make it out this far. It's of important scientific record to stay exactly where they are. Picard doesn't agree and he turns his attention back to the Traveler. Troi announces that Kosinski is gone, explaining that it is her opinion that the man will attempt to keep them there because this represents the opportunity for him to step out of mediocrity; to make a name for himself in history. Contacting Tasha, Picard orders an all out search for Kosinski.

Tasha and Geordi locate and immobilize Kosinski. Once informed of this, Picard opens an inter-ship communiqué, informing the crew that they should concentrate on the Traveler and his task, and clear their minds of everything else. Working together is the only way to get them back home. Again the Enterprise jumps, but this time they are successful at getting back home, but at the cost of the Traveler – he's gone.

Later, Wesley is summoned to the bridge, where Picard, recognizing his contribution to this latest mission, makes him an acting ensign, adding that the boy will have to *earn* the position of full ensign.

[NOTE: *While this draft is satisfactory, it is not nearly as effective as the final version, this despite the fact that the stories follow each other fairly closely. The filmed "Where None Have Gone Before" is more streamlined. The illusions are handled far more effectively, and the charac-*

ters are developed more fully. As stated earlier, we get a better understanding of Wesley Crusher, and there is more of a mystery surrounding the Traveler.

Once again, the transformation that this story went through from initial outline to aired episode is quite a fascinating one, with the two having only the barest of similarities to each other, but both working effectively.]

"LONELY AMONG US"

Michael Halperin's original outline for "Lonely Among Us," dated May 26, 1987, sets the tone right at the outset for what is to follow, as he notes, "Although great strides have occurred since space flight began, small glitches continually emerge in the matrix of 24th-Century human, alien and computer interaction. Those errors may even appear in the coolly efficient propulsion system of a ship like the Enterprise."

The story begins with the Enterprise thrust into an emergency situation, as Picard is informed that the ship's dilithium crystals are breaking down because of a defect in their original structure. They quickly determine that the closest place they can go to repair the damage is Capella V, which is some 72 hours away. The ship has barely enough power to make the journey – if that much. En route, they come across a cloud in space "which appears as a flickering tree-like structure." It is Worf's opinion that they should study this phenomenon. Picard agrees, provided it does not slow down the starship. Worf suggests a photon torpedo be fired into the cloud, in the belief that sensors will take readings of the energy levels given off.

[NOTE: A glitch in the machinery was eventually dropped from the storyline, and for good reason. The 24th Century, as postulated by Gene Roddenberry and the others involved with the show, is not the kind of place for "mechanical screw-ups." In addition, the "tree-like structure" of

the cloud sounds a bit similar to the crystal-being that was eventually utilized in the episode "Datalore." Finally, it is, to coin a phrase, illogical to have to use a photon torpedo to gather sensor information on the cloud. Ship's sensors could, and already have at many times in the past, provide the same kind of readings.]

First Officer William Riker and ship counsellor Deanna Troi stare at the cloud through the ship's main viewscreen. She finds it holds a similarity to a symbol of Betazoid philosophy which is akin to the Burning Bush. Moved by this sight, Troi begins to emit her feelings, which Riker picks up on. For an instant, as Halperin writes, "Riker senses her desire to reach out." It seems that their old feelings are brought back to the surface, albeit momentarily, but it is Riker who draws back. The time, apparently, isn't right.

The captain gives the order for Worf to launch the photon torpedo. It is launched and explodes, thus erupting the cloud and creating a light show unlike any they had ever been witness to before.

[NOTE: At the time of the writing of this treatment, the Riker/Troi relationship was still being dealt with, although it would not end up in final form in this episode. This was one annoying part of The Next Generation's first season; they never seemed to know whether they wanted the characters linked romantically or not. One episode they really felt for each other, while in another you get the feeling that they are merely co-workers. This lack of continuity was something of a problem for regular viewers of the series.]

Geordi LaForge and a "grunt" take a shuttle to the exterior of the Enterprise to repair the tractor beam emitter, which is apparently jammed into an "open position." As they do so, they are completely oblivious that a particle from the gas cloud is heading right towards them. The grunt, attached to the shuttlecraft via a lifeline and working on the physical repair of the tractor beam, is struck by the alien energy. He is instantly in trouble, and it is up to Geordi to save him. As LaForge reaches him, the grunt seems to go crazy, struggling as though he's attempting to escape from enemy hands. Geordi finally subdues him, and brings him back inside the shuttle. Signalling for aid from the starship, Geordi is taken by surprise when he sees an aura around the grunt's body.

As the vessel pulls into the shuttle bay, it is greeted by Tasha Yar, Beverly Crusher and Troi, the latter of which picks up, via her empathic abilities, that the grunt feels like a frightened child. Tasha takes the man to an area called a "high security sick bay," and unbeknownst to anyone, a "mild electric charge" passes from the grunt to her.

On the bridge, Troi details to Picard the situation in the shuttle bay. The captain considers this for a moment, and then asks Crusher to give the man a full physical, and Troi to examine his psychological history to see if there's anything in his past which would lead to such a psychotic episode.

The scene switches to the gym. According to the script, "(The gym is) filled with the most radical, advanced devices for fitness. Geordi and Wes use the machines which engage in motivational dialogue resulting in a running battle of words as the equipment attempts to get them to do more reps. Tasha teaches a class in self-defense. Everyone dresses in modified karate uniforms appropriate for the time."

Everything is fairly normal as Tasha demonstrates some specific defensive moves, when she suddenly seems filled with anger. Then Geordi sees the aura around her as she takes her partner's "attack" too seriously and defends herself by using a death grip. Before it takes full effect, she is yanked away from the man by Wes and Geordi, among others. A moment later, she is back to normal, unable to explain what had happened.

Elsewhere, Troi is studying the grunt's psychological profile, finding nothing that would indicate his state just a short time earlier. Meanwhile, Riker is informed of the situation in the gym, with the result being that he and Troi view Tasha in sick bay. It is Troi's professional opinion that Tasha may be in desperate need of some time off from duty. Both Picard and Riker concur with this assessment. Then Geordi informs them of the aura which suddenly appeared, and then disappeared just as quickly.

The grunt is signed out of sickbay. As he begins down the corridor towards the turbo lift, he is under the "distant control of the Entity which now possesses Tasha."

[NOTE: This tractor beam business comes completely out of left field. We're never told what the problem is, or why it exists. Between this and the dilithium crystal breakdown, one begins to get the impression that this new and improved Enterprise has more than a few bugs to work out. By the same token, we now see why a photon torpedo was used earlier: it was necessary to blow up the cloud so that a particle of it would head towards the Enterprise. The shuttle just happens to be there and the grunt just happens to be working on the tractor beam emitter so that he can conveniently be struck by the particle. Just a wee bit contrived.

Interesting, though, is the fact that the alien entity transfers from one person to another, leaving each host under its influence. In the aired episode, the ship is infected by actually passing through the cloud, and the "possession" of the crew only occurs to one person at a time. In addition, it's nice to see other sections of the ship, such as the gym. This would have given a more detailed look at the many functions the Enterprise serves. It's unfortunate that this particular detail would be lost.]

As Troi and Riker study Tasha, the former states that she senses a great deal of confidence from Tasha, but this could conceivably be attributed to the woman overcoming her horrible background. When she is released from sickbay, Troi suggests that it's possible she may be suffering from an undetected virus, pointing out that it has happened before (and would, unfortunately, happen again).

In sickbay, Wesley Crusher discusses Tasha's situation with his mother. She tries to quell his concern, pointing out that all examinations indicate that it was only a temporary condition, and it's unlikely to occur again. Having no choice but to accept this, he departs for the Navigation Room to continue his studies. Once there, he helps Worf continue to chart the gas cloud they "detonated," and once the Klingon leaves, Wes punches up a holographic star chart and begins to study it.

Later, on the bridge, Riker reports Troi's opinion that there may be a virus on board the Enterprise. Picard orders Beverly to immediately begin a run down of all symptoms, suggesting that this disease may have been brought aboard from the shuttlecraft and that it has been incubating ever since. Worf arrives and punches up all the information he has gathered on the cloud. Moments later, Data, having completed his analysis, explains that this strange alien phenomenon is generating a tremendous field of gravity, the likes of which he has never seen before. In addition, he adds that if the Enterprise had gotten any closer to it, "they would have lost precious fuel in an attempt to counteract the force." Picard asks Worf to continue building enough of a case to prod Starfleet into further investigation.

In an area called "cleaning rooms," both Tasha and Geordi go through the decontamination process. Afterwards, Tasha is grateful that Beverly has deemed her normal. As they touch, however, the alien energy passes on to the doctor.

At the same time, the infected grunt is making his way through the ship, studying everything that he possibly can. In sickbay, the alien-controlled Beverly receives the mental images of everything the grunt sees. Contact, however, is broken when Wes enters sickbay, and it's only a short matter of time before the entity passes from mother to son.

[NOTE: The one comment that needs to be made about this section is that the characters really don't seem to be working in their field of expertise. For instance, Worf is constantly doing the kinds of things that Data should be doing. A phenomenon of this sort, really should be the primary function of the ship's science officer. Also, why is Troi deducing that Tasha might be the victim of a disease rather than Beverly coming to this conclusion? Also a bit disconcerting about this story thus far is the means by which the alien travels. It is precisely the way the disease of "The Naked Time" of the original show and "The Naked Now" of the new series made its way through the ship.]

The alien-controlled Wesley is back in the navigation room, continuing to study the star charts. Utilizing the computer, he/they begin to plot out the Enterprise's return course to the cloud. This is intercut with computer control, where the grunt is beginning to manipulate controls. Back in navigation, Data enters the room, studies the star chart and asks Wesley what the youth is doing. The proposed flight lines suddenly vanish from the screen, and Wes seems to be himself again. The android states that it's time for their chess lesson. They proceed to the Rec Room, where they engage in a holographic game of three-dimensional chess, the pieces to which they move by manipulating hand-controllers. At that time, Wes begins asking Data some pretty basic questions about the ship, such as the propulsion systems, its full capabilities, etc. Data is, admitt-

edly, surprised to hear such questions, having believed that the boy was fully versed in the answers. Wes states that he is only aware of the "broad strokes," and would find it extremely beneficial if Data would broaden his horizons, so to speak. Data, being the kind of "person" he is, happily obliges.

On the bridge, Riker informs Picard that the Enterprise is right on schedule in its approach to Capella V, which is currently standing by to initiate crystal repair. Back in the rec room, Wes actually wins the chess match, which stuns Data. This is the first time that anyone has beaten him at the game. Wes chalks it up to having such a good teacher. The two shake hands, and the alien passes on to Data. From there, the possessed android goes back to the bridge and is asked for information by Picard. Data has difficulty responding with his usual efficiency, and Troi senses a feeling of great anxiety. Riker laughs this off, pointing out that as a machine, Data does not experience great anxiety. She's not entirely convinced. Suddenly Data essentially goes crazy, and is held down by Worf, which allows the alien to pass on to the Klingon. Data seems back to normal and thanks Worf for his help. Worf nods in a gesture uncharacteristically mellow for him, and goes back to his station.

[NOTE: Again, the biggest complaint here is that the characters are behaving so unnaturally it is incredible to think that no one is suspicious of them. That's not saying much for a crew who is supposed to be Starfleet's best.]

Picard, not comfortable with the

way Worf is behaving, orders him to sickbay. The Klingon refuses, stating that he wants to stay at his post. Security guards are summoned, and they escort him. As they depart, Troi states that she's sure something or someone is aboard the ship affecting the crewmembers. Picard finds this hard to believe, pointing out that they have not beamed down to a planet for quite a while. Why, he proposes, would a stowaway wait for such a long period of time before making his presence known. Despite this, he realizes that something is affecting his crew, and his primary concern becomes finding this intruder. Contacting Beverly, he's told that she still hasn't found anything medically wrong with anyone.

Troi admits to Riker that from each of many people she is picking up the feelings of two. In other words, it's as though two personalities are inhabiting a single body. The commander says that schizophrenia ended on Earth years ago, and that she's probably just being over-concerned.

She departs, and a little while later Data goes over to Geordi and describes the bizarre feeling he experienced, adding that he felt a distinct sense of loneliness and a desire to be with his own kind. It's very confusing. Both of them discuss this with Picard, who is now convinced that Troi is right. Riker is concerned, stating that she has gone to see Troi.

Riker goes to the counselling room where Troi informs him that Worf is going to be okay. They hug each other, with Riker feeling remorseful that the time never seems right for them, and she reminds him of the time they spent together before they said good-bye. The commander smiles, stating that he wishes they could relive that moment. Troi has an idea, and leads him to the holodeck, where they recreate the environment of Earth's Monument Valley. They embrace compassionately, forgetting about their "professional" relationship, and begin making love. As the treatment states, "As they do, the Entity fluctuates between them as if the two were one."

[NOTE: Somehow this entire relationship, particularly the climax . . . no pun intended . . . between Riker and Troi, seems very much like the Decker/Ilia relationship in Star Trek: The Motion Picture, which was particularly true of the premiere episode, "Encounter at Farpoint." Unfortunately this element was quickly dropped. Unfortunate because it would have added a continuing level of conflict between the characters, which is something that the show is in desperate need of.]

On the bridge, Data informs Picard that the computer controls seem to be decaying, possible due to the breakdown of the dilithium crystals. He suggests that they be re-routed until the specific problem is discovered. Picard agrees.

Riker enters the bridge and gives Data the order to alter the ship's course *back* to the cloud. The android responds immediately, initiating warp nine, which will burn the ship's fuel (One wishes that the word fuel would stop being used for the ship's propulsion system. As it is, it connotes the image of the starship pulling into a gas station, with Picard

saying, "Fill 'er up."). Picard demands to know why Riker has given such an order. Troi arrives, and states that the alien now has Riker under its control. Picard wants to talk to it directly, and Riker seems to go into a trance, with the alien using his mouth to speak.

The Entity explains that it does not wish to destroy, but would, instead, rather live. There are only two choices that it has: it either self-destructs or destroys the Enterprise. Picard tries to have the ship reverse itself again, but to no avail. The alien has complete control, and tells him as much.

As the ship is approaching the gas cloud, Troi states that the alien has experienced something that it may not be able to understand fully — love. It agrees that the emotion is rather confusing, yet strangely exhilarating. Picard interjects that perhaps both races could learn about each other.

In the holodeck, the alien-controlled Riker recreates the internal structure of the cloud — "a galaxy-sized crystalline structure of enormous beauty." The Entity leaves Riker's body and appears as "a crystal of fluctuating light." It goes on to explain that it must be returned to its home environment shortly or it will perish. There is no way for it to make the journey without the starship for the simple reason that it has no other form of propulsion. Picard cannot accept this, arguing that the life of one surely cannot be worth the sacrifice of 900. The alien, in turn, will not accept that logic, stating that the Enterprise had invaded its world by detonating a torpedo in the cloud. According to the script : "More than a

single individual will die when the Entity's energy fades. It represents the sum total of eons of evolved intelligence. The Enterprise will have destroyed a higher-level inner universe." The captain, it argues, is responsible for getting it home. While Picard agrees with this, he also points out that he is responsible for the lives of the Enterprise crew and that the species known as man is no longer a destroyer.

The alien actually understands what the captain is saying, having experienced the bond of love these humans feel for each other, such as the kind that exists between Beverly and her son as well as that between Riker and Troi.

"Humans," Picard details, "don't have the cold luxury of a non-emotional existence. However, they do have compassion. We must trust each other in order to accomplish the saving of the Enterprise and you."

Picard's plan is to use the "slingshot effect" (last utilized in Star Trek IV: The Voyage Home to propel the old Enterprise backwards in time) to return the ship to Capella V at an earlier time with minimal fuel loss. The momentum of their trajectory will provide enough "push" to the alien to send it back to the cloud. The alien says that it will share its newly accumulated knowledge of humans with the consciousness of the cloud. Perhaps their next contact with each other will be under better conditions.

The slingshot effect is completed, the entity sent back to its own area of space while the Enterprise speeds towards Capella V.

[NOTE: Despite the fact that the outset of this story gives the impression that the alien is taking over the crew one by one, initiating an Invasion of the Body Snatchers-type scenario, this ending works quite well. It's refreshing to have an alien desperate to survive, as opposed to one wanting to conquer all of humanity or to destroy the species because of its savage-like nature.

This said, however, it has to be stated that this treatment has a number of problems, the majority of which have already been discussed. The characters simply aren't as bright as we know they are. They do some pretty ridiculous things, or miss the obvious.

Dorothy Fontana eventually did a substantial rewrite of this treatment, although she maintained Halperin's themes and basic story. In the aired version, the Enterprise is escorting two alien races who hate each other to another planet. Murder is most definitely on their mind, and it is up to the starship's crew to keep the peace. This sounds somewhat similar to the original show's "Journey to Babel," and it is. Fontana wrote that episode as well.

Rather than send a photon torpedo into the cloud, the Enterprise actually passes through it. The alien entity enters through the ship's computer systems, then takes over Worf's body, moves to Beverly's and then, finally, to Picard's. One major difference between treatment and episode is that people do not remain under the control of the alien once it leaves their body.

Eventually the alien, still in Picard's body, has the ship go back to the cloud, and then transports itself into it as pure energy. It is up to the crew to find out precisely where in the cloud it had beamed in to, so that they can, hopefully, retrieve Captain Picard. Naturally they are successful in this attempt.

All in all, this was a fairly good episode with an original premise. If nothing else, it at least was proof that Star Trek: The Next Generation was finally beginning to establish its own identity without the stigma of constantly being compared to the original.]

"JUSTICE"

Original series story editor John D.F. Black's effort for this new version of *Star Trek* was "Justice," the first draft treatment of which is dated January 5, 1987.

Both Deanna Troi and Beverly Crusher highly recommend shore leave for the families on board the U.S.S. Enterprise. It is their professional opinions that a Class M planet should be found as soon as possible so that families can experience a true Earth environment, "where wind and rain are non-simulated, and trees house real bird nests and a child's hands are really soiled by dirt and not a manufactured biochemical compound." Captain Picard agrees with their assessment, but points out that they are in the midst of an urgent mission.

The Enterprise has been ordered to investigate the planet Llarof, an experimental Earth colony practicing the pure democracy of the ancient Greek principle of "demos." The last contact with the planet had come some eighty years ago, and that message itself had so much interference that it was hardly intelligible. The captain adds that if the planet checks out okay, it just may be able to serve their R&R needs as well.

As the starship goes into orbit, all attempts at communication with Llarof prove fruitless. Scanners establish that the planet is inhabited by a city state form of civilization, but with absolutely no communication outside its atmosphere. The captain and Number One discuss the situation, with Riker stating that although he may be bringing his Away Team down to paradise, their sudden appearance could frighten the natives. Further discussion reveals that this colony had been established by Kirk's Enterprise some one hundred and fifty years earlier (this figure would eventually be lowered to seventy five) and there's been no communication since.

An Away Team consisting of Riker, Data, Troi and Geordi beam down. What they discover is an extremely long line of people, who, it turns out, all hope to fill three open slots in the police department. Troi senses a great deal of fear, as does Geordi (apparently at this early stage the character of Geordi LaForge was to have abilities to "sense" beyond his blindness handicap). Riker decides to split up the Away Team to see if they can discover exactly why there is such a great deal of fear amongst the people.

Moving away from the others, Riker and Troi are walking down a street when a police officer pulls to a stop and asks why they are walking, as all the other people in the area, who are in prime physical condition, are running from place to place. Thinking quickly, Troi says that she's twisted her ankle. The cop seems to understand this, adding that they had better keep to the right as the law demands. Then he adds something about how lucky they are that this isn't "the day." Naturally this is a bit confusing to them.

Data and Geordi are walking through an industrial area, when two youngsters approach, one of them nearly knocking them over with a stolen motorcycle. One of the kids drops the vehicle, is not apologetic at all for nearly hitting them, and adds the statement, "Why should I care? This isn't even the day." And they depart, leaving the Enterprise men rather confused.

Soon thereafter, the Away Team beams back aboard, with Data "borrowing" the motorcycle for scientific and historical study. They move to the bridge, where Picard is awaiting a report from them. Troi discusses the fear that she sensed, adding that it is not an imagined fear, but, rather, a very real and intense one. The captain and shipboard experts have been studying the planet from their vantage point, and have located the center of government for Llarof. It would seem that the planet is still operating under a pure democracy, as it is still following the constitution as drafted by the first citizens. They bring up the phrase "the day," and ask Picard if he and the others came up with any reference to it, but the captain has not. Tasha (still referred to here as Macha Hernandez) enters the bridge and is horrified to learn which planet they are orbiting. Apparently Llarof's chief export had been terrorists and weapons, which were supplied to the renegades on her home planet. These supplies stopped some eighty years ago, as told to her by her grandfather, and there's been no communication since.

[NOTE: Thus far, we see a nice building of suspense as the Away Team tries to figure out the situation on Llarof, and being a bit thrown "off course" by the use of "the day" in sentences. One thing that would eventually be dropped is the idea that this colony had been established by Kirk's Enterprise. A reading over *the first draft treatments of many stories initially penned for* The Next Generation *utilized the same idea, that something Kirk and his people had done in the past was having some sort of ramifications in the future. Thankfully this was dropped, as it was decided that this new version of the show should have its own identity.]*

Picard eventually decides that the best thing they can do is establish contact with the planet's government, explain the mission of the Enterprise and find out what the planet's situation is. Deducing from his words that the captain means to beam down, Riker says that he cannot allow it. This is a potentially dangerous situation, and he will not risk Picard's life. Picard ultimately agrees, granting his first officer the diplomatic powers necessary for him to meet the government leaders.

Contact is made with the chief executive of Llarof, Trebor. Riker and Tasha beam down and are brought into Trebor's office by armed guards. They meet him and his first assistant, Reneg. Trebor is thrilled to meet people from the Enterprise, but is quick to add that the problems of some eighty years ago have been eliminated. At that time, terrorism had run rampant on the planet with everybody living in fear of violence, but then the people of Llarof elected to side with law and order as opposed to madness. The result: unbridled justice, "firm and immediate – and chance." Both Riker and Tasha want to know how justice and chance possibly intertwine. Trebor only smiles and changes the subject. A banquet has been planned for the Enterprise.

Trebor and Reneg could beam aboard, which is what they would prefer to do as no one on the planet has been aboard a spacecraft before. It seems that all vessels were destroyed eighty years earlier to prevent criminals from fleeing.

The banquet is held on board the Enterprise. Riker and Tasha excuse themselves to change for dinner, while Picard begins a tour for Trebor and Reneg. At the banquet are the Away Team, the two men from the planet, as well as Beverly and her *daughter* Leslie. Tasha, still curious about the conversation on the planet earlier, once again brings up the issue of justice and chance. Finally he explains that at a randomly selected time each day computers are triggered, a particular quadrant is chosen at random as well as a specific time span, which results in the aforementioned "the day," when there is only one punishment for any crime: the death penalty. This, naturally, stuns the people of the Enterprise, whose shock intensifies when they learn that the police force are fully vested with the power to determine whether or not a crime has been committed. These crimes can include speeding, and the passengers in the car would be sentenced as co-conspirators and put to death as well. When an area is not in the midst of "the day," the law duplicates that of Earth.

Trebor is so proud of his planet, that he suggests to Picard that he allow the families on board the Enterprise to beam down for shore leave privileges. Tasha is furious, snapping that they are not going to stand by and have their children executed for throwing a piece of paper on the

ground. Trebor says that those areas will be made immune to chance selection, which is always the situation within the capital area.

[NOTE: A little bit more of the mystery unfolds, and thus far it is quite effective. There is something truly frightening about the leader of a planet who can speak so casually of a justice system in which those guilty of, or thought to be guilty of, crimes are exterminated in a way that is similar to our stepping on a blade of grass.]

After the banquet, those attending want to know what can be done about Llarof. Picard is a bit surprised by the question, pointing out that they have no right to interfere with this society's way of justice. The Prime Directive forbids this. He is asked about the idea of shore leave, and is again told by Beverly and Troi that the crew is in desperate need. Ultimately he agrees to it (and this becomes the story's first major problem. No captain worth his rank would allow his people to beam down into so potentially hazardous a situation. It just isn't believable).

Beam down starts, with families experiencing the natural environment of Llarof, and some of the children experiencing real snow and forests for the first time (apparently this was when the Enterprise was supposed to be in the midst of a twenty year mission, hence there were children who had never been off the ship before).

Back on the Enterprise bridge, Aspect Experts are concerned with the prison system on Llarof. Each building is built to hold somewhere between twelve and nineteen thousand people, and yet there are only twelve in each. Picard suggests that Riker beam down and talk to Trebor about the situation, and discover why there are only twelve people in each prison.

Elsewhere, an Enterprise security guard named Tenson is watching some children play, when he hears the sound of screaming. Looking away from the kids, he sees four natives being chased by a pair of cops. Contacting Tasha to inform her of the situation, Tenson is told *not* to interfere. No sooner have these words been said, than two of the kids slip, fall and start rolling down a snowy slope. Tenson sets off in pursuit.

They end up between people fleeing and the two cops pursuing them. The kids are fighting with each other when one of the cops, Siwel, raises his weapon. Tenson pleads that they are from the starship and they're immune, but the man will not hear of it. He pulls the trigger and kills the security officer. The other officer, Oitap, screams to the shooter that those people were off-limits, and with that reluctantly kills the offending officer, as the law dictates.

[NOTE: In the aired episode, no one from the Enterprise was actually killed by the police of this planet. By doing so, the earlier draft gives a much more tangible sense of the justice system on Llarof. It's one thing to talk about exterminating people for the barest of infractions, but quite another to actually see the process in action.]

Riker is meeting with Trebor to discuss the prison situation, and at this time neither is aware that Tenson

was killed. Trebor explains that the prisons are usually full, but on the days that those quadrants are chosen by the computers, those people are put to death for their crimes. The twelve people in each are merely the guards, who await the arrival of more prisoners. Then the man is privately informed of the incident that has taken place. He breaks the news to Riker, adding that it was a tragic accident, and that the officer guilty of this offense has already been put to death. Number One insists on speaking to Oitap, which Trebor, naturally, agrees to.

Throughout the planet, panic is spreading to all Federation personnel as the news of Tenson's death reaches them. They are rushing to be beamed back aboard the Enterprise. Meanwhile, Oitap is running to one of the prisons, tears streaming down his face, ignoring his communication device which is constantly beeping and calling out his name.

When all visitors have been beamed aboard, Tasha requests permission to go down and retrieve Tenson's body. The captain disagrees, saying that he will beam down to do so. Trebor, on the surface, is not comfortable with this, and he tells Riker so. The transporter could easily beam the body back up to the ship, so why should Captain Picard go through the trouble of coming down to the surface? Riker tries to detail their devotion to honor, and that Tenson deserves better than just a simple beam up. This is beyond Trebor's thinking. Then, because Oitap has not shown up, Trebor puts all territories in the vicinity of Tenson's killing on "day" status, although Picard will be immune to this.

Picard and an honor guard appear at the site of Tenson's body. The captain lifts the corpse up in his arms, and the three bodies are transported up. The police are agitated at this, wondering why those visitors deserve special treatment.

Drawde, the warden of one of the prisons and also a close friend of Oitap, says that the man must respond to Trebor, as "day" status has been levelled all around them and many innocent people may die. With this realization, he doesn't waste a moment. Oitap, it seems, is really a man of peace, and cannot live with the ramifications of his silence. He contacts Trebor.

From the Enterprise, Tenson's body is sent into space. Tasha points to his death as justifiable cause for Federation intervention on Llarof. Picard does not concur. The Prime Directive is still in effect.

Oitap is put in "irons," and taken to Trebor's office. Both Trebor and Reneg stay in the room as Riker begins his interrogation, learning of the situation wherein Tenson was murdered by another officer, and Oitap, in an act of retribution, took the officer's life.

Later, Riker and Reneg are alone, with the latter filling in some of the planet's history for the commander. Because the world of Llarof could not afford to lose its doctors, scientists and others considered in an elite class, the immune status was created. Then this status moved was given to the governing body, and the system of elections that had been established was abolished. Immunity began to be handed down from generation to generation as with royalty.

The people became fearful, and that fear began to rule their lives. No one had the nerve to challenge the government or to demand a return of the elections. Reneg adds that just about every family has experienced at least one death under this system, and that, in his mind, is enough for revolution.

Riker wants to know if he's expecting the Enterprise to intervene and help the cause, because if that's the case, then he's in for a disappointment. Reneg smiles, and says that he does *not* want intervention, unless a full-scale war breaks out between the people and the government. He has a plan, but he promises both Riker and Picard that he will avert his plan if it looks as though it will result in the slaughter of innocent people. The captain makes his position clear: even counseling Reneg could be seen as an act of interference. Riker must beam back aboard. He does so, while wishing the man the best of luck in his efforts.

Once Riker is gone, Reneg moves to the computer controls and begins initiating his own programming. Drawde, at the prison, gets a signal and says to his guards, "It's started."

Aspect Experts on board the Enterprise notify Picard that all parts of Llarof, with the exception of the government area, have been made immune. Picard wants the area studied carefully. Riker is concerned that Reneg is in jeopardy, but the captain refuses his request to provide aid. The Aspect Experts state that there is combat in the government area. Picard contemplates this for a moment and then, and we quote, "reminds Riker of a sub-paragraph in

the mission orders – that a starship captain has the latitude to decide that observation of an election procedure is necessary to assure it is fairly held. Since no opposition party apparently exists on Llarof, then Reneg, committed to elections, can be considered to be campaigning." To this end, Picard suggests that Riker and Tasha beam down as "observers." Grateful for this opportunity, they depart for the transporter room.

Riker, Tasha, Data and Geordi materialize within the computer center, where Reneg has stationed himself. Reneg admits that he has no battle experience, and accepts Riker's offer to "quiet the situation." He *allows* the guards to enter, and a battle ensues, which quickly ends with the Enterprise personnel disarming them. Data guards them as the others run out to a corridor where more combat is going on. Again, they are able to disarm those people fighting, and return to the computer center. Data informs Riker that Reneg has gone off to deal with Trebor in the oval office.

By the time Riker arrives there, Trebor has a weapon aimed at Reneg, and is screaming at him for attempting to destroy their "natural" system of government. Unwilling to allow Riker to interfere, Trebor aims the weapon at him, which gives Reneg the opportunity to rush the man. The weapon is turned back, and fired at Reneg, who collapses to the ground. Riker leaps at Trebor and a vicious fist fight ensues, which Riker ultimately wins. Doing so, he contacts Beverly Crusher and requests that she beam down for medical assistance, which she does.

"I'm not dying," says Reneg. "I won't let myself die now. Not until it's over."

Days later, families are once again beaming down to Llarof's surface for shore leave. On the bridge, Picard is amused by the fact that the election process has begun on the planet's surface, and that the candidates are down to five, two women and three men. Reneg's platform is simply justice for all, one person-one vote, etc.

"His opponents are calling him a pacifist, or a liberal conservative," Picard tells Riker. "It sounds like home to me, Number One."

[NOTE: This version of "Justice," for the most part, would have worked as an effective episode of The Next Generation. *The theme, as previously discussed, is fascinating, and the idea of immune status being handed down from generation to generation like royalty is simply wonderful. However, it's not surprising that considering Gene Roddenberry's determination to stay as far away from the original* Star Trek *as possible, the ending was dropped. Riker and his Away Team serving as "observers" of the situation, who actually play a part in the revolution, is right out of the old show. Captain Kirk often reinterpreted the Prime Directive to fit his way of thinking, a perfect example of which is "A Taste of Armageddon," in which the Enterprise comes across a pair of planets who have been engaging in a computer war for centuries. The computer targets certain areas, and those people living there would voluntarily walk into disintegration chambers, so that the society itself would continue. Kirk*

took it upon himself to destroy the disintegration chambers, thus forcing the two cultures to do away with their war. This was, really, a flagrant violation of the Prime Directive, and would have been equally as erroneous in "Justice."]

In John D.F. Black's second draft treatment for this story, dated February 17, 1987, Captain Picard is already aware of some of Llarof's conditions, explaining that the society was based on the Greek principle of democracy and that it is apparently crime-free. He has always found this planet to be rather fascinating. Riker and Data inform the captain that some of the children on the ship are involved in a historic study of manned flight, and will be flying models of all sorts of airborne vehicles. Could they conduct these studies on Llarof? The captain does not see this as a particular problem, provided that the planet turns out to be all that it is supposed to be and that the government approves of such a visit.

Trebor and Reneg beam aboard the Enterprise for their first meeting (which is opposed to what happens in the first draft, where Riker and company transported down to the planet's surface). After some conversation, Trebor says that the children are welcome to beam down, provided they are with proper supervision. It is Reneg's suggestion that the Enterprise personnel wear their own clothing as opposed to those worn by the Llarofians, and that they stay in what is termed "relatively unpopulated areas."

Later, Trebor and Reneg are in the midst of an argument, in which Trebor refuses to suspend "the day" during the visit by these strangers, and he will not allow any tampering to take place with the random selecting of the computers. He will, however, grant those visitors immune status.

As was the case with the first draft, the Away Team beams down, finds everyone running to different places, sees the long line of people trying to fill the openings in the police force, are exposed to the reference of "the day," and say that the planet looks okay for the children. They start beaming down. The scene with Tenson plays pretty much the way it was written before, except that Beverly's *son* Wesley is with Tenson's group, and is one of the kids to go rolling down the slope in front of the police officers. Panicking, Wesley climbs the ridge and starts running away.

The Away Team transports back up, just as the news of Tenson's death reaches Trebor from Reneg, who suggests that they will have an official from the Enterprise come down to speak to Oitap and proceed with an official inquiry. Trebor says that before the Enterprise can be contacted, they must locate and question the youth who witnessed this (Wesley).

On the Enterprise bridge, they are discussing the sociological structure of Llarof, which Riker feels is as near perfect as society can be. Troi does not agree, pointing out that the "sublimated emotional pitch is volatile. Like a living volcano that is dormant, it is only a matter of time until it erupts." She honestly believes it is just a question of *when* aggressive violence will resurface.

Wes is moving through the woods when he is suddenly surrounded by six police officers. He tries to run away but is grabbed, accused of resisting arrest and taken away.

Reneg contacts Picard and tells him that Wesley has been taken prisoner, and about the death of Tenson. He recommends that the captain send down a security team to rescue the boy by force. The Prime Directive rears its ugly head again, and Picard requests that Wesley be released after interrogation. Reneg says he can make no such promise. Beverly, who has heard all of this, demands that Picard get her son back via the transporter, but he says he will not.

Again on the surface, one of the kids launches his model of a V-2 rocket. It explodes and accidentally injures one of the police officers. The children, Tasha and three security guards are arrested for this act. Only an eight-year-old child, Alba, who was up in a tree at the time, is not arrested. She climbs down, moves to where the shore leave parties were to contact the starship, and does so. She is brought aboard, tells Picard (which is pretty amazing for an eight-year-old) that the others were arrested and tells him what direction they were moving off in.

Tasha, the security officers and the children are very uptight about their current situation. She is admittedly having a tough time keeping the children from breaking down and crying.

It is Riker's recommendation that they beam everyone aboard and then discuss the situation with Trebor. Picard will not do so for the same reason as before. However, Riker is given permission to beam down to "discuss" the situation with Trebor face to face. Data and Geordi accompany him. They appear in the prison where everyone is being held, and an alarm sounds. Guards arrive, but then so does Reneg, who tells the guards to back off and takes the three men with him. When they're alone, Reneg details the law of "the day" that governs the planet (which was discussed in the summary of the first draft of this story). The child who launched the rocket that injured the police officer will be tried, but everyone else will share her sentence. It is in keeping with their system of guilt by association. He adds that the other children were approached *after* Wes was captured, but no one was informed of this. The reason? Reneg was hoping that such an action would provoke a reaction from the Enterprise. He believes it is time for a revolution so that real justice can exist. He honestly believes that if given the choice, the people of Llarof would want to do away with the system.

While Riker can understand this, he still doesn't know why Reneg wants the Enterprise to take action. His reason is that the children *will* be sentenced to death and will perish unless Picard intervenes. The thought is that the people who agree with Reneg will support the starship's actions, and this in turn will give them the nerve to stand up for their own rights. And if the captain refuses to play into Reneg's plans, it will only be a matter of time before Starfleet hears of what happened and they send other people in to "correct" the situa-

tion. If need be, he will have these children murdered so that the revolution will live.

Picard, who has been listening to the whole conversation via communicator, orders the Away Team beamed back aboard. Later, Data states that he has studied everything about the planet's law and that the children are entitled to defense from someone aboard the Enterprise. It is decided that Riker will serve as counsel.

In the Llarof court room, a device is used on all witnesses to determine whether they are telling the truth. Oitap testifies, explaining why he killed his fellow officer, stating that the Enterprise people were immune. Trebor congratulates him and then has him placed under arrest for gross misconduct. Then Wesley is called to the witness stand, and his testimony reveals that the officer who was wounded by the child's rocket was in the area *after* Wes had been captured, which, essentially, means that he had no right to be there. Riker then calls Reneg as witness. The man initially refuses. Nervously, Reneg claims that in his position he is in possession of confidential information, which would be revealed to the device. Riker says that he will submit all of his questions to Trebor for approval, which is acceptable to all. The questions are approved. Riker begins the questioning and Reneg is forced to tell the truth of his secret intentions. Trebor accuses him of treason.

"You are confusing dissent with treason," Riker counters.

"To disagree is righteous, to attempt to draw the Enterprise into Llarofian internal affairs is treason."

The case against the children is dismissed, and they are beamed aboard the starship. Reneg is found guilty of treason and sentenced to death. Trebor executes the man right there and then.

The Enterprise breaks orbit from Llarof. On the bridge, Riker tells Picard that Reneg was right in his feelings concerning the planet's structure of law. Picard concurs, while simultaneously pointing out that it is not their place to judge. Perhaps, he reasons, the people would have wanted to leave everything exactly the way it was.

"Perhaps they'd rather risk being legally executed for dropping a piece of paper on the sidewalk," Picard muses, "to live without fear of being raped or robbed or murdered in their sleep. In any case, they have a right to their own system of justice."

[NOTE: This version of "Justice" works far better than the first draft does, and it does end on something of a downbeat note, which the original Star Trek was able to pull off wonderfully. The courtroom scene serves as a better setting for the conclusion of the episode than an action-filled revolution between the factions, with the Enterprise crew taking part. The death of Reneg, if filmed, would have been shocking to the audience. This was terrific drama. The only bit of business missing is Riker's guilt for having the man confess the truth and then being killed for it. One would imagine that the commander would at least feel pity towards the other man.

Writer Worley Thorne, who had penned the "Are Unheard Melodies Sweet?" script for the proposed Star

Trek II series of the mid '70s, was asked to take "Justice" to the next stage of development. His first draft treatment is dated March 16, 1987.]

Once again, the Enterprise is in desperate need of shore leave, and they come to the same Class M planet. Riker, who has taken an Away Team down to the surface, finds that the planet is virtually crime-free, and that politically it is a full democracy. Children, under security supervision, are beamed down to play, with the captain ordering that they stay away from populated areas.

[NOTE: Not to break up the story analysis so soon, but there is absolutely no way that the captain of a starship would allow people to beam down for shore leave without first establishing contact with the government.]

Tasha, security officers and children beam down to the planet's surface, where the children immediately start playing in a field. A child named Marta is flying a radio controlled airplane, which veers the wrong way. She runs after it, unbeknownst to security in the area. As the youth looks for her model, she comes across a transparent globe which flashes a series of holographic numerals. Marta then catches sight of her plane, buried in a flower bed. She climbs a small fence, but is stopped by a passing citizen. This man grabs the plane, but a horrified look crosses his face when he realizes that he's picked some "public" flowers as well. He tells Marta to run, and he does the same. It is just a matter of seconds before police officers arrive on the scene in their vehicles. Admitting his crime, the man is

disintegrated. Marta watches this from a relatively safe distance, her face a mask of terror.

Marta runs and finds Tasha, and wraps herself tightly around her waist. The police reach them, and warn Tasha to get away from the child or she, too, will be destroyed. A weapon is leveled at her, and she reacts violently, disarming one of the officers, and starting to beat the other two. The children in the area run away. Then additional officers arrive and disintegrate a pair of security aides. Making a mad dash for it, Tasha reaches the children and they continue to run. She tries her communicator, but it has been smashed in the battle.

The police utilize "mechanical bloodhounds" to chase after these violators. Once they've gone, Riker and Geordi appear. Geordi's unique vision sees the residue aura of the Enterprise crewmembers who were disintegrated.

Tasha and the children reach an area near a river. They are all weary and hungry, with some of them unable to continue. Tasha carries the smallest child, and they continue across the bridge. Once across, she pulls out her phaser and disintegrates the bridge. They then proceed to a house, with the sound of the mechanized bloodhounds not too far behind them.

From the Enterprise, Data announces that by studying occurrences on the planet's surface, he has discovered that the police serve as judge, jury and executioners for any infraction, including the one detected: the picking of flowers. Picard is astounded, as is Beverly, but

Data points out that this system of "the day" has resulted in a law-abiding society. Their primary concern is Tasha and the children.

The children are eating within the house, while Tasha stands guard by watching out the window. An old man walks in, stating that he has left a false trail for the police. He also seems very excited to be dealing with the "criminal" element. The Security Chief is curious as to why the old man helped them, and his response is that he couldn't stand by and watch the deaths of all those children. In response, one of them hugs the old man, who develops tears in his eyes.

Riker and Geordi follow the infrared trail left behind by the group. They arrive at the location where the bridge had been, and they have the Enterprise beam them to the other side. The police arrive, and are stunned. How did those strange visitors get where they are? The duo continue, but come across a police roadblock, and are told that they are being placed under arrest. Riker wants to know what the charge is, and, before there is a response, phasers are used on stun. The two men leap into one of the police vehicles and drive off in it. There is a high-speed chase (who ever said that there would never be a car chase in *Star Trek*?). Riker ultimately loses control of the vehicle, and it careens down the riverbank, the result being that both men are thrown free. Geordi lies on the ground, stunned, while Riker's upper body is submerged. Geordi tries to help, but can't, as he blacks out. The commander's body is carried away by the river's current as Geordi's body is beamed aboard the Enterprise. On the starship, panic is setting in. They can't locate Number One.

Riker is eventually found by a beautiful woman named Nydia, who has been bathing naked in the river. She swims out to his body, and pulls him to shore.

Data enters sickbay to see his friend, Geordi. The two begin to talk, with the android admitting that he has been thinking an awful lot about Tasha, believing that he is deeply in love with her (ugh … this is too much to accept, and one can only be grateful that it was eventually dropped from the storyline). He expresses his feelings, and Geordi responds by telling him that he is more human than he thinks.

Nydia is mending Riker's wounds, and making love to him. Elsewhere, Tasha has led the children to a dark cave, where they're resting. Utilizing her phaser, she blasts a hole in the roof of the cave, thus allowing fresh air to enter.

On the bridge, Data wants to beam down to conduct a search. Picard refuses, and Data responds in an uncharacteristic way which causes the captain to raise an eyebrow. A moment later he apologizes.

Riker awakens to find the woman beside him. Riker tries to remember where he is, and can't. He eventually passes out again.

Enterprise sensors have detected a power source, and they eventually locate a satellite which is apparently supplying the entire planet with power. After careful examination, Data determines that this is the source of the random selection

of times and locations for what he terms police sweeps. In his opinion, a society capable of working with such a clear cut "efficiency" is one which would undoubtedly result in a highly law-abiding population. Picard cannot accept this as a rational move, pondering the price those people must have paid. What could their past have been like if they were forced to resort to such actions? Data begins absorbing information on the history of this world, and is joined by Wesley.

Tasha sees that Marta still has her radio control from her airplane. She takes it from the child and begins tinkering with it, hoping that she will be able to adjust it to something that the Enterprise can pick up (how on Earth she eventually does it is beyond me), and ultimately they start detecting a Morse code signal.

Once again Riker awakens in Nydia's bedroom, and the woman proclaims her love for him. He says that he would love to stay with her, but he can't. He has responsibilities elsewhere. But he will never forget the time they've shared together. He leaves and then contacts the Enterprise. Picard says there's a mission for both him and Data, and the android transports down to the planet's surface. With him is an ancient Earth-style radio receiver, which will, hopefully, lead them to the signals they've been receiving on board the ship. Eventually they come to the conclusion that the code is coming from a cave, and are transported there. They enter the cave, and find themselves surrounded by police officers, who expect him to sacrifice himself for the good of the law. The

commander says he cannot do so for only one child has been charged, and they do not have any say over his actions for the simple reason that he has *not* been charged with any crime. They claim he resisted detainment, and he counters that he had not been charged with anything, so how could he be resisting? Somehow this results in a stalemate.

Picard wants everyone beamed aboard, but the materials of the cave are apparently blocking out their scans, so it is impossible to get a proper fix.

After conferring, one of the cops tells Riker that he can take everyone with him, with the exception of Marta and Tasha. Riker cannot accept this, instead demanding a trial. The officer agrees, but points out that if the human does not prove his case, then he will be disintegrated with the others. Data, believing he's more expendable, asks that he be the one to defend them, to which Riker replies in the negative.

The courtroom scene takes place, with Riker defending Marta and Tasha, and Nydia serving as the prosecution. Her argument is simple: the child broke the law and has to be punished. Riker's argument (in an effort to make the "sweeps" period pass over them, thus sparing everyone) is that the evidence – the flowers that were picked – is not in the courtroom. Nydia protests this.

"This will be murder," says Riker, "if you harm any of us. You don't care about justice. All you care about is whether your system works. It matters not at all to you if you convict the innocent."

The judge ignores this, believing

there is no fault with their system. A vote, via devices hooked up in every home, is to take place. The tallies start to come in, with it looking as though those thinking the Enterprise personnel are guilty are edging out those believing they're innocent.

On the Enterprise, Data figures out how to tap into the satellite, and he uses the Enterprise to power it up in such a way as to speed the numbers on the holographic globes, thus accelerating the sweeps period. Before the final vote comes in, sweeps is over and, therefore, the case against the starship people is summarily dropped and everyone lives happily ever after . . .

[NOTE: One can detect a somewhat sarcastic tone to this summary, but for good reason. It is hard to believe that John D.F. Black was dropped from his own story, and that this one was developed instead. The original idea commented on our current society, taking a dark look at what happens when a society reaches its saturation point with terrorism; the action that those people feel they have to take in response. This version of the story is much ado about nothing. In addition, the love scenes, or corresponding dialogue, are awful. The only comment Worley Thorne's story makes is on the network sweeps period, which in the television industry is life and death. Such a statement on the medium was handled in a better fashion in the original series' "Bread and Circuses" episode. Of course it should be pointed out that this was Thorne's first draft treatment, and that by the time he got to first draft teleplay, the story improved drastically, and then, in turn, lost quite

a bit in quality when turned into an actual episode. In terms of quality, this story really was a roller coaster ride throughout its development, proving that there was little justice in the world for "Justice."]

In Worley Thorne's second draft treatment, dated April 6, 1987, the Class M world the Enterprise comes across is named Selene V, "a planet with a reputation for being free of crime, but about which little else is known."

In an amphitheater on the planet's surface, Riker and his Away Team are meeting with the natives, who are physically fit beings adorned in athletic attire. They contact Picard and tell him that the planet is a paradise. The captain, in turn, grants shore leave for some of the children, including Marta. Things play out like the first draft with the model plane flying into the flower bed, and the citizen removing it and accidentally pulling up some of the flowers. Police arrive, and instead of disintegrating him, they use a device which shrinks the man to tiny size, then encase him in a transparent golden globe. He tries to speak, but his voice is little more than a squeak. According to the outline, each human is a galaxy unto himself, with much space and relatively little matter. The Selenes have discovered how to compress molecules closer, the globe itself a by-product of the excess energy employed. Marta, again, has witnessed the way in which the police deal with violators.

Marta runs to a member of Enterprise security, Harris, and he is also shrunken and encased in a small globe. On the bridge, Data picks up the series of squeaks from a commun-

icator and is a bit puzzled as to its source. Picard orders a check of all crewmembers down on the planet.

Marta continues and meets up with Wesley and Tasha. Meanwhile, Riker and his team come across a display of extremely lifelike figurines in globes, unaware that these were once living people.

Soon thereafter, Tasha, who resists the police, is miniaturized, encased in one of the globes. On the bridge, they pick up Harris' voice again, finally recognizing it, and are stunned to hear that he is extremely giddy about the whole situation. Children are appearing in the transporter room, only to be followed by the small globe containing Tasha.

Eventually Picard learns how the Selenes are dealing with crime: it's still the "day" system. Now the ship is trying desperately to save Tasha. Later, Harris dies within the globe, and Picard is forced to oversee the funeral ceremony. The unvoiced fear is that Tasha will be next. Eventually they beam a magistrate up from the planet's surface. Nydia, the magistrate, is angry that they've stolen property from the planet, namely the globe housing Tasha. Riker is furious, stating that it's a human being they're talking about, and not some object.

What follows is that an angry Nydia beams back down, followed by Riker, who tries to use his charms to get her to help him enlarge Tasha again. Lots of breast-feeling and lovemaking ensues, with this woman actually falling for Riker, and then growing angry that he wants her to help him save Tasha.

We end up back at the trial, but this time Picard is handling the defense of his people, and it is he who will be turned into a globe if he is not successful. The captain is ultimately able to prove that the police hunted Tasha at a time when the sweep was legally over, and therefore, on that technicality, she cannot be sentenced to die. The court agrees with this, Tasha is freed, the charges are dropped against Marta, and the Enterprise departs for its next mission.

[NOTE: This writer is shaking his head while reading this storyline, still bothered by the fact that much of the original concept has completely vanished. The bit with shrinking of people and placing them in globes ... it's the kind of thing that would make up Saturday morning television, not Star Trek. The heart has been taken out of the premise of this story. There is no real sense of jeopardy here.]

Thorne, whose name would ultimately appear in the aired credits for this episode, turned in his first draft teleplay of "Justice" on July 29, 1987. This time out, the Enterprise is attempting to negotiate a treaty with the members of the Edo star system so that they can rescue a pair of scientists in a Federation Science Observatory that will soon be under the threat of an ion storm. The source of escape would be through Edo space, but as his log points out, "Edos are isolated, suspicious people. All prior negotiations with them have failed." The leader of Edo has agreed to meet with Picard on Alba 2, a neutral planet, and the meeting will be mediated by that world's First Councillor. When the captain voices some concern about the situation, Data points out that

crime on Alba 2 is practically non-existent. Troi is hopeful that they will be able to establish trust between their two races, but Riker doesn't think this is likely. It turns out that he had encountered them several years earlier, and found them to be an arrogant, self-important people who believe their culture is far superior to all others.

The Enterprise receives a communiqué from the Charles Drew, a medical evacuation vessel that is attempting to rendezvous with the observatory. Picard asks Captain Wilheim Van Hoeck how the journey is going, and is told that it's "bumpy," and that it would be a big help if the Enterprise was able to establish a treaty. Picard informs him that he's doing his best. From there he goes to the transporter room, where he beams down to the surface of Alba 2. The Councillor is the party who will serve as mediator between the Federation and Edo.

Picard, Riker, Tasha and Troi beam down to the surface and make their way through the streets. Just as they notice that everyone runs from place to place, they are greeted by Rivan and two monitor aides, who are in prime physical condition, and lead them all on a brisk jog to a place known as The Chambers. Shortly thereafter, they meet up with the First Councillor who greets them warmly. The representative from Edo is late in arriving (supposedly purposely so), so Picard takes the opportunity to contact the ship. After speaking to Data, he talks with Beverly, who tells him how important it is for some of the children to get shore leave. Picard asks the Councillor if this is okay, to

which he replies in the affirmative – provided they follow the behavior code which will be transmitted to the Enterprise. This is acceptable to all.

On the ship Data begins reading all of the Alba 2 laws at superhuman speed. An astounding thirty nine seconds later he completes this chore, contacts Picard and tells him that there does not seem to be anything out of the ordinary about Alban laws. Permission is granted for shore leave, although Picard requests that Tasha beam back up so that she can supervise the security teams accompanying the children.

Tasha leaves, and the ambassador from Edo, Amyx, arrives. There is some hostility between him and Picard, but the captain quickly discovers that a firm hand will serve him best in these meetings. A discussion ensues between them in which the female Amyx wishes to know why the Federation wants to extend its grasp to this part of the galaxy, to which Picard replies that this is merely for scientific research and nothing more. As the conversation goes on, it's obvious to all that it is extremely strained. This is *not* going to be an easy negotiation.

Outside, Marta sees some flowers that she thinks looks pretty. She picks one, ignoring the sign that says she shouldn't do so, and starts to walk away. She is confronted by Rivan who asks if she did what he saw her do, and she says yes. Tasha and Wes approach, and are told by Rivan of the seriousness of this crime, and are stunned to hear that judgement will be passed at that exact moment.

Data receives a transmission from Van Hoeck, who claims that the ion storm is intensifying. Passage has to be granted quickly, or the scientists aboard the observatory are doomed. When told of the captain's meeting, the man says he will try again at a later time.

Rivan questions Marta, and the child admits everything that she did. Rivan passes sentence, which is, of course, death. Tasha fights back and it comes down to a showdown between her and Rivan, as they level weapons at each other. Geordi comes up, and a weapon is aimed at him as well by one of Rivan's assistants.

At his station, Data has been listening to all that's been going on. A crewman suggests that they just beam the child and the others up, but Data points out that such an action would be a direct violation of the Prime Directive.

In the council chamber, the debate between Picard and the representative from Edo is heating up, with the latter stating that humanity is a violent, savage race and a barbaric one. Picard is then contacted, and asked to come out to the park area where the incident had taken place. He, and everybody else from the meeting, arrives there in short time. The captain is told of everything that transpired, and filled in on the random selection of Albian law.

Picard is granted a bit of leeway in terms of time, and goes back up to the Enterprise to figure out what he can do without violating the Prime Directive. While there, he is contacted again by Van Hoeck, who says that time is running short and whether or not a treaty is negotiated, he is going

to have to make an attempt to save the two scientists. Finally Picard, completely exasperated, says to Beverly, "Does it come down to that? We sacrifice a nine-year-old to get a treaty to save two, possibly three, others?" There is no answer to the question.

Picard and his top officers attempt to act out the trial they know is coming, looking for something they can use as a legal loophole to get them out of this situation. In the midst of this, they are contacted again by the Charles Drew, its captain saying that they are moving through Edo space and are being tracked by a battle cruiser, which is arming photon torpedoes, but does not fire. Picard tells him to take no evasive action, and he will see what he can do planetside. Picard decides that there's only one thing he can do, and it will be quite a gamble for his career and any hopes of negotiations with the Edos.

Everything else, for the most part, follows the previous treatment, although the scenes are considerably longer. Picard does indeed go to court, and tells them that he admires their system of justice, but, he adds, "To pay back the removal of a flower with death . . . to destroy a young life not lived. Punishing not only this girl, but a mother, a crew, a captain — who've learned to love her. It is unthinkable. I cannot participate by obeying my directive. In this one instance, I must disobey."

Guards move in to arrest him, but first he gives Marta's coordinates to Data, and the child is beamed away to safety. The First Councillor is angry over this move, believing that Picard has betrayed them. He says

that the captain should leave, and tell the Federation not to send any other emissaries in the future. The transporter effect begins, but takes Amyx aboard as well. Once this is done, he shows her the monitor which displays the image of the Charles Drew traveling through Edo space, pursued by a native battle cruiser. Amyx is shocked to see this.

"War," says Picard. "Or the beginning of one. A Federation ship is already in your space. Yours in pursuit. It may already be too late. While you drew out our talks, while you suspected the worst and failed to recognize our genuine needs, your 'prophecy' (of war) may have become self-fulfilled."

Not wanting war, and the savagery that would accompany it, she uses a secret code to contact the ship, and tells it to veer off. Ultimately, the woman agrees that an open line of communication with the Federation would be beneficial to both sides.

Later, Riker informs Picard that he has had an in-depth conversation with Admiral Wythe-Jones, who has been informed of everything that happened. The Admiral wishes him to know there will be an official inquiry, but also that this mission was a job "well done."

(NOTE: This version of "Justice" was a bit more complex and more interesting than the previous two attempts by the writer, and for that he should be commended. The problem, however, is the same as with the treatments: the core of John D.F. Black's original concept is, for all intents and purposes, gone. This story just becomes another mediocre adventure aboard the starship Enter-

prise. The characters are handled very nicely, though, and the dialogue is quite natural.

Worley Thorne would ultimately do the final script as well, but, unfortunately, that one would fall far short of his own first draft teleplay. As aired, "Justice" seems to be just another episode preoccupied by sex, combined with an alien muckity-muck with a booming voice pulling the strings.

The Enterprise has just set up a colony on another planet, and the crew are investigating this unexplored Class M world they have come across. It happens to be Edo. They beam down, go through essentially the same adventure – although there's a lot of hugging and love-making going on all around them – and Wesley is the one who accidentally falls on some plants and is sentenced to death. Picard is caught between saving the boy's life and attempting to live up to the Prime Directive. The people of the planet, who are not driven by any form of malice, beg Picard not to upset the natural balance of their civilization. The unseen alien seems determined to allow the human boy to die, perhaps as a lesson to the others, but Picard's words about true justice apparently arouse something in it, and they are beamed back aboard the Enterprise.

There are some nice moments in the final version of "Justice," and the script does manage to hold up, but the episode seems to come across as an ad for "Club Med in Outer Space."]

"THE BATTLE"

Herbert Wright's "The Battle" originally began as a script treatment by the late Larry Forrester entitled "Ghost Ship," dated April 16, 1987.

The Enterprise is providing relief to another starship which has been patrolling the territorial "line" separating Federation space from that of the Ferengi Alliance. The other side is being guarded by a war ship from that race. On the Enterprise bridge, Data is filling Picard in on the background of the Ferengi ship, identifying its captain as Bok and filling the captain in on the ship's various capabilities, armament, etc.

On the Ferengi ship, Bok surprises his crew, particularly first officer Kazago, by opening up communication with the Federation ship and requesting contact with Picard. Riker is immediately wary of a trap, but the captain decides to accept the communiqué. Utilizing an exterior ship viewer, Bok replaces his own image with that of a another craft. Picard is stunned, recognizing it as his old ship, the Stargazer.

Shortly thereafter, Picard and Riker are discussing the mysterious reappearance of the Stargazer, as the vessel was captained by Picard in a fierce battle against the Ferengi nearly a decade earlier. It was a battle in which the captain truly distinguished himself, but ended with his abandoning the burning ship. Riker is preparing an Away Team to beam over, and Picard admits that he is extremely envious. Still, procedure must be followed.

Bok toys with a small machine called a "trauma recall unit, which produces a beam that probes to the core of a person's mind, stimulates secret guilts and fears and uses them as a weapon, breaking down willpower." Kazago discusses the device with his captain, and is shown a brain chart taken of Captain Picard, culled from the memory banks of the Stargazer, which were raided by the Ferengi once the ship was abandoned. Bok obviously hates Picard for something, which disturbs Picard's first officer, although the man will not say anything about it. But as he watches his captain, he begins to figure out the pieces of the puzzle: why the Stargazer was towed to the borderline of their territory and why Bok has been devoting such an inordinate amount of time to this brain machine, which, according to the story treatment, has been banned.

The Enterprise Away Team arrives on the Stargazer, and immediately discovers that the ship's memory banks are completely empty. They are even more surprised that the ship still has power, although some answers are revealed as Data takes note of obvious repairs which were initiated. His thought, however, is that such repairs may have been necessary to tow it to the borderline.

Picard, meanwhile, is trying to rest, but he is the victim of a savage migraine headache, and is experiencing flashbacks to the final battle he fought while aboard the Stargazer. Both Beverly Crusher and Deanna Troi enter the room, attempting to get the captain to submit himself to medical and psychological examinations. What they find, however, is the captain in the midst of this bizarre flashback. Then, he collapses.

While Picard is regaining consciousness in sickbay, Troi informs Dr. Crusher that right before he collapsed, she sensed a profound sense of hatred envelop him. She is unable to give any more detail, but emphasizes her belief that the captain's life could be threatened. Her words do not go over lightly. Then Picard awakens completely.

After instructing Data to research Bok's background, Riker proceeds to Picard's cabin, where the captain has gone to from sickbay. They discuss the final struggle of the Stargazer. Picard describes the battle in which a Ferengi ship began a suicide attack, but was destroyed by his quick thinking and not a little bit of luck. Picard is admittedly confused that the memory keeps reoccurring, adding that he does not feel guilt for what happened. Still, he says, memories of the deaths of all of those people, whether they were enemies or not, have never left him. He wants to beam over to the ship, believing that such a visit will rid him of the nightmares he's experiencing. Riker does not like the idea.

On the Ferengi ship, Kazago is discussing the situation regarding his captain, who he loves like a father, with the chief medical officer. Something, he says, is definitely wrong with him, but he can't put his finger on it. The doctor assures him that he will investigate the situation.

[NOTE: One important thing can already be pointed out: Larry Forrester apparently felt it necessary to devote a significant amount of story time to the Ferengi, going aboard their vessel and providing conversations between them. This is

important, because it provides some insight into this race, in some ways mirroring relationships on board the Enterprise, and helps to elevate them above the role of stock villains. The Ferengi were never very popular, mostly because they were played for laughs after being built up to supposedly represent an awesome threat to the Federation. In providing this counter-balance between them and "us," Forrester was establishing a situation much like the original series episode "Balance of Terror," which introduced the Romulans.]

By the time Picard returns to the bridge, his mind is obviously occupied elsewhere. Alarm spreads throughout the crew when he refers to Geordi as a member of the old Stargazer crew. He catches this a moment later, and concern is etched on his face. Elsewhere, Data has collected all available information on Bok, and tells Riker that the Ferengi had a large role in the treaty developed between both their peoples. He insists that there is absolutely nothing that would indicate nefarious intentions on their part or that he had ever encountered Picard in the past.

Back on the Ferengi ship, the medical officer admits to Kazago that Bok will not undergo an examination, and in that case there's nothing the doctor can do about it. Apparently the Ferengi don't empower their chief medical personnel with the right to *force* a captain to undertake an exam, or relieve him as unfit for command. Moments later, Bok informs his first officer that he should watch for the moment that the Enterprise crosses into Ferengi territory. Kazago considers this for a moment, and comes

to the horrible realization that somehow his captain is attempting to use the brain device to draw both Picard and his ship into a situation where they would be able to open fire. Something must be done, he notes to himself, or else it could result in an intergalactic war. He takes an awful chance by contacting Riker.

In the ensuing conversation (which Riker has Troi mentally eavesdrop on), Kazago speaks cryptically, comparing the Stargazer to "the wooden horse." He adds that Riker should remind his captain that broaching the Ferengi territorial line would be considered an act of war, and that both he and Bok would be deemed enemies of peace. A grudging respect develops between the two first officers as communication is closed. Troi tells Riker that she sensed only sincerity in the Ferengi's words.

Trying to come to grips with what he's been experiencing, Picard has the holodeck convert to a serene country setting. He is surprised to be joined by Beverly and Wes. The boy starts asking the captain questions about the capabilities of the Stargazer, which Picard does his best to answer, although he never mentions the final battle. Beverly listens to the conversation intently, and finally asks Wes to go find some wood for a cooking fire. Once the youth has departed to carry out his assigned task, the two adults begin talking about the death of her late husband, Jack Crusher, who was serving under Picard on the Stargazer when he met his demise. Picard is the one who brought home the man's body, and even though she had never held the captain responsible, she admits that

the event has created something of a barrier between the two of them. Picard considers this statement, and replies that he finds it strange that Jack's death is not weighing as heavily on his mind as the battle aboard the Stargazer does. Then he says that he almost feels as though his subconscious mind were being driven towards that particular memory by an unseen force. This strikes a chord with Beverly's memory. As the treatment notes, she recalls research concerning "a device that could rummage around in a person's brain, select traumatic memories, experiences influencing the person's whole life, and recreate them, breaking down the personality – even to the point of madness, with past and present inextricably tangled, indistinguishable." Research was eventually abandoned in the belief that such a device was more appropriate for the more barbaric past.

[NOTE: The issue of Jack Crusher's death and the fact that Picard brought his body home to Beverly and Wes was supposed to be one of the most important aspects of, and ties between, these three characters. It was dealt with slightly in the premiere episode of season one, "Encounter at Farpoint," and has only been touched upon peripherally in a couple of other episodes. Ironically, an early draft of the fourth episode, "Where None Have Gone Before," dealt with the issue in an illusionary, and powerful, sense – see the previous volume in this series for full details – but it never made it to the air. Then, again, in "Arsenal of Freedom," Picard and Beverly are trapped in a cavern and are struggling to stay

alive. An early draft of that had them deal with their true *feelings for each other, but that, too, was dropped in the final episode. Now that Gates McFadden has been, unfortunately, removed from the show, we'll never see this element developed any further. This is truly a shame, as it was a relationship which was never allowed to reach its full potential.]*

On the Ferengi ship, an angry Bok confronts Kazago. He knows his first officer has spoken to Riker. As a result, he is confined to quarters.

Picard awakens in his quarters after another flashback. He lies there for a moment, tries to orient himself, gets dressed and departs. His face has an angry look to it. He makes his way to the bridge, where he has communication immediately opened with Bok. A barrage of questions about the Stargazer and this situation are launched. Bok remains calm, telling him that as an "act of goodwill," the Ferengi have decided to return the ship to its former captain. This, we learn, is a lie, as we cut to Kazago, who indicates that this is a complete lie. The channel is closed, and Picard turns to Riker, asking if it's possible that the vessel is not really the Stargazer, but another ship holographically designed to resemble it. Riker thinks that this is a distinct possibility, and restates his position that Picard should not beam over, as he has been talking about doing. The captain leaves the bridge, makes his way to the transporter room and beams over, much to the horror of the bridge crew, as they are informed of this event.

Bok, who is in his quarters with the brain control device, is watching the image of Picard, obviously delighted. He has his ship (somehow) jam the Enterprise transporter system, and then begins utilizing the device in his hands.

Upon realizing that the transporter is blocked, Riker attempts to contact the Ferengi vessel, but is completely ignored. Weapons are locked on to the ship, and Riker gives the order for the Enterprise to broach the border, which he does with much trepidation. On the Stargazer, Picard is in the midst of a powerful mental struggle, juggling the past with the present and trying to secure his real "location." Images of the battle come to his mind again, only under Bok's "direction," the Stargazer attacked a Ferengi ship which was under a flag of truce, thus resulting in its destruction. One sentence echoes in his mind: "The commander of that ship was my son . . ." This from Bok.

Kazago has heard what's going on, and driven by his sense of duty and devotion, he gets the attention of the ship's doctor and proclaims an emergency situation.

The mental game continues, with Bok essentially controlling Picard's every move. The battle plays out as it did nine years earlier, only this time the Enterprise appears on the viewscreen, but to Picard it looks like the Ferengi vessel. The plan becomes clear: Picard will use his old ship to destroy his new command, and all those aboard. Using communicators, Riker is able to patch in to Picard, desperately trying to make the man realize the truth of the situation. Tense moments pass. Beverly's voice joins that of Will. It's starting to work, but not quickly enough. The Stargazer

fires its weapons, striking and starting to weaken Enterprise shields.

Kazago enters Bok's quarters and quickly places the captain under arrest, claiming him to be incompetent. Bok is not that bothered, feeling that his revenge will be complete: an explosive charge has been rigged on the Stargazer, and it will detonate in approximately sixty seconds. Kazago contacts Riker and warns him, suggesting that he beam his captain back aboard the Enterprise. Beverly continues talking to Picard, and it seems to be having the desired affect. They manage to "unjam" the transporter and whisk the captain aboard just as the Stargazer explodes.

When all is well, Riker contacts Kazago and expresses sincere appreciation from both himself and the Federation. Perhaps a new era of cooperation has been born.

[NOTE: The majority of story elements from this treatment would eventually make it to the aired episode, albeit in a much more detailed form. Again, the one aspect which would not, but should have, is the development of the Ferengi as loyal officers and creatures with some sense of honor. This would have made them more, if you'll pardon the word, human, and, in turn, much more realistic.]

Herb Wright took the Larry Forrester story and did the rewriting and expansion process, producing a first draft teleplay dated September 1, 1987.

Picard, who is still suffering from severe headaches, is scheduled to meet with Bok in a neutral area. What is most bizarre, is that the Ferengi asked to meet with Picard specifically, rather than just a representative of the Federation. Communication is opened, and Bok requests permission to beam over to the Enterprise. Troi immediately senses deception on the Ferengi's part. Riker picks up on this, and adds that there has never been a time when a member of the Ferengi Alliance has set foot on a Federation vessel. Picard considers this, while simultaneously trying to ignore the headache which continues to plague him, and suggests that they beam over to Bok's ship. Surprisingly, the Ferengi agrees, which makes everyone on the Enterprise bridge instantly suspicious. Picard states that they will beam over in one hour's time.

Moments later he is in sickbay, being examined by Beverly. Data is there as well, discussing the situation concerning Bok. While Picard is trying to figure out how the alien knew him, Beverly is more interested in convincing the captain that he's human, whether he likes it or not, and as such he has got to rest before he does himself in. "Contrary to popular conjecture," she says, "you were not built to go twenty five hours a day."

Then she "pops" a pill in his mouth which is designed to relieve stress, at least temporarily. Picard immediately feels back to normal. From there, Picard and Data proceed to the transporter room, where they join Riker, Tasha Yar and Troi. The Away Team beams over to the Ferengi ship and rematerialize on what appears to be the Enterprise bridge. They are, obviously, stunned. At that moment, Bok and several other members of his crew, including Kazago, join them. Indicating around them, Bok says that

this copy of the Enterprise bridge is merely a holographic image designed to "make them feel at home." Geordi scans the area, and takes note of a silver-sphere near the science station.

Bok seems to be "dancing" around the subject of their meeting, and as Picard tries to guide the conversation back on its proper path, he finds his headache from before returning. At that moment, the main viewer is put into operation, revealing a Constitution class starship circa the late 23rd Century. Picard immediately recognizes it as the Stargazer.

[NOTE: Already from the treatment we can see some significant differences, the primary one being that Picard joins an Away Team on an actual beam over to the Ferengi ship. Also, the Stargazer is classified here as a Constitution class starship, which means that the original plan must have been to use the Enterprise model from the feature films in an effort to save on the budget. Eventually they would make this an original design.]

Bok says that the derelict floated into Ferengi space, and he would like it removed. Therefore, he asks that Picard tow it away from them.

Once the Away Team returns to the Enterprise, Picard puts Data in command of the bridge and tells him to alert the captain as to when the Enterprise is in the vicinity of the Stargazer. Then Picard and Riker go to the ready room, where the former begins discussing his tour of duty as captain of the Stargazer. He details how his ship was the victim of an unprovoked attack from an alien vessel, which eventually turned out to be one from the Ferengi Alliance. The battle came

to an end with the "Picard maneuver," whereby the ship, utilizing warp speed, appeared to be in two places at one time. This distracted the Ferengi, and allowed the Stargazer to launch its weapons, thus destroying the enemy vessel. His ship, Picard adds, was on fire, and the surviving members of the crew had to escape via shuttles. No sooner has he finished this tale than Data signals that they are approaching the Stargazer.

[NOTE: Picard's tale is a fascinating one, and the idea of the Picard maneuver is really quite wonderful. The dramatic device of using a holographic device to create a reproduction of the Enterprise bridge instead of one belonging to the Ferengi was undoubtedly done in order to save money on the episode's budget. Additionally, in the aired version Bok beamed over to the Enterprise rather than our people beaming over there.

As often as things change between first drafts and the final version, they just as often do not alter all that much. The latter is the case with "The Battle." Basically the storyline follows the treatment quite closely, albeit in expanded form and, in turn, the aired episode is rather similar to Herb Wright's first draft teleplay. As often seems the case with Next Generation *teleplays, the early drafts seem to have much more character interaction than the shows themselves. This was no exception, particularly where Picard and Beverly Crusher are concerned. There are some really nice moments where they begin to explore their true feelings for each other, and during one sequence in* particular they are seconds away from kissing, when Data interrupts them. While dropped from "The Battle," a very similar occurrence would take place in Tracy Torme's "The Big Goodbye".

As aired, "The Battle" is a delightful episode of the series, and one which is highly original as well.

Director Rob Bowman manages quite a bit of suspense, and Patrick Stewart is great as Picard, particularly during the moments where he is interacting with the "ghosts" of his former crew aboard the Stargazer. Considering that he acted alone, and the other images were superimposed later, this was quite an acting feat that he

pulled off. All in all, "The Battle" works quite well, with the only complaint being the treatment of the Ferengi. Quite frankly, they are not frightening at all, and do not seem to hold much of a threat – with the exception of Bok's mind device.]

"HIDE & Q"

Perhaps one of the biggest surprises coming out of the first season of *Star Trek: The Next Generation* was the growing popularity of John DeLancie's characterization of Q. This threat to the Enterprise began as little more than a rip-off of Trelene from the first series, but ended up leaping off the scripted page in the premiere episode "Encounter at Farpoint," and, then again, in "Hide & Q."

The first treatment for the latter story, written by Maurice Hurley and dated June 30, 1987, begins much as the aired episode did with the Enterprise en route to an emergency situation where it must provide medical assistance, when the infamous Q grid blocks their passage. Everyone on the bridge recognizes it immediately. Then the alien himself appears. Q reveals that he has arrived to provide test number two for the crew, the situation at Farpoint serving as the first. If they are successful once again, then humanity will be off for a great adventure. Picard protests, stating that they don't have the time for this nonsense, because they have dying humans that must be saved.

"Your species is always dying," Q dismisses his protest.

At that moment, his outfit changes to one of a gunslinging cowboy. "Let's stop the bull," he says. "It goes like this, Slim. We're gonna find out – here and now – if you can dance, and if you can . . . we ride on from here."

Anger swells in Picard, but before he can explode, Beverly contacts the bridge, asking if they should continue to prepare for their mission. Picard answers in the affirmative, resulting in Q commenting on the on-going confidence of the human spirit. Then it comes to him. The test will have something to do with teamwork and cooperation. With that, the bridge crew suddenly finds itself on a barren planet filled with fog and smoke. The image is a dangerous one.

"Can you forget your own petty needs for the common good?" asks Q. "Can you sacrifice when you know that another will not just survive, but benefit greatly?"

[NOTE: These points seem rather moot, as Picard and his people seemed to have proved themselves sufficiently in "Encounter at Farpoint."]

The game he comes up with is hide and Q, in which the crew will have to seek him out. At that moment, we move to the bridge, which only Q and Picard have transported to. Q does not want Picard to join in the games, because he knows what the captain is capable of doing, and he wants to study how the rest of them will do without his leadership. The captain does not seem concerned, having faith in his crew.

Q appears on the planet's surface again, pointing out to the Enterprise personnel that the last time they encountered each other, no one died. This time, someone is going to "bite the dust." But who? Worf says that it will be him as he moves in for the kill. Q effortlessly grabs someone's phaser and fires it, stunning the Klingon. Q actually seems disappointed that the weapon was only set on stun.

Meanwhile, Picard is alone on the bridge, unable to leave or contact anyone else. He tries to make a captain's log, but finds himself unable to. Then he hears Q's voice doing so.

On the planet, everyone is attempting to out-think Q, but they find themselves unable to do so. There is no apparent logic to his thinking, so he could conceivably be hiding anywhere. Then again, he could be somewhere obvious. Then again, he could be anywhere . . . it's a circle. They do realize that Q is after something, hence this test, but until they find out what, all they can do is play out the game and begin seeking him. As the conversation continues, Riker takes note of the fact that Data hasn't added anything, which is quite out of character for him. Data turns around, but everyone is stunned to see that it is actually Q in the android's uniform. Riker proclaims they've found him, but Q laughs this off, stating that he hasn't hidden yet. And now there's a new element to the game: they have to find Data as well. As an afterthought, he says that they can find Tasha too, and in a flash she's gone.

Tasha appears on the bridge, joining Picard. Q then materializes, stating that he thought the captain might have been growing lonely. The alien is growing angry that his people are handling the situation much too calmly. Then he becomes what is described as a "cosmic biker."

"They aren't even trying," he explodes. The image on the viewscreen becomes that of the Away Team on the planet. As the focus shifts, they enter a primitive, yet futuristic, town which bears some kind of resemblance to a western setting. On the bridge, according to the story treatment, "Picard realizes that Q has thrown him a clue. Somewhere in the verses of Shakespeare is the answer. He runs them. Until one jumps out. One line and Picard makes the connection. It tells Picard all he needs to know."

As they enter the town, they find themselves unsettled by figures which move around in the shadows, as well as inhuman sounds. Q apparently has allowed communication to be reopened, as Riker is contacted by Picard. The captain says that he believes he has figured out Q's purpose, but the game must be played out until the end. Remembering Q's words that one of them would die, they realize that if it's going to happen at all, this will be the place. They then find themselves in a series of situations where they willingly help each other, obviously putting their lives on the line to save the rest of the Away Team.

Picard continues to order them on, despite the danger, which causes them to wonder why he is doing so. They are concerned, but the captain is, for some reason, calm. Then the Away Team appears on the bridge. Picard explains that he came to the realization that Q would not actually harm any of them, nor allow them to be harmed on the planet's surface. "Once Picard realized that he controlled the game," Hurley writes, "all he had to do was have the courage to push." Riker wants to know the reason for this, and Picard compares him to a child who has no idea how to make friends, so he plays games with them. He assumes that Q has a favor to ask, but is unable to just come right out and ask it. The Enterprise continues on its mission.

Picard goes to his cabin, where he finds Q sitting in a chair, reading Shakespeare. Q wants to know how the captain knew he was there, with Picard responding that this was the most perverse place the alien could be (the reason for this deduction, however, is never explained). Finally Q explains his purpose: there are a total of three Qs, and the planet they reside on is dying. They need to relocate. This confuses Picard, as the Qs can obviously move themselves. Why do they need the aid of the Enterprise and his people?

Quite frankly, says Q, they don't know where to go. Of all the species they have found in many dimensions, none compare to man, hence their reason for seeking out Picard. The Enterprise, he believes, will be able to find them a suitable planet to settle on. Then they have to transport the people from their planet. How many people, Picard wants to know.

"A little over a hundred thousand," says Q.

"How many over?"

"One point eight million." Q adds that his native planet has many resources, the majority of which have not been discovered by the Federation as of yet. Whatever place is chosen must provide the same isolation that the race now has, for they are not interested in alliances. They are merely asking for Picard's assistance in this matter, and it is a *sincere* request . . . perhaps the first of its kind made by Q.

The captain nods, stating that this particular request will have to be discussed with Starfleet Command.

The treatment ends with the statement that "the story of Q is not over."

[NOTE: After an intriguing beginning, this treatment for "Hide & Q" falls apart at the end. Besides the fact that it really has no conclusion, the idea that Q needs the Enterprise's help to move their people is a bit hard to believe. With everything we've seen this alien capable of doing, there's no way you could convince anyone that they couldn't replenish their world. In the interview with actor John DeLancie which follows, the actor states that he thinks it might be interesting for Q to come to Picard needing something, but this just isn't acceptable.

The final draft of the script, written by Gene Roddenberry and C.J. Holland, is far more effective. Q still appears in the same way that he does in this treatment, but his purpose is quite different. He offers the crew a wondrous gift beyond their imagination. It turns out that after the Farpoint mission, the Qs became intrigued by humanity, and were able to foresee a future where mankind would surpass them in terms of overall achievements as a species. To study the race better, Q's intention is to turn Riker into one of them, and to this end he provides the commander with the same powers that he has. What we see is a perfect example of power corrupting absolutely, a theme which is slightly reminiscent of the second Star Trek pilot, "Where No Man Has Gone Before." One cast member compared the story to the last temptation of Christ, and that may not be too far from the truth, as Riker is torn between remaining human and something akin to being a God.

As an episode, "Hide & Q" is really quite good, allowing both Riker and Q to come into their own.]

"HAVEN"

When *Star Trek: The Next Generation* was first starting to come together, the producers of the series began an intensive search for stories to launch this new version of the classic SF television show. To this end, they contacted, and were contacted by, numerous writers, and rapidly purchased a wide variety of story ideas. The writers themselves were oftentimes cut off at the outline stage.

This practice was, in some cases, quite a mistake, as witnessed by John D.F. Black's original concept for "Justice;" and in others, such as the initial outline for "Haven," entitled "Love Beyond Time and Space," quite justifiable.

That treatment, written by Lan O'Kun and dated February 11, 1987, begins with a young man named Victor Flambeau, sleeping restlessly, with voiceovers detailing a conversation between him and a woman named Aseea, who claim that they have waited their entire lives to be together, and that it will only be a short matter of time before they are united. Victor's mother approaches his sleep chamber and starts awakening him, stating that the "ship's waiting."

Victor awakens and tells his mother about the dream, which they both mention is an old, recurring one. In the ensuing conversation we learn that he is a Lieutenant in Star Fleet, and that he will be serving on a world known as Silver Major, an extremely cold planet. Louise is obviously bothered by his going there, but he tries to calm her.

"Don't be sad," he says. "This is

what I've always wanted. What I've trained for."

And that's how the teaser ends.

[NOTE: One point which should be made at the outset is that any person wishing to write for Star Trek *should know that it is absolutely imperative that the pre-credit sequence somehow involve the Enterprise or her crew. This is a lesson that can be learned from watching any episode of either the original or animated series.]*

The Enterprise is approaching Silver Major, with Picard's log informing us that they will reach a fantasy world known as Tannenger within a week. He wonders about that planet, and a person known as Ootel. Will the Enterprise be welcomed with open arms, or not?

We learn that the captain is relaxing in his bathtub, where he is recording his log, and adding that Commander Riker has been bombarded with requests by "half the male crewmembers" of the starship to join the Away Team to Tennenger. While he states that he doesn't blame them, who will they speak to? Where will they land? Those are the questions which must be answered before they are able to make any such decisions. The recording screen goes out. At that moment, Riker's face appears on the viewscreen (geez, not exactly a lot of privacy for the captain of a starship. He can't even take a bath without people being able to see his business). The commander states that Picard's God-son, Victor, will be arriving along with his parents and Deanna Troi's mother. The captain considers this and adds, "Who'd have ever believed this?" The conver-

sation is obviously bothering Riker. The channel is closed.

Geordi and Data are in the Enterprise mess hall, with the former eating dinner and the latter accompanying him for conversation. They are discussing the benefits of being human, as well as the benefits of being an android. Their conversation is interrupted by Macha Hernandez (eventually Tasha Yar, but, in this case, a male). He starts ribbing Data, referring to him as "the beautiful Andrew Android." But there is no insult intended.

Riker and Troi run into each other in a corridor, and start to discuss the current situation. In their conversation we learn that Deanna was destined to marry Victor since the time they were children. "I joined Star Fleet because he had a God-father who was a legend," she explains. "I wanted to please him. To show him I'd share his loves – live his dreams. It was an act of faith. When I was assigned to the Enterprise, I couldn't believe my good fortune."

The two of them obviously care deeply for each other, but she has to live up to Betazoid tradition and accept this marriage arranged by her and Victor's parents. Riker wants to know if she's actually looking forward to this, to which she responds in the affirmative, adding that she's waited her whole life to meet Victor.

[NOTE: In the aired version of this story, Deanna was very much against the idea of the marriage, but, as is the case here, she was planning on going through with it for the sake of tradition and honor. The bit about Victor's God-father being a legend of sorts, which led to her joining Starfleet, is a very nice touch.]

In the shuttle bringing Victor to the Enterprise, the young man is asleep, and once again dreaming of Aseea. As he moans, his father reaches over and awakens him, asking if he's alright. His mother is not feeling well at all, never having liked to travel by rocket (and one must ask why she's didn't simply beam over). Mrs. Troi approaches them and utters a stream of honest/sarcastic comments towards the couple, coming right out and expressing her belief that they haven't aged well at all over the past twenty five years.

On the bridge of the Enterprise, Riker announces that the starship is in orbit around Silver Major and that it will be fifteen minutes before they rendezvous with the shuttle, and pick up the passengers, including one Rolf Roessinger, a businessman who Riker has no desire to meet. "He's a pitch-man, a hustler, a profiteer, not to mention a loud mouthed, irresponsible . . . "

Picard interjects, ". . . president of a consortium of three space companies who want to open a direct route from Earth . . ."

". . . to Paradise. Paradise found – Paradise Lost. The universe an extension of Earth – filled with souvenir stands . . . I am not taking that man to Tannenger."

[NOTE: Quite frankly, who the heck does Riker think he is in this scene? Is he forgetting that Picard is the captain of the ship? It's one thing to offer your informed opinion about a situation, but quite another to state categorically what you will or will not do. Plus, the bit about Roessinger wanting to extend Earth's souvenir stand mentality to outer space is a

mistaken one. As established by the original series, our planet is supposed to have evolved far beyond that way of life, therefore rendering this kind of conversation senseless. This is the kind of basic Star Trek information that, again, someone attempting to write for the show should certainly be aware of.]

In the Enterprise gym, Macha is in front of a group of children. In his hand is a bottle containing a fly, and he explains that the lesson has everything to do with reflexes. He lets the fly out, and with a karate chop, swats it. The children seem to be stunned by the speed by which he moves.

[NOTE: It's necessary to interrupt again to emphasize the inaccurate view the author has of the Star Trek universe. We don't swat flies in the 24th Century. Certainly that sounds somewhat simplistic, and perhaps an overstatement of 24th Century man's view of the world around him, but we have been led to believe that all life forms are precious. Thus, Hernandez killing a fly, as insignificant as that act may appear to be to us, is something we would never see an instructor teaching children on the Enterprise.]

This lesson is interrupted by a communiqué from Geordi, who explains that the shuttle is docking. As the passengers start unloading, Riker meets with Roessinger, who immediately starts complaining about the flight. The two men depart to meet with Picard, while Mrs. Troi meets Deanna, and the two of them begin conversing telepathically. Victor and his parents are the next to step off of the shuttle. He and Deanna look at each other, a couple destined

to marry, and in his mind he hears the echoing voice of Aseea asking him where he is. It's obvious that Deanna is not the woman from his dreams. While they begin to talk to each other, the impression we get is that the in-laws are already bickering.

On the bridge, Picard and Riker are in the midst of a conversation with Roessinger, who is describing Tennenger as a world whose music "promotes tranquility." Deeming the planet an Eden in Space, he unfolds diagrams of a resort area he would like to build, which would be akin to the vacation spots in the Bahamas of some three hundred years earlier. He's quick to add that he is thinking in terms of the private sector, but it would seem that the military is trying to take full control. Picard finds himself getting annoyed at the man, but the conversation is interrupted by Data's arrival with Victor, thus the captain is able to shift the focus of conversation. He embraces Victor, and greets the in-laws.

Later, Victor and Deanna try to get to know each other, but it's clear that she is not the woman of his dreams. They discuss the future, life on the Enterprise, and other such matters.

Riker stops by Deanna's office later on when she is meeting with Geordi. According to the treatment, "there is a 'moment' between them before Riker excuses himself and departs." Deanna describes to Geordi how difficult it is to end a relationship with someone like Riker. It's his suggestion that she confront Victor with her true feelings.

Elsewhere, Victor has opened up to Data, describing the situation about the woman of his dreams. Data considers this, and suggests he talk to Deanna, while adding, "Of course I'm not human and you have to weigh where this advice is coming from." Victor agrees with his suggestion.

[NOTE: The characterization of Data as presented here is fairly unlikable. This guy is nothing but a mope, constantly moaning about how wonderful it would be to be human, and how inferior he feels, despite his superior abilities. While this is good characterization material in small doses, on a constant level it comes out as nothing more than whining and complaining.]

Finally, Victor and Deanna start discussing the truth of the situation, with his noting the woman of his dreams. She can sense that he's still thinking about her. They nonetheless try to look at the future, with Deanna noting that once every thirty days Betazoid women are absolutely irresistible to men, so on that day he will have to lock her away. The interplay between them continues.

At dinner, Mrs. Troi starts a fight between Victor's parents, and then goes back to eating her meal. Back to Victor and Deanna, and we see they are getting along much better, continuing to look at the future.

Later, Picard is in his quarters, playing the trumpet for relaxation (an analogy is drawn to Sherlock Holmes playing the violin), when Riker stops by to announce that a smaller ship is approaching the Enterprise. It is captained by Ootel, who his bringing his granddaughter.

In their sleep chambers, Victor's parents have decided to release their son from the bond agreement, as they do not want to have Mrs. Troi as

a member of the family. Deanna comes to see Victor, and before he can tell her this, she has already sensed it. Nonetheless, Victor asks her to marry him, which she agrees to. Picard will be delighted to marry them.

In the meantime, Roessinger has contacted the President of Star Fleet, who, in turn, has spoken to Picard, informing him that the Tannenger project is an extremely important one, and that the captain should do whatever he reasonably can to assure its success. Shortly thereafter, Riker announces that Ootel's ship is docking on the Enterprise.

Ootel comes to the bridge, where he meets with Picard and tells him that he may have strong enough influence to work out the Tannenger situation. Ootel and his family are invited to the wedding of Victor and Deanna, an invitation they happily accept. Ootel says that he's only brought his granddaughter, and he agrees to go and get her.

Victor is getting dressed for the ceremony, and while he's staring into the mirror he hears Aseea's voice asking, "Where are you?" This changes his whole expression. In her quarters, Deanna, too, is getting ready, when she feels the presence of someone who is confused as to her location. Stepping into the corridor, she catches sight of Aseea, and invites her to Victor's quarters, opens the door, sees the expression that passes between the two dream lovers, and moves back into the corridor, "silent tears running down her cheeks." Data comes back, sees Victor and Aseea in a passionate embrace, moves back out to the corridor and tries to console Deanna.

Picard is informed of the fact that Victor and Aseea want to stay together aboard the Enterprise, and the captain goes to speak to Ootel about this. The old man will hear none of it, telling Picard that he must deliver his granddaughter if he wants the agreement with Tannenger to work out. Picard meets with Victor, tells him this and adds that there is no alternative. He can take Aseea back home. This stuns Victor, who wants to stay aboard the Enterprise. Picard suggests that the young man follow his dreams.

Later, Picard performs the marriage ceremony between Victor and Aseea, adding that "Their love gives us all hope that somewhere, somehow, in the worlds we know, or in some place yet to be found, there is a love for us."

Victor bids a farewell to his parents and then one to Deanna. He and his bride depart with Ootel, whose ship breaks away from the Enterprise. Riker puts his arm around Deanna's shoulder as the story ends . . .

[NOTE: Not a hell of a lot to recommend this version of the story which would eventually become "Haven." Many of the story ideas and much of the dialogue presented strike one as being very much like a soap opera, and not particularly effective.]

O'Kun's second draft outline, dated March 30, 1987, is pretty much the same as the first one. The one addition is that a ship from the doomed planet of Xelephian, containing a crew of plague victims, is headed for Tannenger in the hope that the mythical powers of that world will cure them of their illness. The primary difference between this version of the story and the aired one, is that the planet will indeed cure them of their sickness, and after much cajoling, Picard and Ootel agree to aid them in the fulfillment of their goals. While this draft was a considerable improvement over the first one, it was destined to get much better.

Writer Tracy Torme, who would pen a total of three episodes during *The Next Generation*'s first season and achieve the position of Executive Story Editor, was assigned the task of turning "Love Beyond Time and Space" into "Haven."

While much of Lan O'Kun's story beats would make it to the air, the entire tone of Torme's piece was more in line with the rest of the series. The characters were considerably more realistic, and the story a more moving one. Victor becomes Wyatt Miller, who, like his predecessor, has come to the Enterprise to marry Deanna Troi, but is surprised to find out that she is not the woman of his dreams. That woman, known here as Ariana, is aboard the plague ship of the Tarellians, who are hoping that Haven will provide them the cure they so desperately need. Wyatt, an aspiring physician, realizes that his destiny lies on the other vessel, so he beams himself and medical supplies over there. But so contagious is the crew of that ship, that the young man has now isolated himself there for the rest of his life . . . or until he is able to discover a cure. He confers with the bridge crew of the Enterprise, hoping that his parents and Deanna can understand his rationale for this seemingly insane action. Surprisingly, everyone does, finding it a particularly noble act.

Ironically, as well as unfortunately, Torme's script for this episode turned out to be better than the aired version. Much of this blame perhaps falls on Majel Barrett's somewhat overbearing performance of Mrs. Troi, a role played so broadly that there is little the audience can find to identify with. Some of the humor as intended by the writer does not work on film the way it should, and he ended the script with our people on the surface of the truly beautiful and awe-inspiring planet of Haven. Torme's treatment ends with our people in a building on Haven. They are about to beam up to the ship when Data suggests that they at least take a step outside. As the treatment notes, "We stay on their faces as they do so. Soft colors reflect on their eyes as they look at Haven in stunned disbelief . . . Geordi is a bit sad. He can sense the colors, but he can't really see them. He asks his friend Data to describe the color of the sky. Data's description is right out of a dictionary. Troi interrupts (softly): 'It's blue . . . dark blue . . . the color of love.'"

It would have been a nice moment. As it stands, "Haven" falls somewhere in the middle of the show's success level during the first season.

"THE BIG GOODBYE"

One of the original *Star Trek*'s most popular episodes was "A Piece of the Action," in which Kirk and company beam down to a planet whose society is based on Chicago of the 1920s. So significant was this particular show to the producers, that it paved the way for numerous visits to Earth-like planets, mirroring such situations as Nazi Germany, Ancient Rome, the Old West and so on. Granted that this thematic device quickly became a cliché, but oftentimes it worked quite well.

Bearing this in mind, it's no surprise that *The Next Generation* episode entitled "The Big Goodbye" has proved to be one of the more successful presented during the first season, even going so far as to win the coveted Peabody Award.

In the case of "The Big Goodbye," Co-Executive Producer Maurice Hurley came up with the concept of several crewmembers being trapped in an artificial world created by the holodeck. That premise, originally called "Homicide," had our people get involved in a 1930s mystery. Writer Tracy Torme was again contacted and given the assignment of fleshing that premise into a an outline and then a script.

His first draft outline, dated August 17, 1987, begins with Captain Picard attempting to learn the official greeting he will use when meeting the Jarada, so that the Enterprise can pass through the territory of that alien race. Deanna Troi, who has been coaching him for many hours, suggests that he take some time out to relax in the holodeck. The captain

considers this for a moment and agrees. Going there, he programs a Raymond Chandler-like environment (which Torme refers to as Chandlerland), in which Picard is playing the fictional role of one Dixon Steel (eventually this character would become Dixon Hill).

The year the holodeck has recreated is 1941, and Picard approaches Steel's office where he meets a beautiful woman, whose name is Mrs. Black. She is desperate for his help, stating that someone is trying to kill her. Allowing himself to slip completely into character, he fixes a drink for her and she begins to detail her current situation.

Elsewhere on the ship, we learn that there is something of a strained relationship between Tasha Yar and Data, resulting from their passionate rendezvous in "The Naked Now." While it's uncomfortable for her to be around him, he is under the illusion that they now have a lifelong bond. "You made me a man," Data says. In all honesty, she would rather forget that the entire incident ever took place.

The two of them, along with Geordi LaForge, are enroute to a meeting. Geordi tries to clarify the situation for Data, but he fails to see the logic. The subject is dropped.

[NOTE: Torme has gone on record as saying that he felt the show needed more inter-ship conflict. The reader can only assume that this bit of business between Tasha and Data was his attempt to create an underlying tension between these two characters. Too bad that this, or something like it, never made it to the air.]

Still in Chandlerland, Picard, playing the role to the hilt, escorts the woman out of his office, assuring her that he will do what he can to help her. Once she's gone, he approaches a wall with a blue streak, to exit the holodeck. There is a knock upon the door. Picard sees the silhouette of someone and tells that person to come back later as he leaves the room. Still within the holodeck, we see a character, who's supposed to be a takeoff of Peter Lorre and referred to as such, step into the room, wondering where Dixon Hill has gone.

Going to the briefing room, Picard joins the others for the meeting, first informing them of his experience "back in time." Troi in particular is pleased to see him so exuberant. He wants to go back, and would like to dress the part and have others join him as well, including a literature expert named Hall. He makes note of the woman who had asked him for help; a woman who was so "incredibly alive, her kiss was so real; yet a simple push of a button ends her existence."

We learn that this isn't quite so, as the body of the woman is found in a "rain soaked" alleyway, two bullet holes in her back.

[NOTE: This scene never made it to the final version, although it is certainly an interesting one, illustrating that something is indeed very wrong in the holodeck as the computer seemingly refuses to shut down the imaginary world it has created from the pages of ancient Earth literature. Of course with the bit of Lorre entering the room once Picard disappears, it may have been deemed a bit of

overkill. Picard would later learn that the woman had been killed, although we wouldn't see the corpse.]

Still in the midst of the meeting, Data puts on a tape of the last encounter between members of the Federation and the Jarada. In that meeting, we see that the aliens are snake-like humanoids. The Federation captain begins the extremely difficult greeting, but stumbles on some of the bizarre inflections, infuriating the Jarada, who break up the meeting. The image disappears. This was not something that Picard needed to see. The android is apologetic, to which Picard replies that there is nothing for him to apologize for. In fact, since they have some extra time before the meeting, he invites Data to join them on their expedition to the "past." That evening, Data studies everything available on the world of Dixon Steel.

Next day, Picard, Hall and Data, dressed properly, get set to enter the holodeck. Tasha Yar will join them later. Rather than appear outside Steel's office, they materialize outside a newsstand, where Data is quick to comment on the news of the day. No sooner have they arrived, than Lieutenant McNary, a friend of Steel's, approaches and finds himself with no choice but to arrest the detective for the murder of Mrs. Black.

Later, Tasha materializes in Chandlerland, and goes to the police station, where she meets up with Data and Hall, and is told of the current situation with the captain. They're all rather excited about the detail of this place, believing that the captain must be having a great time. In the interrogation room, the questions are coming fast and furious, but Picard

maintains his good spirits. McNary tries to get the other cops to lighten up.

Meanwhile, Riker arrives on the bridge upon receiving news that a trio of Jarada vessels are approaching, stating that they await the words of Captain Picard. They will not show themselves visually until they are greeted in the proper manner. Riker states that they are several hours early, but the aliens are already insulted, having been communicated to by a "mere" second in command. Riker, doing his best to keep his temper under control, has Worf proceed to the holodeck in order to get Picard back up on the bridge.

In the interrogation room, Picard has finally had enough of the questioning session. He gets up to leave, but is thrown back in his seat. Deciding that the best way to deal with the situation is to stay completely in character, he responds to them in kind.

"I'm sick of staring at your ugly mug," he says defiantly. "If you monkeys got somethin' on me, go ahead and book me. Otherwise, I'm goin' home."

Ultimately they decide that he can go, while they tell him not to leave the city. As the captain starts to leave, McNary suggests that he work with them, so as to make it easier on himself. Picard says that he'll think about it. The treatment notes that "He and the others walk out of the police station and find themselves in Dixon Steel's hallway. Everything in Chandlerland is surrealistically interconnected due to space limitations in the holodeck. None of the computer created characters realizes this, of course."

[NOTE: This is a fascinating as well as logical point made by the treatment, and something that is never touched upon on the air. It only makes sense that there be an economy of space, given the limited amount of space occupied by the holodeck.]

Tasha (incidentally, in the aired version Beverly Crusher would essentially replace Tasha in these sequences, which allowed for a bit of romantic interplay between the doctor and Picard) reminds the captain that the time is approaching for his communication with the Jarada, and there is still studying to be done. The captain agrees with this, and the group proceeds to Steel's office and exits from the holodeck. Unfortunately when they get there, Peter Lorre (who would eventually be renamed Leech) is waiting for them. Choosing to ignore him, they proceed to the wall, but Lorre, angered, pulls a gun and demands that they deliver to him "the Bird" (a reference to The Maltese Falcon, which this entire Dixon Steel story is a take-off of; a reference which would not make it to the air). Tasha, having had just about enough of this man, moves quickly, disarms and slaps him. Lorre is angry and makes the threat that the Fat Man will get back at them. Picard brushes this off, as he leads everyone to the exit. But, then, nothing happens. The exit refuses to open.

Picard suggests that there may be wiring in the room which will unlock the door, and has everyone begin a search for it. They are stopped from this task by the arrival of Greenstreet (eventually renamed Redblock), who demands to know where the object he seeks is. Playing along, Hall says that if the man is looking for a falcon, then he's liable to be in for a major disappointment; he'll never find it. He then proceeds to verbally threaten Greenstreet. One of the man's thugs doesn't take kindly to this, and fires his gun. Hall is thrown backwards, blood flowing freely from his wound. "But," he whispers in shock, "they're not real." He dies a moment later.

[NOTE: Much of this plays exactly as it would on the air, with the exception that the Hall character would be wounded, but live. By the way, the sequence with Hall getting shot, as described above, sounds a bit like the moment in Westworld when the Yul Brenner Gunslinger robot fires a real bullet into James Brolin, who stammers, "I'm shot," before collapsing to the ground.]

Lieutenant McNary, who has heard the gunshot, enters the room and is disarmed by Greenstreet's people. Turning his attention back to Picard and the others, Greenstreet says that if they tell him where the object is, they can all go free. McNary doesn't buy this for a second and says as much. Data points out that they are completely unable to help him in his quest for the simple reason that Greenstreet and the others are not real. Naturally they do not accept this despite Data's attempts at explaining the workings of the ship's computer.

Enterprise bridge: the Jarada have surrounded the starship on three sides. Worf states that they have found the "glitch" in the holodeck,

and that it will take extreme caution not to cause greater problems. Riker, considering the deadly situation the starship is rapidly finding itself in, orders Worf to begin the unravelling of the wires so that the captain can be found. The Klingon sets about his task (in the aired version Worf would be aided by that boy genius, Wesley Crusher).

Back in Steel's office, no one believes this talk of a holodeck. Outside the room, Worf is working on the wires. There are some sparks, and the inhabitants of Steel's office suddenly find themselves in an arctic wasteland, before returning to the comfort of the office again. This has stunned all of the computer-generated people, who don't quite know what to make of the situation. So moved by this is Greenstreet, that he attempts to make a deal with Picard. Data can find the wires they seek, provided that he and his men can go with them. This is acceptable to the captain, but only after his own people have left.

On the bridge, Riker receives a communiqué from the Jarada, who state that they have never been so insulted. An attack is the only way to restore honor. This will, however, be averted, provided that Captain Picard greets them.

Data finds the wire, makes the necessary corrections and the blue streak appears on the wall once again. The door opens, and Greenstreet moves ahead to step through, ordering his people to kill the Enterprise crew members as soon as he's gone. Lorre joins him. But no sooner have the two of them stepped out

into the corridor than they begin to disintegrate, thus "proving that computer images can only exist in a computer world."

A fight breaks out in Steel's office while Worf, still on the outside, continues working. The lights go out in the office and come back on. Objects are winking out of existence. Tasha takes on one of the gunmen. McNary is shot in the shoulder during the action. Finally, when everything calms down again, Picard and his people get ready to "go home." The captain is sorry to say good-bye to McNary, who asks, "Tell me something . . . when you're gone, will I still exist? Will my wife still be waiting for me at home?" Picard simply does not know the answer to those questions. They bid each other farewell, and the holodeck goes black.

Picard arrives on the bridge and flawlessly greets the Jarada. There is a moment of silence. Finally, the aliens state that the captain has honored them, and for that the Enterprise may pass in peace.

[NOTE: Even in the outline form, this was quite an effective story. The final moment between Picard and McNary is very touching, and works quite well in the aired version. The only problem not satisfactorily answered here, or on the air, is the nature of the holodeck screwup. One can chalk it up to being nothing more than a McGuffin, designed to propel our people into this story.

All in all, "The Big Goodbye" was one of the first episodes to really turn out to be a winner, helping to establish Star Trek: The Next Generation with an identity of its own.]

DATALORE

"Datalore," which was written by Maurice Hurley and Robert Lewin, began as a treatment titled "Apocalypse Anon," dated July 22, 1987. As the story commences, the Enterprise is doing its best to prevent the destruction of a planet. A specialist named Minuet is arriving via shuttle, and once docked she and Picard go off for a private meeting. Eventually we learn, by way of Picard's explanation, that the planet in question served as a galactic dump site for waste-product from fissionable material. Due to incompetent handling, the situation is extremely precarious, with the planet threatening to blow at any moment, thus possibly destroying other planets in the vicinity. Minuet has to go to one location in particular to utilize special equipment, which is why, we are told, she didn't use the transporter to come on board. The Away Team, led by Riker, is given the task of making sure she reaches her destination.

Riker details his MO and she modifies the plan, saying that they should move in small groups, like mountain climbers. Then, the treatment notes, "Riker's . . . professional admiration for her, at first wary, now grows, solidifies and intensifies when he sees the way she handles herself."

While preparations are made for beam down, Riker invites Minuet to dinner in holodeck two, where he programs a romantic atmosphere. They eat and dance, and by the time he is summoned to the bridge, it's obvious that he's grown very attracted to her. Riker excuses himself,

bumps into Troi in the corridor and the Betazoid's empathic abilities pick up his feelings, and she grows a bit jealous.

Meanwhile, Minuet goes to her quarters. Data shows up a little while later, excited that she is an android and curious as to why she has kept this a secret from everyone else on the ship. Minuet explains that she is a disaster expert, and believes that coming across as a human allows human beings to more readily trust her. This is sound logic for Data, who is "proud" to be working with her.

Picard and the Away Team spell out their plan and start to put things into motion. Tasha prepares "mobile force fields" to be used on the surface, while Beverly Crusher, who is expecting to have to deal with radiation burns, is in the midst of setting up a mobile medical station. Geordi is gathering provisions, while Wesley has developed a "self-propelled carrier," whose purpose is to supersede exhaustion by somehow allowing them to avoid contact with any surface.

[NOTE: It's easy to see why this was eventually dropped. Quite frankly, it would have been too expensive.]

While Riker and Data are making their preparations, the commander mentions his feelings for Minuet, describing her as "the most wonderful woman he's ever met." He also points out that he knows Data would not comprehend the emotion he's talking about, and on seeing the android's confused expression he changes the subject. Riker enters Minuet's quarters to give her a protective suit for their mission, and then

rejoins Data in the corridor. It is just a moment before Data asks the commander whether or not he's aware that Minuet is an android. This, of course, comes as a complete shock to Riker. Data apologizes for stating the fact so bluntly that it may have hurt him. Riker dismisses the sentiment, saying that he needs to be alone.

Ultimately Riker goes back to Minuet's quarters and demands to know why she didn't tell him. Their conversation continues, with her giving the same reason she gave to Data. Eventually Riker says that it doesn't matter to him that she's a machine. Minuet has opened up feelings in him, and he wants to give their relationship a chance to develop . . . despite what she really is. Minuet isn't so sure, explaining that she cannot respond like a human female, but Riker says that he will teach her how to be human. "All relationships are chancy," says Riker. She considers this and then admits that she admires him and would like to give it a chance.

[NOTE: We have to interrupt here to say one thing: are you kidding? It's just too impossible to believe that Riker would a) fall in love so quickly and b) be willing to continue with the romance once he's discovered that she's a machine. Undoubtedly this is the reason the idea was ultimately dropped. Of course it should be pointed out that Minuet makes it to the air in "1010101," as a holographic image that Riker falls in love with. She is part of the programming supplied by the Binars, and used as a distraction so that Riker will not catch on to the fact that the aliens are essentially kidnapping the Enter-

prise. At least in that situation it works far more effectively than it could have possibly worked here.]

Later, Riker meets with Picard, wanting to know why the captain didn't inform him as to Minuet's true identity (which seems a rather moot point when bearing in mind the previous scene). Picard wants to know if Riker is too emotionally involved to continue with the mission. The commander replies in the negative, stating that he allowed personal feelings to cloud his judgement. It won't happen again. This is good enough for Picard.

The Away Team is broken into two groups, the first with Riker, Minuet, Tasha and Data, and the second with Geordi, Beverly and two members of security. Team number one beams down and finds itself within a turbulence so powerful that it leaves them "stunned and inert inside the forcefield."

Back on the bridge, scanners indicate that a change in energy levels on the planet may cause it to explode at any second. The starship immediately pulls back, effectively stranding the Away Team. As a study of the situation commences, Picard is informed that the energy unleashed on the planet during the beam down was enough to disrupt the delicate balance. Additional equipment, as well as a rescue team, will not be able to be transported down for fear that it will trigger the explosion that will destroy everyone.

Wesley Crusher comes up with the idea of constructing a transporter relay station which, despite the fact that it's extremely dangerous, should be able to beam up the Away Team in two stages. Picard considers this

for a moment, and realizes that it's a better solution than anything they've been able to come up with.

Tasha and Riker work at expanding the forcefield's radius, but Minuet says there is no more time. She must bring her equipment into play or it will be too late. Riker says that her walking out of the forcefield (and exactly how she'll do that neat trick is never really explained) will be suicide, but she logically points out that it is simply what she was programmed to do. Her arm pierces the forcefield and is immediately disintegrated. Riker pulls her back in.

Although "angry" that Riker allowed his feelings for her to interfere with the mission, she comes up with an alternative plan: they will use the carrier device, created by Wesley (does anybody besides this kid create anything?), which will move the equipment, and a small forcefield will be used around her and Tasha. Data protests this, saying that the two androids are more expendable than any of the humans. Riker, in turn, protests this, but Data finally gets his way.

Data and Minuet, protected by a forcefield, go on with their plan, en route expressing their mutual respect for each other. Eventually they reach the proper location, with Minuet explaining that depositing a "neutralizing agent" there will balance the energy mass of this unstable world. She moves out of the forcefield, does what she has to and is almost instantly destroyed. Data contacts the Enterprise and requests that they be beamed up. Before this can happen, and just prior to the planet exploding, all the destructive energies are imploded and the planet

stabilizes. The Away Team is beamed back up.

Riker and Troi meet alone later, with Deanna stating that Riker is over both Minuet and her. It is a moment which probably severs all romantic ties between the two, although they'll always be friends. It just doesn't seem likely that their love will ever rekindle. Deanna exits the room, leaving Riker alone.

[NOTE: It's obvious that this draft was attempting to provide a bit more depth to some of the main characters, which is certainly applaudable. The only problem with the way it is handled is that Riker's irrational love for an android becomes the most important element of the story as opposed to the mission at hand. In this show's format, this is not exactly the best way to work. The story itself should be the main focus, with the characterization being carefully layered in. As it stands, this was only a fair effort. As is often the case with stories by Maurice Hurley, the pacing is off. Things build one way, and then we cut to a dialogue scene which doesn't really move the story along. Thankfully "Apocalypse Anon" would come a long way before it made it to the air.]

The second draft treatment, now titled "Datalore," dated August 13, 1987 and with the writing credits reversed, begins with Data practicing human expressions in his mirror when he is summoned to the bridge by Lieutenant Worf. Arriving there he learns that the Enterprise is receiving a signal from Kiron III of the Kappa Rho star system, which is Data's home world – the place of his birth.

Both Riker and Picard are

awakened, and are on their way to the bridge. Everyone is wondering why they are suddenly receiving a signal now. In addition, preliminary ship scanners have detected a single giant snowflake some one hundred miles tall. Data muses over the idea of "going home," which gives him cause to pause. Rather a human thought, he nearly smiles.

The Enterprise eventually locks into orbit, and an Away Team is transported down to the surface. Data experiences something akin to deja vu, but really doesn't remember much of what they're looking at. They begin tracking the distress signal, move beyond the remains of the colonists and go to what is described as an empty crypt. Certain clues (and we're never told what they are) indicate that this place was once Data's, but he has no memory of it. The search continues some miles away where they find another crypt, in which there is a female body, obviously, by the color of her skin, an android along the lines of Data. As they near, she suddenly comes to life (activation?) and moves out of the crypt. The woman is eventually introduced as Lore and upon meeting Data "there is ... something immediately comfortable and familiar between them."

The Enterprise people try questioning her, but it soon becomes apparent that she does not really have a lot to tell them. Meanwhile, on the bridge, the snowflake discovered earlier is being studied, and it seems to be made of formaldehyde. Back on the planet, Lore takes everyone to an underground cavern where humans in suspended animation are

discovered. The crypts open and the people revive, while Lore searches for something – even though she doesn't know what it is. The colonists, much as is the case with the Away Team, try to gather information as to their surroundings. Like Lore, they are unaware of who or what saved them while the other colonists perished.

Everyone moves to the surface and stares at the snowflake. It's pointed out that the two androids in particular are intrigued by it because it's quite possible that somehow it was responsible for their creation. Then Picard warns them that the readings are changing and says that they should stay away from it for the moment.

The colonists explain that they would like to rebuild this world, and Riker responds that the Enterprise would be happy to provide any aid that it can. They begin looking around the area, while Data and Lore get involved in a conversation, with the former describing life with humans aboard the Enterprise. The conversation continues when they're alone, with Data trying to explain love and sex, as he's discovered from the humans.

The order comes down from Enterprise for them to investigate the snowflake. Data wants to stay behind with Lore, but Riker says that he's needed. So Lore asks for and receives permission to go along with them. As the Away Team approaches the crystal, the bridge crew grows apprehensive because its structure is becoming "more chemical than crystalline."

Everyone actually enters the crystal and they are surprised to hear

a serene music which lulls them, causing carelessness and resulting in their being trapped. Data and Lore try to help and as they do so come to the conclusion that this crystal is what was responsible for the death of the colonists. Since they are immune to the music which affected the others, they can only assume that the colonists were trapped in the same way. The duo (somehow) manage to get the Away Team out of the crystal. Data contacts the starship and ask that they be transported over to the colonists. This done, the colonists want to know if the Enterprise is going to rid the planet of the snowflake. The request is piped through to the Enterprise, but Picard states that the Prime Directive prevents him from doing so. Of course they are outraged at this, wondering if the captain is intending to let them get out like their fellows had years earlier. Picard believes that he can come up with an alternative way of dealing with the situation, and if he is unable to do so then he will beam the colonists aboard, even though he knows that's not something they would want. They are not pleased at this turn of events.

In the cave, a member of security explains to Tasha that he experienced some kind of mind drain while they were within the crystal. This is confusing to them, but the information is transmitted to the Enterprise. Ship scanners indicate that the crystal seems to be searching for life forms, so it's probably not a good idea to beam anybody up at this time.

While they're in the cave, Geordi begins to examine one of the colonist's crypts and discovers a button with an arrow next to it. Lore sees this, reaches over and presses the button, explaining that this was what she was looking for earlier . . . even though she didn't know it at the time. This action has an instantaneous affect on both androids, as their eyes "light up" and they begin explaining their origin, which had been deeply buried.

"Together," Lewin and Hurley write, "they now tell the colonists and the Away Team how they were saved and created by a vessel of androids who discovered the Snowflake was killing the colonists and draining their minds."

Apparently the androids considered humans "valuable," so they created Data as a preserver of their minds. Discovering additional humans, they put them into suspended animation and followed through with Lore, whose purpose was to help them. It was the opinion of the androids that the snowflake would have left this world within twenty years, which is why the distress signal was timed to go off in exactly that amount of time. Obviously their deductions were wrong. Picard is told of all this, and deems it necessary to beam everybody aboard the Enterprise.

Lore admits that she doesn't want to go aboard, believing that she will be out of place. Data tries to assure her that everything will be alright, and that together they will someday become human. Everyone recognizes a definite relationship developing between the two of them.

Aboard the Enterprise Picard comes up with a plan to beam everybody up at one time, thus not allowing the snowflake to capture

anyone. But on the planet the snowflake (one wishes they would have come up with a different name for this thing) begins to make a "sweep" over the planet's surface, looking for life forms. Everyone is beamed up at the last possible moment.

Once on board, Theron, the leader of the colonists, gets into an argument with Picard over his beaming them up from the planet. The captain doesn't have time to argue the situation, as he has developed a plan which he is still trying to put in effect. Picard has the Enterprise move towards the snowflake, which apparently extends into the stratosphere, and then moves just out of its reach. The flake, a rather uppity entity, rips itself from the ground and begins pursuing the Enterprise for a game of "space-tag." Ultimately they elude it, and the snowflake goes off into space, vanishing quickly into the distance. A triumphant Picard believes that some day, perhaps in a millennium's time, "all the intelligence it has gathered and digested will blossom forth in some magnificent way."

The colonists, who are extremely grateful, want to beam back down to the surface so they can rebuild their world. Lore says she must join them, and asks Data to come down to the planet and live there with her. Picard overhears this, and tells Data that he will not stand in the science officer's way if this is what he wants. Data does not want to do this, as much as he cares for Lore. Ultimately he is an officer of Starfleet. The two androids kiss good-bye as Lore and the colonists beam back home.

[NOTE: A massive improvement

over the first draft treatment, "Data-lore" would have made a truly exciting episode, with some nice characterization for Data, as well as some true suspense and the opportunity for great special effects. One major problem, however: why in God's name would Picard lead the snowflake into space so that it could move off to other star systems and threaten other worlds? The Prime Directive is one thing, but hasn't he caused the death of millions by this action? With the exception of this rather major point, the story is terrific, and one can only wish that this was the version that made it to the screen.]

In the revised draft, dated August 27, 1987, Enterprise is en route to Starbase 64 for supplies, when Wesley makes the discovery that the ship will pass by Kiron III, Data's home world. Riker gives the boy permission to tell Data this information. Picard says that the Enterprise should take readings on the planet before they continue. Data is delighted.

The starship nears Kiron III, when sensors detect a smaller alien vessel which approaches, veers off and is gone. The only information they can gather from ship computers is that it is known as the Pikril and that it is something of a ghost-ship which vanishes and reappears.

There are no life forms on the planet, but an Away Team is assembled anyway, with Picard taking the lead this time. As in the previous draft, they enter a cave, but this time they find astronomical charts which are evidence of an interest in the universe around the colonists, who seem to have died suddenly, while in the midst of their everyday activities. Their search continues, until they find a dismantled android which looks exactly like Data. Needless to say, this is stunning to them – especially to Data.

They beam up to the Enterprise, bringing the other android along, convinced that there's a good chance that the expertise of the starship crewmembers will be enough to bring it to "life." While this is being done, the Pikril appears momentarily, causes the starship to go to yellow alert, and then disappears once again.

Eventually the other android is activated, and Data helps it get to its feet. It immediately begins to articulate, slowly at first, and identifies itself as Lore. It rapidly becomes apparent that Lore learns quickly, as he is soon speaking and moving around just fine, and without assistance. They take notice of a slight tic in his face, but aside from that he seems perfect, an image driven home as he actually *laughs* with delight at being alive. Everyone is taken by his charm.

Later, it's decided that Lore will "bunk" with Data, and he is given details about all aspects of starship life, including bridge operations. Soon thereafter there is a meeting called in the ready room, wherein Picard recommends that Lore be brought to a scientific starbase as soon as possible so that he can be studied. Data doesn't agree, wanting to help raise his "brother" himself. Lore's opinion is asked, and he states that he will abide by whatever they decide, and then excuses himself to allow them to discuss the situation without his sitting there, possibly adding pressure.

Back on the bridge, it becomes obvious that Wesley and Lore are hitting it off, and Lore quickly demonstrates that his mind can work even beyond Data's, which is quite a surprise in itself. Picard is concerned . . . actually, curious, as to the reason for the difference between Lore and Data, believing that the former is fairly close to being human in his attitude. He also wants to figure out exactly what had happened on Kiron III that resulted in the death of the colonists.

Back in the ready room, Picard asks Data and Lore to piece together what they know of their native planet so that perhaps they can figure out exactly what happened. The conversation is interrupted by the reappearance of the Pikril, which scans the starship, but refuses to acknowledge all attempts at communication. Lore gets permission to sit at Ops, and uses the ship's various capabilities to get a reading on the other vessel. He learns that there are no life forms aboard and that the weapons systems indicate that they are there merely for defensive purposes, and that the ship itself is designed merely to gather information (although no one really questions exactly how Lore was able to determine these rather amazing revelations).

As Picard's meeting continues, we learn that the colonists died quickly, with Data deducing that a "higher power" might have desired the things that they had been working on. Lore disagrees, stating quite simply that the colonists were bad and were being punished. The captain wants to know how Lore came to this conclusion. He doesn't know, but

it would seem the logical conclusion. Data, it seems, had explained to him that "good creates good and bad creates bad . . . if nothing happens without a cause there is no reason to think otherwise." Data clarifies, explaining that the definition and good and bad is applied to humans, who are capable of both. Lore says he has something new to think about.

Time goes on, and it would seem (at least in Data's eyes) that everyone is taking to Lore at the expense of Data. The android looks up the word jealousy, and then talks to Deanna Troi about it, wondering if he is, indeed, jealous of Lore. She tries to rid him of this concern.

The Pikril makes another appearance and disappears. Lore thinks it is dangerous, while Data believes it is benign. An argument starts between the two and they are granted permission to go off to work it out between them. They make their way to the mess hall, where Lore drops something into Data's food, efficiently causing him to stumble around. Managing to pull himself together somewhat, Data returns to his position on the bridge.

Pikril makes another appearance and comes even closer to the Enterprise than it had before. Data begins acting erratically, and moves away from his console. Lore moves in to replace him, but Worf gets to the seat first. Data is given permission to go to his quarters, where he begins the process of reprogramming himself.

On the bridge, Picard wants either Geordi or Beverly to check on Data, but Lore volunteers to do so. Geordi wants to go, but the captain elects to send the android. Lore goes to Data's quarters, and recommends his "brother" terminate himself because he is not functioning properly. Data says that there is an "isotope" within him which is the cause of the problem, and he wonders aloud if Lore would like him *not* to recover. Lore responds in the affirmative, stating that he would like nothing better than to live Data's life on board the Enterprise. He has no interest in being dropped off at a Federation starbase. Lore starts to move out, and Data tries to stop him, but is slammed against a wall, and slumps to the floor unconscious. Lore takes his phaser and leaves the room. Lore returns to the bridge just as the Pikril reappears, and he suggests that shields be raised. He claims that the other ship is automated and that something has gone wrong with it and destruction is the only solution. Data suddenly appears from within the turbolift and states that he needs Lore's help. In a moment the two androids are on the turbolift, and the door closes. Soon thereafter a communiqué comes from cargo deck four, where the two of them are in the midst of a savage fist fight. Tasha, Beverly and Picard arrive there, about to help. Data warns them back, stating that Lore will kill them if they interfere. Lore raises his phaser to fire, but Data

hurls a "piece of heavy equipment," which forces him down to the ground. Lore is suddenly dying (again, why?), but he manages a phaser shot at Data. As other people arrive, it seems that both androids have died.

Meanwhile, the Pikril has vanished again, while Picard starts thinking about Data's funeral. Wesley enters the bridge with a will that Data had left in the boy's quarters, and in that will, if they choose to use it, is a method to bring him back to "life." Beverly and a team of technicians work on bringing him back, while the alien vessel reappears and is hovering a short distance away from the Enterprise. The operation is a success, and Data is brought back.

Later, the group is in the observation deck and Data is detailing the real situation with Lore. At that moment, a tractor beam is emitted from the Pikril, and a robot is at the window, waving at them. It then goes back to the Pikril, which is gone in an instant. As this happens, an image appears on the viewscreen, and everyone begins to watch.

On the bridge, Picard explains that the robot on board the Pikril had to learn their language, which is why it continued to appear, absorb information, return to its master and reappear once again. Apparently that

race was the one that built Lore, and wasn't satisfied with the results and constructed Data instead. Assuming that Enterprise was heading towards Kiron III, the Pikril was actually sent out to *protect* the starship from Lore. Finally, he adds, "These superior androids noticed the colonists on Kiron III being killed by some still unknown . . . entity; and all they could do was try to save the memories of these good people."

[NOTE: *While this version of "Datalore" was okay, it was destined to improve greatly by the final draft. As aired, the show successfully combined elements from both versions of the treatment, as Lore, who is played pretty much as written, is actually working in cahoots with a crystal-like/ snowflake alien which is the one that destroyed the colonists and is determined to destroy all life on the Enterprise. Much of the episode's success must be directly attributed to actor Brent Spiner, who so magically created the distinct personalities of Data and Lore and really made you believe that they were two different people. Of all the science fiction shows that have used the good/evil-twins story premise, it somehow seems appropriate that it was* The Next Generation *which came closest in quality to the original* Star Trek's *handling of the idea.]*

A letter to The Next Generation *from Gene Roddenberry, the creator of* Star Trek
[From the Press Kit for Star Trek: The Next Generation*)*

Good wishes from a television dramatist who lived a hundred years before your time. I create science fiction tales set in your 21st Century and beyond for television and movie audiences. These are tales which reflect the affection and optimism I have for the human creature. I welcome this opportunity to share my perspectives with you.

For many living now, today is a time of fear and even despair. Some believe that life has become too complex for us. Or too artificial. Or that this era's nuclear missiles, its waves of hysterical nationalism or quarreling superstitions mean a violent end for the human creature, perhaps as soon as the close of our present century.

I believe the complete opposite to be true. The present tumult in our world is the natural and understandable result of a vigorous intelligence moving out of the savagery of our lifeform's childhood. Instead of humanity's demise, our era seems to be filled with evidence that we were meant to survive and evolve much further.

For example, a recent flood of remarkable human happenings include a primal invention as revolutionary as the discovery of fire, the wheel and language. We call it the *computer*, an astonishing device which handles information at near-light speed and in ways suggests humanity has been gifted with the perfect servant. Next, largely because of the computer, we have begun to recognize that the human brain is an equally astonishing device whose ten *billion* or so neurons appear to interconnect into a potential of *trillions* of thought patterns. Rather than being unable to handle the complexities of today, the combination of computer and brain appears to be doubling human knowledge every six or seven years, leading us toward knowledge and ability our ancestors would have considered godlike.

Which means that the human future is not for the fainthearted. The most dramatic happening in our era has been our first efforts to move out from our home planet. Our first moon visits are remarkably similar to the early sailing craft that visited the American New World. Bold children, both! Those early sea voyages found a wilderness as forbidding to them as the moon's landscape seemed to us much later on.

I find it equally remarkable that, so far, no other intelligent life forms seem to exist on those worlds overhead. In fact, everything about our sun and its planets proclaims "RE-SERVED FOR HUMANITY." What a lovely educational arrangement for the offspring of our fertile Earth-egg planet! Having left childhood behind as we move out from our home planet, humanity is ready for the stretching and learning of adolescence.

What better place to evolve into adulthood than in our own solar system? There exists, out in our own "backyard," an incredible treasure house of eight other planets, plus dozens of moons and other raw material – plus the almost inexhaustible energy of our hydrogen furnace sun with which to shape those materials to our needs.

All of which makes it interesting that the galaxy's other stars are, for now, inconceivably distant. Even traveling at light speed, most range from thousands to millions of years away. In its own way, this fact is as heartening as the apparent absence of other intelligent life on the worlds circling our own star. If our universe is a gigantic life and intelligence-creating machine as some believe, what better way of protecting life forms than a system of natural laws which protects them from one another until they become adult and capable of understanding the master plan?

One obstacle to adulthood needs to be solved immediately: we must learn not just to accept differences between ourselves and our ideas, but to enthusiastically welcome and enjoy them. Diversity contains as many treasures as those waiting for us on other worlds. We will find it impossible to fear diversity and to enter the future at the same time.

If the future is not for the fainthearted, it is even more certainly not for the cowardly. One of the saddest spectacles of our time is to watch the leaders of Earth's nations meeting together clumsily and embarrassedly, exchanging slogans containing grains of friendship and understanding, yet fearful that this might constitute some awful blasphemy. Those who insist theirs is the only correct government or economic system deserve the same contempt as those who insist that they have the only true God.

As I began by saying, I am a television dramatist who lived many years before your time, and I realize that the future will be infinitely more complex than anything I am able to imagine. I hope, however, that by your time some small truths will be found in the rough sketch of tomorrow that I offer here. If not, at least you may find this a pleasant and entertaining tale.

* * *

The preceding was taken from "In 'Open Forum'" sponsored by Volkswagon and appearing second in a series in Time Magazine.